AICT 2017

The Thirteenth Advanced International Conference on Telecommunications

June 25 - 29, 2017

Venice, Italy

AICT 2017 Editors

Kevin Daimi, University of Detroit Mercy, USA
Sergei Semenov, Huawei/HiSilicon, Sweden

Printed from e-media with permission by:

Curran Associates, Inc.
57 Morehouse Lane
Red Hook, NY 12571

Some format issues inherent in the e-media version may also appear in this print version.

Printed by Curran Associates, Inc. (2017)

International Academy, Research, and Industry Association (IARIA)
412 Derby Way
Wilmington, DE 19810

Phone: (408) 893-6407
Fax: (408) 527-6351

petre@iaria.org

Additional copies of this publication are available from:

Curran Associates, Inc.
57 Morehouse Lane
Red Hook, NY 12571 USA
Phone: 845-758-0400
Fax: 845-758-2633
Email: curran@proceedings.com
Web: www.proceedings.com

TABLE OF CONTENTS

AICT 6 / ESTDETDEC: CHANNEL ESTIMATION, DETECTION AND DECODING

AICT 2017

Forward

The Thirteenth Advanced International Conference on Telecommunications (AICT 2017), held between June 25-29, 2017 in Venice, Italy, covered a variety of challenging telecommunication topics ranging from background fields like signals, traffic, coding, communication basics up to large communication systems and networks, fixed, mobile and integrated, etc. Applications, services, system and network management issues also receive significant attention.

The spectrum of 21st Century telecommunications is marked by the arrival of new business models, new platforms, new architectures and new customer profiles. Next generation networks, IP multimedia systems, IPTV, and converging network and services are new telecommunications paradigms. Technology achievements in terms of co-existence of IPv4 and IPv6, multiple access technologies, IP-MPLS network design driven methods, multicast and high speed require innovative approaches to design and develop large scale telecommunications networks.

Mobile and wireless communications add profit to a large spectrum of technologies and services. We witness the evolution 2G, 2.5G, 3G and beyond, personal communications, cellular and ad hoc networks, as well as multimedia communications.

Web Services add a new dimension to telecommunications, where aspects of speed, security, trust, performance, resilience, and robustness are particularly salient. This requires new service delivery platforms, intelligent network theory, new telecommunications software tools, new communications protocols and standards.

We are witnessing many technological paradigm shifts imposed by the complexity induced by the notions of fully shared resources, cooperative work, and resource availability. P2P, GRID, Clusters, Web Services, Delay Tolerant Networks, Service/Resource identification and localization illustrate aspects where some components and/or services expose features that are neither stable nor fully guaranteed. Examples of technologies exposing similar behavior are WiFi, WiMax, WideBand, UWB, ZigBee, MBWA and others.

Management aspects related to autonomic and adaptive management includes the entire arsenal of self-ilities. Autonomic Computing, On-Demand Networks and Utility Computing together with Adaptive Management and Self-Management Applications collocating with classical networks management represent other categories of behavior dealing with the paradigm of partial and intermittent resources.

The conference had the following tracks:

- Wireless technologies
- Optical technologies
- Signal processing, protocols and standardization
- Trends on telecommunications features and services
- Trends on protocols and communications models

- Channel Estimation, Detection and Decoding

We take here the opportunity to warmly thank all the members of the AICT 2017 technical program committee, as well as all the reviewers. The creation of such a high quality conference program would not have been possible without their involvement. We also kindly thank all the authors that dedicated much of their time and effort to contribute to AICT 2017. We truly believe that, thanks to all these efforts, the final conference program consisted of top quality contributions.

We also gratefully thank the members of the AICT 2017 organizing committee for their help in handling the logistics and for their work that made this professional meeting a success.

We hope that AICT 2017 was a successful international forum for the exchange of ideas and results between academia and industry and to promote further progress in the field of telecommunications. We also hope that Venice, Italy provided a pleasant environment during the conference and everyone saved some time to enjoy the unique charm of the city.

AICT 2017 Chairs

AICT Steering Committee
Kevin Daimi, University of Detroit Mercy, USA
Eugen Borcoci, University "Politehnica" of Bucharest (UPB), Romania
Carlos Becker Westphall, Federal University of Santa Catarina, Brazil
Tulin Atmaca, Telecom SudParis, France
Mariusz Głąbowski, Poznan University of Technology, Poland
Mario Freire, University of Beira Interior, Portugal
Ioannis Moscholios, University of Peloponnese, Greece
Masayuki Murata, Osaka University Suita, Japan
Wenzhong Li, Nanjing University, China
Ali Houssein Harmouch, Lebanese University, Lebanon

AICT Industry/Research Advisory Committee
Mayank Raj, IBM, USA
Sergei Semenov, Huawei Technologies, Lund, Sweden
Dragana Krstic, University of Niš, Serbia
György Kalman, Norwegian University of Science and Technology, Norway
Seema Garg, Nokia, India
Runxin Wang, Vmware, Ireland
Sungsoo Choi, Korea Electrotechnology Research Institute (KERI), South Korea
Motoyoshi Sekiya, Fujitsu Laboratories Limited, Japan

AICT 2017
Committee

AICT Steering Committee

Kevin Daimi, University of Detroit Mercy, USA
Eugen Borcoci, University "Politehnica" of Bucharest (UPB), Romania
Carlos Becker Westphall, Federal University of Santa Catarina, Brazil
Tulin Atmaca, Telecom SudParis, France
Mariusz Głąbowski, Poznan University of Technology, Poland
Mario Freire, University of Beira Interior, Portugal
Ioannis Moscholios, University of Peloponnese, Greece
Masayuki Murata, Osaka University Suita, Japan
Wenzhong Li, Nanjing University, China
Ali Houssein Harmouch, Lebanese University, Lebanon

AICT Industry/Research Advisory Committee

Mayank Raj, IBM, USA
Sergei Semenov, Huawei Technologies, Lund, Sweden
Dragana Krstic, University of Niš, Serbia
György Kalman, Norwegian University of Science and Technology, Norway
Seema Garg, Nokia, India
Runxin Wang, Vmware, Ireland
Sungsoo Choi, Korea Electrotechnology Research Institute (KERI), South Korea
Motoyoshi Sekiya, Fujitsu Laboratories Limited, Japan

AICT 2017 Technical Program Committee

Ghulam Abbas, GIK Institute of Engineering Sciences and Technology, Pakistan
Michele Albano, University of Pisa, Italy
Petre Anghelescu, University of Pitesti, Romania
Tulin Atmaca, Telecom SudParis, France
Ilija Basicevic, University of Novi Sad, Serbia
Carlos Becker Westphall, Federal University of Santa Catarina, Brazil
Ilham Benyahia, Université du Québec en Outaouais (UQO), Canada
Stefano Berretti, University of Firenze, Italy
Robert Bestak, Czech Technical University in Prague, Czech Republic
Antonella Bogoni, Scuola Superiore Sant'Anna-TeCIP Institute, Italy
Eugen Borcoci, University "Politehnica" of Bucharest (UPB), Romania
Larbi Boubchir, University of Paris 8, France
Alexandros-Apostolos A. Boulogeorgos, Aristotle University of Thessaloniki, Greece
Christos J. Bouras, University of Patras, Greece

Copyright Information

A Security Architecture for Remote Diagnosis of Vehicle Defects

Kevin Daimi
Computer Science and Software Engineering
University of Detroit Mercy
Detroit, USA
email: daimikj@udmercy.edu

***Abstract*—Remote vehicle diagnostics within the auto industry will soon become a reality. Currently, all maintenance work including diagnostics is being performed by dealership. With the new setting of remote vehicle diagnostics, manufacturers will take the lead in the diagnostics process to improve their products and customer satisfaction. This paper proposes a high-level architecture for the remote diagnosis of vehicle defects. It then sets the ground for securing such an architecture due to the fact that safety and privacy of drivers and passengers are extremely challenging with the manifestation of security breaches.**

Keywords—Remote Vehicle Diagnostics; DTC, ECUs; Telematics; Security Architecture; Security Policy

I. Introduction

Modern vehicles utilize a number of buses in the in-vehicle networks. These buses include Local Interconnect Network (LIN), Controller Area Network (CAN), Media-Oriented System Transport (MOST), and FlexRay. LIN handles the lowest data-rate functions, such as door locks, climate control, and mirror control. CAN fits medium speed applications including body systems, engine management, and transmission. High-speed data rates are dealt with by MOST, and therefore, it is convenient for multimedia and infotainment. Finally, safety-critical applications, such as steer-by-wire, stability control, and brake-by-wire are managed by the FlexRay [1]-[5]. Connected to these buses are various Electronic Control Units (ECUs). Modern-day vehicles are furnished with over 80 embedded electronic control units (ECUs), which oversee an enormous part of their functionality. This functionality spans a broad collection of tasks including overseeing door looks, climate, sunroof, body systems, transmission, advanced safety and collision avoidance systems, and pressure monitoring systems. On each ECU, a dedicated and independent firmware runs to control these tasks. ECUs acknowledge signals from various sensors located at various parts and in different components of the vehicle. Using these signals, ECUs control various critical units in the vehicle [6]-[10].

The entire network, including the buses and the ECUs, demands protection against security attacks. Some analyses of the buses, especially the CAN bus, have spotted various vulnerabilities in the available in-vehicle network protocols [11] [12]. All the potential attacks on cellular networks will find their way to the vehicle and can impact the ECUs. Therefore, it is critical to enforce the security of the buses and ECUs when remotely diagnosing problems of various parts of the vehicles controlled by these ECUs.

Vehicles experience various defects. Some of these defects are considered safety-critical, while others are non-safety critical faults. Examples of these defects include problems with fuel consumption system resulting in fuel leakage and possibly a fire, broken or stuck accelerator controls, unexpected rupture of the engine cooling fan blades, improper operation of windshield wiper assemblies, wiring system problems that result in a fire or loss of lighting, a defect in child safety seats, inadequate operation of air conditioning and radio, ordinary wear of shock absorbers, batteries, brake pads and shoes, and exhaust systems, and excessive oil consumption. The vast majority of vehicle defects result in issuing Diagnostic Trouble Codes (DTCs), which are collected by the Electronic Control Units (ECUs) overseeing the operation of these components. Faulty ECUs or bus errors can also result in defects including many of the stated defects above. Currently, all repairs and maintenance are performed by vehicle dealerships. A future trend within the auto industry would be to execute these fixes remotely. This approach will save auto manufacturers a huge amount of money including penalties payed as a result of casualties arising from these defects and from recalls, help manufacturer discover potential recalls ahead of time, and improve their products using the big performance data that will be available. Dealerships' time will be saved through receiving the diagnosis and fixing procedures directly from the manufacturer site. Vehicle owners will feel safer, have increased trust in their vehicle's manufacturer, and save considerable amount of time including the time spent at the dealership. Obviously, for systems providing remote diagnosis to be productive and efficient, security is inevitable.

Pant, Pajic, and Mangharam [13] utilized an automotive ECU architecture for communications between the vehicle and a Remote Diagnostics Center to diagnose, test, update and verify ECUs' firmware. Their diagnostics scheme concentrated on both real-time and non-real time defects, and involved a decision making function to perceive and isolate faults in a system with modeling uncertainties. The suggested framework incorporated in-vehicle and remote diagnostics with the goal of making vehicle recalls management cost-effective. They only used three units in their approach. Their scheme completely ignored security enforcement.

A development of a prototype application for remote vehicle diagnostics, based on the Diagnostics over IP (DoIP) protocol was presented by Johanson, Dahle, and Söderberg [14]. Basic manipulation experiments with synchronous remote diagnostics read-out and control were portrayed. Various safety related concerns requiring closer investigation before a visible exploitation of remote diagnostics services becomes feasible were ascertained. Furthermore, a taxonomy of vehicle diagnostics applications was postulated. This was proposed to interpret the divergences between synchronous (online) and asynchronous (offline) setups in local and distributed settings. Their system merely dealt with remote vehicle diagnosis with no reference whatsoever to securing the remote vehicle diagnostics.

Ferhatović, Lipjankić, Handžić, and Nosović [15] introduced the implementation of a straightforward system for the diagnostics of vehicle faults. Their implementation deployed the standard diagnostic trouble codes and relied on a client-server setting. They presented some functionality and algorithms for that purpose. The communication link between the client and the server was achieved through mobile phone. There was no connection with the manufacturer site. Furthermore, securing the diagnostic process was not an option.

Oka, Furue, Bayer, and Vuillaume [16] introduced an analysis of the security properties for remote diagnostics with some overview of possible attacks. They investigated and categorized diagnostic services and examined mainly their suitability for being remotely performed. They later pinpointed relevant security properties for each of the suitable diagnostic service category. They indicated they will consider the security between the ECUs and telematics module and between the telematics module and the OEM server. However, no message was encrypted and no key management system was provided. Furthermore, authentication, integrity and confidentiality was loosely mentioned. They used only three components, ECUs, telematics module, and OEM server.

This paper presents a security architecture for remote vehicle diagnostics. The architecture includes a number of components. The vehicle site has three components: ECUs, Driver Interface Unit, and the Telematics Module. The Telematics Server, Diagnostics Engine, Knowledge Base Manager, and the Performance-Historical Data Manager reside at the manufacturer site. There are also two external components: Dealership Control Unit, and Supplier Control Unit. The heart of this architecture is the Security Engine. The remainder of the paper is organized as follows: Section II will discuss the use case scenario for the architecture. Section III will introduce the security policy. The remote vehicle security architecture is presented in Section IV. The paper is concluded in Section V.

II. Remote Diagnosis Scenario

Figure 1 is used to explain the remote diagnostics scenario. This scenario will be carried out without reference to the Security Engine (SE) to better understand the technical concepts of remote diagnosis. In the next section, security will be introduced. The symbols used are collected in Table 1 below. The remote diagnosis scenario is depicted in the following use case:

(1) When a problem occurs, Diagnostic Trouble Codes (DTCs) are generated.
(2) The DTC's are stored in the respective ECU's memory. In other words, the ECUs write down the conditions existing when the fault occurred and store them in their memory. The DTCs could also be distributed among several ECUs.
(3) The Onboard Diagnostic System (OBD-II) has access to these DTCs. Other information is also stored when the trouble occurs. This includes vehicle speed, engine RPM, engine coolant temperature, open/close states of the valves, and vehicle emission-related data required by law.
(4) The Telematics Module (TM) of the vehicle communicates the problem-related information from the OBD-II to the Telematics Server (TS) of the manufacturer.
(5) TS analyzes the uploaded information to see if further details are needed, and adds the vehicle VIN number and the diagnostics ID number (DID).
(6) TS transfers all this information to the Diagnostics Engine (DE) at the manufacture site.
(7) DE receives commands from the Diagnostic Center (DC) to start the diagnosis. The DE is in charge of the actual diagnosis. It behaves like an expert system for diagnosis.
(8) Diagnostics Engine extracts the possible symptoms from the diagnostics information.
(9) DE communicates with the Knowledge Base Manager (KBM) and provides the found symptoms.
(10) KBM consults its knowledge base (KB) to see if a solution can be found based on these symptoms.
(11) If further information is needed, DE will be consulted. It is possible that DE will contact the Telematics Server if it cannot provide what the Knowledge Base Manager asks for.
(12) The Knowledge Base Manger contacts the Diagnostics Engine and provides its findings. Here, either a solution is found or no solution exists.
(13) If KBM is unable to provide a solution using its knowledge base, DE will use its diagnostics algorithms to find a possible solution.
(14) If DE cannot find a solution, it will get in touch with the firmware Supplier Control Unit (SCU) residing at the supplier site to provide diagnostics information and symptoms.

(15) The SCU provides the solution. The solution can be updating the firmware of the ECUs that faced the problem, or completely flashing the firmware of the ECU to install a new firmware.
(16) When the solution to the problem is found by the Diagnostics Engine and that solution does not need the dealership to be involved, the commands to fix the problem are sent to the TS. This is further elaborated in steps 20-21.
(17) The Diagnostics Engine sends the fixes to the Knowledge Base Manager to update the knowledge base. It also sends the diagnostics details including symptoms and fixes to the Performance-Historical Data Manager (PHDM) to update the vehicle's performance and historical data stores. These will be very valuable assets for business intelligence.
(18) If there is a need to have the vehicle's engine turned off, the Telematics Server will inform the TM.
(19) The TM transmits a message to the Driver Interface Unit (DIU) to have the driver turn the engine off. When that happens, the TM informs the Telematics Server.
(20) TS sends messages containing the fixes in a form of diagnostics commands to TM.
(21) The TM communicates with the ECUs in question and the fixes will be applied.
(22) If the solution involves more work than just simple fixes, such as new update and ECU flashing, and there is no Firmware Over-The-Air (FOTA), the dealership must be involved.
(23) If the option of FOTA exists, the TS communicates with the TM to achieve that. In this case, the vehicle must not be running.
(24) If the dealership is needed, the Telematics Server will help the Diagnostics Engine in scheduling an appointment for the vehicle. It will communicate with TM requesting the dealer's name and address, and date and time of the appointment.
(25) The TM communicates a message to the DIU informing the driver of the problem and requesting the name and address of the dealer, and the date and time of dropping the vehicle.
(26) The received information from the DIU is sent to the TS via the TM.
(27) The Diagnostics Engine communicates with the Dealership Control Unit (DCU) at the dealership site. The DCU will receive the symptoms and fixes in addition to the date and time of the appointment. If there is a need to change the date/time, the TS will re-contact the TM. The scheduled date should also give the dealership enough time to prepare spare parts if needed.
(28) The vehicle will be fixed.
(29) If a new update or a completely new firmware is needed as a result of the problem in the vehicle in question, a recall will be issued by the manufacturer for all vehicles of that model and year.

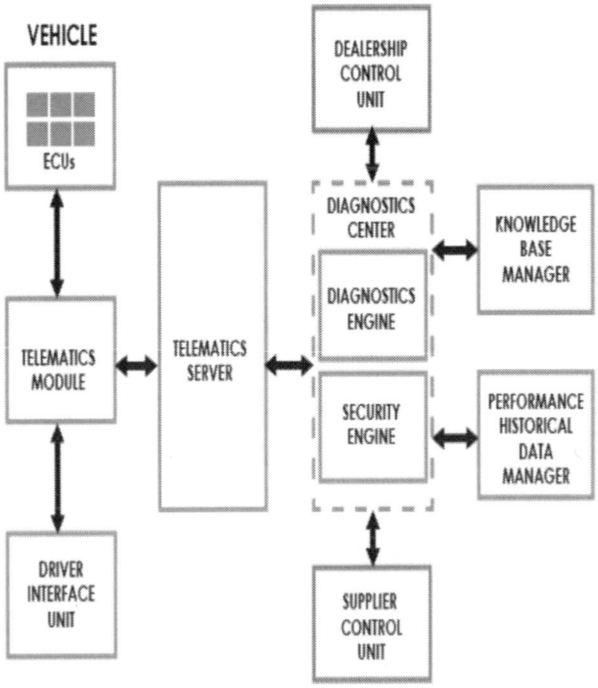

Figure 1. Vehicle remote diagnosis security architecture

TABLE I. SYMBOLS USED

Symbol	Meaning
DTC	Diagnostics Trouble Code
ECU	Electronic Control Unit
TM	Telematics Module
DIU	Driver Interface Unit
TS	OBD-Based Telematics Server
DC	Diagnostics Center
DE	Diagnostics Engine
SE	Security Engine
KBM	Knowledge Base Manager
PHDM	Performance-Historical Data Manager
DCU	Dealership Control Unit
SCU	Supplier Control Unit
OBD-II	Onboard Diagnostic System
VIN	Vehicle Identification Number
DID	Diagnostics Identification
PU	Public key
SK	Symmetric key
PR	Private Key
PDS	Performance data store
HDS	Historical data store
→	Then in Section III, Sends in section IV
← →	Both parties apply security requirements
X_S	Parties communicating using SK
MAC	Message Authentication Code
KB	Knowledge base

III. SECURITY POLICY

Security policies mandate what must be secured, and how to secure them to support the security architecture or the network security. Without a security policy, a network may be compromised. With the intention of safeguarding access to various components of an information system, a network security policy should be developed. It consists of a list of conditions and actions to prevent illegitimate access to private information. Network security management has been focusing on security policies to the extent that security policy repositories are at the core of many network security management systems. A security policy furnishes the basis for system security architecture [17]–[22]. In what follows, the security policy is represented by rules.

IF component = SE → component can access {TM, TS, SCU, DCU, DE, KBM, PHDM}
IF X is an algorithm and X belongs to the list of algorithms {RSA, EEC, AES, SHA-3, HMAC, DDA, CMAC, CTR, CFB, …} approved by SE → X can be used
IF X is a component & Y is a component & X and Y are allowed to communicate & X has algorithm Z & Y does not have algorithm Z → Z cannot be used
IF component = ECU | DIU → only TM can access them
IF component = DIU → ECUs cannot access component
IF component = SCU | DCU → component is not allowed to receive info about driving habits of the vehicle's owner including speed, route and the location of the vehicle when the fault occurred
IF component = TM → only TS can access component
IF component = TS → only TM & DE can access it
IF component = DE → only DCU, SCU, TS, KBM, & PHDM can access component
IF component = KBM | PHDM | DCU | SCU → only DE can access component
IF M is a message & M is sent to DCU | SCU → DCU | SCU cannot deny receiving M
IF M is a message & M is encrypted with PR | M is encrypted with SK → M is authenticated
IF M is a message & M is encrypted with Private Key | MAC(M) is encrypted with PR → M is signed
IF M is a message & X is the sender & Y is the receiver & X encrypts M with Y's Public Key | X encrypts M with SK → M is confidential
IF K is a key & SE did not distribute this key → K cannot be used
IF K is a key & X is a component & K is issued by SE → X must receive the validity period of K from SE
IF X is a component → X must have its own Intrusion Detection System
IF X is a component & A is a malicious activity & X detected A → X must notify SE immediately
IF X is a component & A is a malicious activity & X detected A →X must stop its communication
If X is one of the data stores in {PDS, HDS, KB} → X must be encrypted
IF X = PDS | HDS → X is only accessed by PHDM
IF X = KB → X is only accessed by KBM
IF X is a component & M is a message & M is received by X at time = t & M is received again by X at time = t +1 & … → X must terminate communication
IF X is a component & M is a message & M does not belong to the set of messages allowed for X → X denies M & X informs SE
IF X is a component & Y is a component & X and Y are allowed to communicate & P is a protocol & P approved by SE → X and Y can use P
IF component X belongs to {ECU, DIU, TM} → X's outgoing messages are encrypted with PU
IF component X belongs to {TM, DE, TS, PHAM, KBM, DCU, SCU} → X's sent messages are encrypted with SK
IF X is a component & Y is a component and X communicates with Y and D is an auditor → D may access HDS
IF X and Y are components & A is a malicious activity & X detected M | Y detected M & A is blocked → X and Y may continue their communication

IV. REMOTE DIAGNOSIS SECURITY ARCHITECTURE

The Remote Diagnosis Security Architecture (RDSA) will be explained below using the available communication between various parties. The messages sent will be represented symbolically including the type of encryption. In what follows, (PU, messages) is used to indicate that public key cryptology is used, (SK, messages) implies using symmetric key cryptology. This will be followed by the security requirements (enclosed by parentheses) applicable to the message.

A. The Security Engine

The heart of the remote diagnosis security architecture is the Security Engine (SE). Note that the connection between TM and SE in Figure 1 has been omitted for clarity purposes. The Security Engine is responsible for symmetric keys distribution and management, updating keys, issuing keys for Message Authentication Codes, and ensuring the security policy is not violated. It further controls the cryptographic algorithms and techniques used for encryption/decryption and message authentication. Initially, parties communicating based on symmetric cryptology have a preinstalled symmetric key that will be used just once by SE to forward the newly created symmetric key for each pair of parties. Once those parties receive these keys, the pre-installed ones are discarded. SE also uses the created symmetric keys to communicate the keys needed for message authentication. As part of the security policy, the Security Engine informs each pair of communicating parties what techniques they are allowed to use. The parties can agree on a subset of techniques out of the allowable set of techniques approved by the SE during handshaking. The relationships below illustrate what the SE sends the parties (X_S) communicating using symmetric key.

SE → X_S: (Symmetric Key, MAC-Key, Algorithm Set)

B. TM, ECUs and DIU Communications

The Telematics Module communicates with both the ECUs and the DIU. The public and private keys for TM, DIU, and ECUs are preinstalled at manufacturing time. In addition, the ECUs and DIU have the public key of TM preinstalled, and TM has the public keys of DIU and ECUs preinstalled. To replace the pre-installed keys, ECUs and DIU must change their public and private keys and use the old private key to encrypt the new public key before sending it to TM. TM will create its new public and private keys and forward its public keys encrypted with the old ones to the ECUs and DIU. This procedure will be followed every time the Telematics Module issues a request to replace keys. TM receives messages containing the DTCs and other vehicle status information when the fault occurred, such as vehicle speed, coolant temperature, and engine RPM from the ECUs and OBD-II system. TM and ECUs authenticate each other. The messages containing DTCs and status information are encrypted using public key cryptology. Confidentiality of the exchanged messages is enforced, and the integrity of these messages is verified to ensure the messages have not been modified. On the other hand, the messages sent by TM to ECUs include remediation commands (fixes). These are also encrypted with public key. Confidentiality, integrity, and authentication are required. The same applies to the interaction between TM and DIU. The messages sent by the TM to DIU include problem, turning engine off, providing dealer address, dealer name, date of appointment, time of appointment and appointment details when it is scheduled. The DIU sends engine turned off, dealer address, dealer name, and requested date and time of appointment to TM. They first agree on the algorithms to be used for encryption and MAC, nonce(s), and the allowable waiting time for receiving a message to overcome replay attacks. The relations below exemplify these messages.

TM → ECU: (PU, remediation commands)
ECU → TM: (PU, DTCs, status info when fault occurred)
TM ↔ ECU: (confidentiality, integrity, authentication)
TM → DIU: (PU, turn engine off, request for dealership details, request for appointment details)
DIU → TM: (PU, engine off, dealer details, requested appointment date and time)
TM ↔ DIU: (confidentiality, integrity, authentication)

C. Telematics Server and TM Communication

The Telematics Server is the only component that can communicate directly with the vehicle. Virtually, it can provide various information to the vehicle through the TM. However, only the messages needed for this architecture will be introduced. Confidentiality, integrity, and authentication are also needed. The TS receives problem-related information from the TM. The TM accepts fixes messages, inquiries for further problem information, requests for turning the engine of the vehicle in question off, request for dealership details, and driver preferred appointment date and time. The symbolic representation for this communication is given below.

TS → TM: (SK, fixes, further info request, dealership info request, appointment date/time request)
TM → TS: (SK, problem-related info, dealership info, appointment date/time, engine off, VIN)
TM ↔ ECU: (confidentiality, integrity, authentication)

D. Telematics Server and Diagnostics Engine Communication

This is an internal communication within the manufacturer's site. The Telematics Server supplies the problem related information received from the TM to the DE after adding the VIN number of the vehicle and the Diagnostic ID (DID). The VIN number will help in retrieving further information about the vehicle in question if needed, and DID will designate the fault and will be used for indexing purposes. The TS will also provide further details from the TM if needed by the DE. The Diagnostics Engine will check if a solution exists, try to find a solution, and contact the supplier of firmware if it fails. In any case, a remediation procedure is sent back to TS. This includes fixing commands if there is no need to involve the dealership, request for scheduling appointment for the vehicle, need for further information about the problem, and request to turn the engine off.

TS → DE: (SK, problem-related info, further info, dealership info, appointment date/time preference, engine turned off, VIN, DID)
DE → TS: (SK, remediation procedure, dealership info request, appointment date/time, engine off request)
DE ↔ TS: (confidentiality, integrity, authentication)

E. Diagnostics Engine and KBM Communication

Prior to applying any diagnostic algorithms, the Diagnostics Engine consults the Knowledge Base Manager to see if any solution exists in the diagnosis knowledge base. It provides the KBM with all the symptoms of the problem, which are extracted from the DTCs. The Knowledge Base Manager will reason about its knowledge base using the provided symptoms. If a solution is already stored, KBM will send its details to DE. Otherwise, a "Solution does not exist" message is forwarded. If no solution exists, the DE will try solving it itself. If it finds a solution, it sends this knowledge to the KBM to be stored in the diagnosis knowledge base. In other words, the knowledge base is augmented. The DE will use the VIN number to get any other needed information about the vehicle.

DE → KBM: (SK, symptoms, further info about Vehicle, DE's solution, DID)
KBM → DE: (SK, KBM's solution, DID)
TM ←→ ECU: (confidentiality, integrity, authentication)

F. Diagnostics Engine and PHDM Communication

As a result of various diagnoses, diverse important data is accumulated. Some of this data will be stored in the Performance Data Store (PDS) and the rest in the Historical Data Store (HDS). Examples of the data stored in the Performance Data Store are DTC's, symptoms, various vehicle status information when the problem occurred, solution, vehicle model and year. The HDS will include the above and other communication messages in the architecture. All this information is forwarded by the DE to the Performance Historical Data Manager to be stored in PDS/HDS. These two data stores will accumulate big data that will be used by the manufacturer for a range of analyses and statistics. These analyses and statistics are beyond the scope of this architecture. However, the PHDM does provide some simple statistics on the number of performance records for certain vehicle models and years, and number of historical records for all vehicle models and years.

Performance Data = {DTC's, symptoms, various vehicle status information when the problem occurred, solution, vehicle model, model year}
DE → PHDM: (SK, performance data, all other communication messages)
PHDM → DE: (SK, performance statistics, historical statistics)
PHDM ←→ DE: (confidentiality, integrity, authentication)

G. Diagnostics Engine and DCU Communication

When the problem needs the dealership's interference, the DE informs the Dealership Control Unit at the dealership site. This is an external communication outside the manufacturer site. The dealership receives the diagnosis, remediation procedure, and the needed firmware or firmware fixes. Furthermore, DCU receives the information of the driver and details of the appointment. The dealership submits the details of fixing the vehicle and any possible functions in the vehicle impacted by the maintenance process. If the vehicle cannot be fixed, the DE will re-contact the firmware Supplier Control Unit. Here, the security requirement, nonrepudiation, is required to prevent the dealership from claiming it did not receive the messages sent by DE.

DE → DCU: (SK, diagnosis, remediation procedure, ECU firmware, driver details, appointment details)

DCU → DE: (SK, maintenance details, other functions impacted)

DCU ←→ DE: (confidentiality, integrity, authentication, nonrepudiation)

H. Diagnostics Engine and SCU Communication

When the DE is unable to find a solution for the problem, it contacts the firmware Supplier Control Unit. This is also an external communication that needs nonrepudiation to be applied. The SCU must receive the DTCs, the state of the vehicle when the problem occurred, DE's analysis of the problem and trials stemming from DE's attempts to fix the problem, and vehicle model and year. On the other hand, the SCU provides firmware update, firmware fixes, or new firmware, and affected ECU. Certainly, the vehicle model and year will be attached.

DE → SCU: (SK, DTCs, vehicle state, DE's analysis, model, year)
SCU → DE: (SK, firmware update, firmware fixes, new firmware, affected ECU, model, year)
SCU ←→ DE: (confidentiality, integrity, authentication, nonrepudiation)

V. CONCLUSION AND FUTURE WORK

This paper presented a comprehensive architecture for remote diagnostics of vehicle defects. This architecture is enhanced by adding a Security Engine to oversee and coordinate all possible security functions, procedures, policies, and key creation and distribution. Traditionally, the Telematics Control Unit (TMU) is in charge of telematics. Because TMU is an ECU, all the limitations of ECUs including message size apply here. If TMU is used in the above security architecture, public key cryptology would have been the right choice for its communication with TS because TMU can only handle very short messages. A new trend in vehicle industry is the use of a more powerful unit, the Telematics Module. This is included in the above architecture. A future improvement would be extending the system to deal with the buses defects, especially, the CAN bus errors. Here, another component will be added. For systems of remote diagnosing to be trusted, driver privacy must be enforced when sending the information to the manufacturer site. The next step after expanding the architecture would be implementing it.

REFERENCES

[1] On Semiconductor, "Basics of In-Vehicle Neworking (INV) Protocols," http://www.onsemi.com/pub_link/Collateral/TND6015-D.PDF, pp. 1-27, [retrieved: April, 2017].

[2] Freescale Semiconductors, "In-Vehicle Networking," https://cache.freescale.com/files/microcontrollers/doc/brochure/BRIN VEHICLENET.pdf, 2006, pp. 1-11, [retrieved: April, 2017].

[3] S. Seo, J. Kim, S. Hwang, K. Kwon, and J. Jeon, "A Reliable Gatway for In-Vehicle Networks Based on LIN, CAN, and FlexRay," ACM

Transcation on Embedded Computing Systems, vol. 4, no. 1, Article 7, 2012, pp. 1-24.

[4] The Clemson University Vechular Electronics Laboratory, "Automotive Electronics," http://www.cvel.clemson.edu/auto/auto_buses01.html, [retrieved: April, 2017].

[5] K. Parnell, "Put the Right Bus in Your Car," Xcell Journal, Available: http://www.rpi.edu/dept/ecse/mps/xc_autobus48(CAN).pdf, [retrieved: April, 2017].

[6] D. K. Nilsson, P. H. Phung, and U. E. Larson, "Vehicle ECU Classification Based on Safety-Security Characteristics," in Proc. the 13th International Conference on Road Tarnsport Information and Control (RTIC'08), Manchester, England, UK, 2008, pp. 1-7.

[7] CCS, "Electronic Control Units (ECUS)," 2014, http://www.ccs-labs.org/teaching/c2x/2014s/05-ecus.pdf, pp. 1-27, [retrieved: April, 2017].

[8] STW, "Control System Electronics," 2011, http://www.stw-technic.com/wp-content/uploads/2011/05/controllers.pdf, pp. 1-19, [retrieved: April, 2017].

[9] ETAS GmbH, "Electronic Control Unit (ECU) – Basics of Automative ECU," 2014, http://www.scribd.com/doc/268828296/20140121-ETAS-Webinar-ECU-Basics#scribd, pp. 1-30, [retrieved: April, 2017].

[10] Freescale, "Future advances in Body Electronics" https://cache.freescale.com/files/automotive/doc/white_paper/BODY DELECTRWP.pdf, 2013, pp. 1-18, [retrieved: April, 2017].

[11] T. Hoppe, S. Kiltz, and J. Dittmann, "Automotive IT-Security as a Challenge: Basic Attacks from the Black Box Perspective on the Example of Privacy Threats," Computer Safety, Reliability, and Security, 2009, pp. 145-158.

[12] M. Wolf, A. Weimerskirch, and C. Paar, "Security in Automotive Bus Systems," in Proc. the 2nd Embedded Security in Cars Workshop (ESCAR 2004), Bochum, Germany, 2004, pp. 11-12.

[13] Y. Pant, M. Pajic, R. Mangharam, "AUTOPLUG: An Architecture for Remote Electronic Controller Unit Diagnostics in Automotive Systems," Technical Report, Department of Electrical and Systems Engineering, University of Pennsylvania, 2012, pp. 1-13.

[14] L. Ferhatović, A. Lipjankić, A. Handžić, and N. Nosović, "System for Remote Diagnostic of Vehicle Defects," in Proc. The 17th Telecommunications Forum (TELFOR 2009), Serbia, Belgrade, 2009, pp. 1323-1326.

[15] M. Johanson, P. Dahle, and A. Söderberg, "Remote Vehicle Diagnostics over the Internet using the DoIP Protocol," in Proc. The Sixth International Conference on Systems and Networks Communications (ICSNC 2011), Barcelona, Spain, 2011, pp. 226-231.

[16] D. Oka, T. Furue, S. Bayer, and C. Vuillaume, "Analysis of Performing Secure Remote Vehicle Diagnostics," in Proc. Computer Security Symposium (CSS 2014), 2014, pp. 643–650.

[17] A. Mishra, A. K. Jhapate, and P. Kumar, "Improved Genetics Feedback Algorithm Based Network Security Policy Framework," in Proc. The 2nd International Conference on Future Networks, Sanya, China, 2010, pp. 8-10.

[18] N. Ben Youssef and A. Bouhoula, "Systematic Deployment of Network Security Policy in Centralized and Distributed Firewalls", in Proc. The 2011 IEEE International Conference on Privacy, Security, Risk, and Trust, Boston, Massachusetts, USA, 2011, pp. 1214-1219.

[19] C. Tang and S. Yu, "A Verification Algorithm of Network Security Policy Repository," in Proc. The 2009 International Conference on Information Technology and Computer Science, Kiev, Ukraine, 2009, pp. 297-300.

[20] X. Wang, W. Shi, Y. Xiang, and J. Li, "Efficient Network Security Enforcement with Policy Space Analysis", IEEE/ACM Transcaction on Networking, vol. PP, issue 99, 2015, pp. 1-13.

[21] D. Chemyavskiy and N. Miloslavskaya, "A Concept of Unification of Network Security Policies," in Proc. The Fifth International Conference on Security of Information and Networks, Jaipur, India, 2012, pp. 27-32.

[22] T. Bourdier and H. Cirstea, "Symbolic Analysis of Network Security Policies Using Rewrite Rules," in Proc. Symposium on Principles and Practicies of Declarative Programing (PDPP'11), Odense, Denmark, 2011, pp. 77-88.

Machine Learning Regression-Based Approach for Dynamic Wireless Network Interface Selection

Lucas M. F. Harada and Daniel C. Cunha

Centro de Informática (CIn)
Universidade Federal de Pernambuco (UFPE)
Recife-PE, Brazil
Email: [lmfh, dcunha]@cin.ufpe.br

Abstract—**Battery consumption is a general problem in any portable wireless device and it depends directly on the transmission technology (cellular, Wi-Fi or short-range wireless networks) that is used to send and receive data. When various networks are available, mobile devices should be able to choose which network interface to use based on a variety of factors, such as required bandwidth or energy efficiency. This work proposes a dynamic wireless network interface-selection mechanism focused on minimizing the energy consumption of the mobile device, allowing an increase in battery life. In doing so, Machine Learning (ML) regression-based algorithms are used to predict the energy cost per transferred byte for each type of available network interface using field data. A comparison of the energy consumptions for both the proposed mechanism and the Android native method is performed. Numerical results show that our proposal helps save energy.**

Keywords–Network selection; energy consumption; wireless interface; machine learning; regression.

I. Introduction

In the last decades, mobile communications have evolved from a level of expensive technology used by a few individuals to the condition of ubiquitous systems used by the majority of the world population. The number of mobile subscriptions in 2016 was around 7.5 billion, surpassing the world inhabitants. By 2020, it is expected that about 90% of people above six years old will have a mobile phone and that the global IP traffic will reach 2.7 zettabytes [1].

These forecasting scenarios are related to the evolution of the smartphones that today are equipped with a wide range of sensing, computational, storage and communication resources, functionalities that have allowed mobile devices to perform activities previously restricted only to computers [2]. All these new functionalities presented by the recent mobile devices require better components, such as faster Central Processing Unit (CPU) and larger storage, which have turned smartphones into energy-hungry battery-powered devices.

It is a well-known fact that battery consumption is a general problem in any portable wireless device and it depends directly on the transmission technology (cellular, Wi-Fi, or short-range wireless networks) that is used to send and receive data (see [3] and references therein). Kellokoski *et. al.* [4] analyze the effect of making vertical handoffs on the energy consumption of the smartphones. Since disconnecting from one network to connect to another is an energy consuming activity, the energy consumption related to the vertical handoff process is

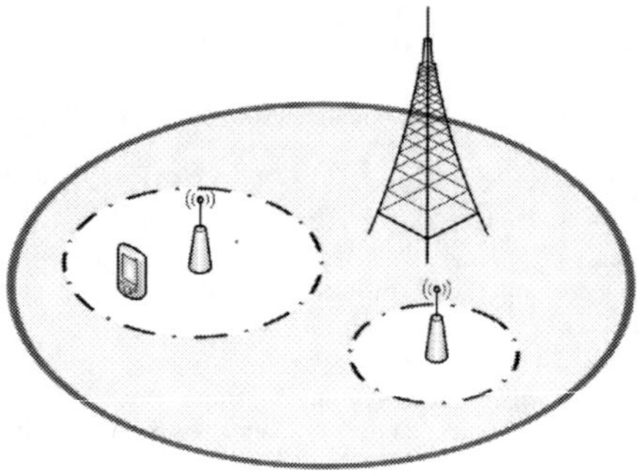

Figure 1. Representation of cellular and Wi-Fi network integration: full line circle – coverage area of a cellular network cell; dashed line circles – coverage areas of the Wi-Fi hot spots.

reasonable as long as the new network to connect to is more efficient than the original one. In [5], a quantitative analysis on how the network quality affects the energy consumption in smartphones for both 3G and Wi-Fi networks is presented. The results show that poor wireless signal strength may increase the energy consumption eight times on Wi-Fi and 50% on 3G.

In face of this, the 3rd Generation Partnership Project (3GPP) started to investigate the possibility of integrating cellular networks (3G or 4G) with Wi-Fi networks [6]. Figure 1 illustrates an example of cellular and Wi-Fi network integration, where the larger circle (with full line) represents the coverage area of a cell of the cellular network, while smaller circles (dashed lines) represent the coverage area of Wi-Fi access points. When various networks are available, mobile devices should be able to choose which network interface to use based on a variety of factors, such as required bandwidth or energy efficiency.

In case of wireless network interface selection, there are two possible approaches: one focused on the mobile device and another focused on the wireless network infrastructure. Most of the network interface selection algorithms proposed in the literature focus on choosing the wireless network interface that delivers the best quality of service, as can be seen, for example, in [7]-[9]. In [7], Abbas *et. al.* propose a decision tree to define the best network interface based on criteria such as locality (at home or away from home), device speed and signal strength. In [8], a fuzzy logic scheme is proposed to select the best network interface. It uses the signal strength for both 3G and Wi-Fi networks to estimate the rates for each interface and use them to select the appropriate option. In [9], Lai *et. al.* analyze the wireless network interface selection as a multi-criteria problem based on an utility function, defined as the user satisfaction regarding the network interface choice.

The central point that motivates this paper is that, as far as we know, there are not many works in literature concerning energy consumption as the main network interface selection criterion. So, this work proposes a dynamic wireless network interface-selection mechanism focused on minimizing the energy consumption of the mobile device, allowing an increase in battery life. For this, Machine Learning (ML) regression-based algorithms are used to predict the energy cost per transmitted byte for each type of available network interface and to choose the most energy-efficient one. Finally, a comparison of the energy consumptions for both the proposed mechanism and the Android native method is performed.

The remainder of this article is structured as follows. Section II presents the proposed dynamic network interface-selection mechanism. Details about the measurement setup and the model tuning are also introduced. Numerical results are provided in Section III. Finally, conclusions are drawn in Section IV.

II. Proposed Dynamic Selection Mechanism

Although most of the network interface-selection mechanisms do not consider energy consumption as their main selection criterion, energy-efficient mechanisms are not a novelty. For example, in [10], an energy-efficient adaptive scheme was proposed based on the mathematical modeling of energy consumption and data transfer delay patterns. However, in our case, we intend to find the most energy-efficient network interface available for the mobile device under a high network traffic, e.g. download a file via browser, using field data. To achieve that, the proposed mechanism estimates the energy cost per transferred byte and uses this parameter as a network interface selection criterion. The estimation of the energy cost per transferred byte is obtained by ML regression-based algorithms.

A. Machine Learning

ML is a form of artificial intelligence by which computers evolve the ability to learn from and make predictions based on data. Today, ML has been used by organizations and academic communities in a variety of ways, including enhancing cybersecurity [11], improving medical outcomes [12], and making automobiles safer [13].

ML algorithms are categorized into supervised and unsupervised learning. In the first category, we have labeled input and output data to provide a learning basis for future data processing. In the second one, we have to draw inferences from input data without labeled response. Considering supervised learning, ML is divided into classification and regression algorithms. The difference between them is that the former aims to classify new data and the latter focuses on estimating a new data continuous variable. Both algorithms depend on training data, i.e., a set of examples with paired input and expected output.

TABLE I. FEATURES COLLECTED FROM THE SMARTPHONE AND THE WIRELESS NETWORK.

Feature Category	**Features**
Battery info*	Battery voltage and current
Execution time info*	Execution time for each collect
Data transfer info*	Number of transferred bytes
Global config.	ADB status, Bluetooth status
Smartphone config.	Accelerometer, Location Manager status
Bluetooth config.	Bluetooth state, Bluetooth discovery state
Wi-Fi config.	Wi-Fi state, signal frequency, link speed
Celullar config.	Network type, connection status and state, RSSI
Process info	Process list, CPU usage

B. Measurement Setup

To begin with, we collected data as a set of features from a Motorola Moto G 2nd Gen. Dual SIM XT1068 [14]. After that, we divided the data into two sets: the first one to generate (train and test) the regression models and the second one to validate our proposal by simulation. The collected features are shown in Table I by feature category, including current and voltage measurements and the value of transferred bytes for each network interface individually. The feature categories marked with (*) are the ones used to calculate the energy efficiency, which will be described later. The number of transferred bytes is measured by the difference of total transferred bytes, value available in Android API, between two collect iterations. Concerning the Wi-Fi signals, the environment in which the data was gathered had six wireless access points, but the device could only connect to one of them. For data gathering, a self-developed app collected the features every five seconds, while the mobile device was held in movement during the entire gathering time to guarantee variable network conditions for both Wi-Fi and 3G interfaces. It is known that the battery voltage drops according to the level of the battery charge in a non-linear way [15]. To prevent that, all measurements had a maximum duration of five minutes and were started with the fully-charged battery.

Considering that modern smartphones have reliable readings from the battery [16], both current and voltage measurements were obtained via software. The voltage measurement was read via the BatteryManager class from Android API [17], while the current measurement was obtained from the Android system files. Based on voltage and current measurements, we define the instantaneous power P_i as

$$P_i = V_i I_i \tag{1}$$

in which V_i is the battery voltage in mV and I_i is the battery current in μA. From P_i, we can define the consumed energy E_c, as

$$E_c = P_i \Delta t \tag{2}$$

where Δt is the time interval in which the power in used. Finally, we can obtain the energy cost per transferred byte C_b as

$$C_b = E_c / Q_b \tag{3}$$

where Q_b is the number of transferred bytes in the time interval Δt.

To verify how the collected features affect the response variable C_b, we apply the Recursive Feature Elimination (RFE)

TABLE II. RANKING OF FEATURES GIVEN BY THE RFE ALGORITHM.

Feature	Ranking
User CPU usage	1
Cellular RSSI	2
Wi-Fi link speed	3
Wi-Fi RSSI	4
System CPU usage	5
Number of transferred bytes	6
Wi-Fi signal frequency	7
Cellular network activity type	8
Cellular network state	9
Cellular network data connection status	10
Cellular network connection type	11
Wi-Fi state	12

algorithm [18]. The objective of the RFE algorithm is to create a rank of all input features from the most to the least relevant of the set when considering the target variable. Table II shows the ranking of features by relevance to the energy cost C_b obtained by the RFE algorithm. To reduce the feature space and, consequently, the computational complexity, we define a threshold rank, where the features whose rank is below the threshold are discarded. The threshold rank was found by testing the models and checking if the accuracy was reduced by removing the last ranked feature. This process was done iteratively. Therefore, the threshold rank was defined as 12 and the 7 least relevant features were dropped from Table II.

Figure 2 shows a diagram that represents the development of the regression model. The features used to train the model are divided into categories, which, in turn, are grouped in two sets (A and B). Even after optimizing the features by the RFE algorithm, it is important to emphasize that some features of the final dataset can not be used as part of the training data. For example, due to limitations of the Android Operating System (OS), during 3G data collection, the Wi-Fi interface must be shut down, otherwise the smartphone will always be connected to the Wi-Fi network. As a result, the Wi-Fi configuration features (features whose rankings are 3, 4, 7, and 12 in Table II) are not included on the 3G training data. Also, the number of transferred bytes Q_b is not adopted as input of the 3G training data, because when both interfaces are available, the collected variable Q_b normally refers to the Wi-Fi interface. Conversely, the remaining features of the set B (except those from the Wi-Fi configuration category) are common to both network interface modeling. At last, since features do not include the energy cost C_b, a parser is applied to generate it (see (3)) for both 3G and Wi-Fi regression models using the features of the set A.

C. Model Tuning

Cross-validation is a statistical method for estimating the performance of a predictive model [19]. The basic form of cross-validation is k-fold cross-validation. In this technique, the data is initially split into k equally (or nearly equally) disjoint data segments named folds. This partitioning allows the execution of k iterations of the technique, where in each iteration, a different fold is used for validation and the remaining $(k-1)$ folds are used for training.

Figure 3 illustrates how the process of three-fold cross-validation works. In each iteration, one ML algorithm uses two folds to learn one model and, after that, the learned model is asked to make predictions about the data in the validation fold. In this work, the following ML techniques are examined: Linear Regression (Ordinary Least Squares, OLS) [20], Random Forest [21], Gaussian Process Regressor (GPR) [22], K-Nearest Neighbors (K-NN) [23], Multi-Layer Perceptron (MLP) [23], and Support Vector Regression (SVR) [24]. To evaluate the ML algorithms, we use four metrics to assess the outputs from the regressors: Mean Absolute Error (MAE), Mean Squared Error (MSE), Median Absolute Error (MnAE) and R^2 score. Due to limitation of space, the mathematical definitions of these metrics were omitted in this work and can be found in [25].

The final step of the proposed mechanism is to compare the estimates of the energy cost per transferred byte of new data for each network interface and select the interface that has the lower energy cost, or equivalently, the higher energy

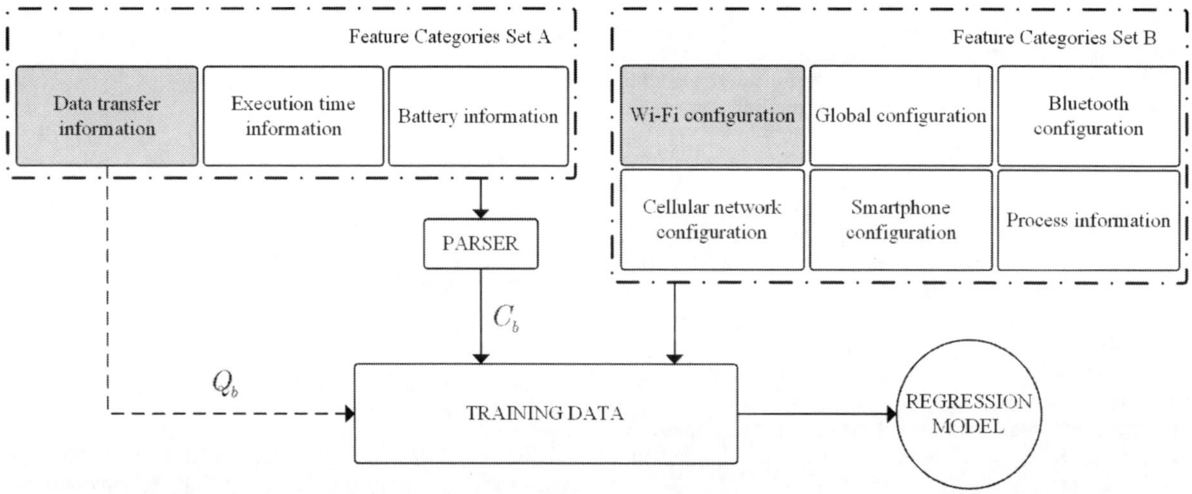

Figure 2. Diagram representing the creation of the regression model. The feature categories marked in grey are only used for the Wi-Fi models.

TABLE III. STATISTICAL ANALYSIS FOR THE WI-FI AND 3G DATA SUBSETS.

Feature	Wi-Fi				3G			
	Average	Minimum	Maximum	Median	Average	Minimum	Maximum	Median
RSSI	-58.55 dBm	-80 dBm	-27 dBm	-59 dBm	-74.11 dBm	-103 dBm	-53 dBm	-73 dBm
User CPU	21.30%	2.00%	41.00%	20.00%	20.61%	6.00%	35.00%	20.00%
System CPU	12.20%	5.00%	22.00%	12.00%	11.56%	6.00%	20.00%	11.00%
Battery current	337 mA	205 mA	483 mA	341 mA	425 mA	326 mA	770 mA	408 mA
Battery voltage	4.20 V	4.17 V	4.24 V	4.19 V	4.20 V	4.17 V	4.22 V	4.20 V
Energy cost (J/B)	2.26e-05	7.46e-07	2.98e-04	1.75e-06	3.87e-06	1.06e-06	2.25e-05	2.92e-06

TABLE IV. EVALUATION OF REGRESSION MODELS FOR WI-FI AND 3G DATA SUBSETS.

Regressor	Wi-Fi				3G			
	MAE	MSE (e+05)	$MnAE$	R^2	MAE	MSE (e+03)	$MnAE$	R^2
OLS	241.48	1.59	170.09	0.41	19.31	0.86	14.31	0.09
SVR	294.64	3.10	145.17	-0.07	19.47	1.32	10.71	-0.05
Random Forest	58.31	0.28	2.62	0.89	14.56	0.70	9.03	0.46
K-NN	61.10	0.38	2.25	0.89	14.64	0.91	7.40	0.38
GPR	329.12	29.7	212.96	-0.08	21.46	1.29	13.84	-0.13
MLP	98.96	0.48	22.73	0.82	13.54	0.40	8.30	0.66

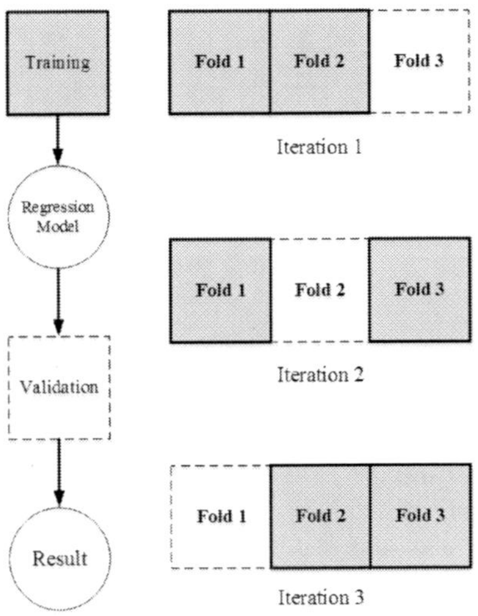

Figure 3. Diagram depicting the process of three-fold cross-validation. Adapted from [26].

efficiency. In summary, the proposed mechanism dynamically finds the threshold where the Wi-Fi interface consumes more energy than the 3G interface, in case of high network traffic.

III. NUMERICAL RESULTS

All models considered in this work are implemented in Python language, utilizing *scikit-learn*, an open-source ML toolbox [25]. The performance metrics of the regression models are evaluated for the ML regression-based techniques mentioned in Subsection II-C.

After the data acquisition, we verify if the final dataset is able to represent different network conditions. From this point, we split the training dataset into two portions (Wi-Fi and 3G subsets), since our objective is to generate an estimation of the energy cost per transferred byte for each type of network interface. Table III summarizes the statistical analysis for both Wi-Fi and 3G data, containing the average, minimum, maximum, and median for Received Signal Strength Indicator (RSSI), CPU usage (user and system), battery information (current and voltage) and parsed energy cost. The RSSI values are within the range described in [8] from very low signal strength (lower than -85 dBm and -95 dBm for Wi-Fi and 3G, respectively) to very high signal strength (higher than -55 dBm and -65 dBm for Wi-Fi and 3G, respectively). Battery information (current and voltage values) is also consistent with the results presented in [5], where the 3G interface drains more energy than the Wi-Fi interface, on average. However, when considering the energy cost per transferred byte, the collected data shows that it is possible for the 3G interface to be more energy-efficient under conditions where the Wi-Fi network has a very low signal strength. The data also shows us that the energy cost for the Wi-Fi interface has a higher variation.

Considering the Wi-Fi subset, we apply the six regressions models previously mentioned. To find the best predictive model for the Wi-Fi interface network, a three-fold cross-validation is executed for each regression model. Table IV shows the evaluation of the regression models for the Wi-Fi subset. The results show that Random Forest and K-NN approaches have better accuracy than the other ML techniques.

To refine the choice of the best regressor for the Wi-Fi network, we compare the order of magnitude of the expected and model responses. Table V illustrates the difference in order of magnitude for Wi-Fi and 3G regressors. For Wi-Fi, the Random Forest estimation have the same magnitude order of the expected response on 82.4% of the cases, a value 1.5% higher than the K-NN estimation. When analyzing situations where the models estimations have a lower magnitude order than the expected response, the Random Forest model is better, with 8.8% against 10.3% for the K-NN model. With this in mind, we define Random Forest as the best regressor to estimate C_b for the Wi-Fi network interface among the investigated options.

Let us now analyze the 3G network interface, where the

TABLE V. DIFFERENCE IN ORDER OF MAGNITUDE FOR WI-FI AND 3G REGRESSORS.

Regressor	Wi-Fi Magnitude order (%)			3G Magnitude order (%)		
	Equal	Higher	Lower	Equal	Higher	Lower
Random Forest	82.4%	8.8%	8.8%	94.6%	0%	5.4%
K-NN	80.9%	8.8%	10.3%	93.3%	0%	6.7%
MLP	–	–	–	98.7%	0%	1.3%

same regression models apply to the 3G subset. Table IV also shows the performance metrics of the regression models for the 3G subset. It can be seen from the results that Random Forest, K-NN, and MLP have better accuracy than the remaining of the investigated ML algorithms. Similar to the Wi-Fi interface, an investigation about the magnitude order of the expected and real responses is executed. From Table V, we can see that the MLP is the best option among the regression models to estimate C_b for 3G network interface.

Defined the best regression model for each network interface individually (1 for 3G and 1 for Wi-Fi), we simulate the behavior of the proposed dynamic selection mechanism using the second dataset defined in Subsection II-B, which is equivalent to a 15-minutes long download. This simulation is performed to compare the energy consumptions of our proposal and the Android native selection mechanism. We should remember that the Android native mechanism always selects the Wi-Fi network interface when it is available. Another relevant keypoint for comparison is that the energy consumed on network interface switching is not considered.

Figure 4 shows the estimated energy cost per transferred byte for Wi-Fi and 3G network interfaces for a 12-minute long segment of the dataset. The whole dataset is not included on the graph to make the lines distinguishable. Note that lower energy cost means higher energy saving. Also from Figure 4, it is possible to see time instants where the 3G energy cost is lower than the Wi-Fi one, implying that the 3G network interface is more energy-efficient and, consequently, its use can extend the battery life. The results show that the proposed mechanism chooses the 3G interface for about 26.7% of the total time.

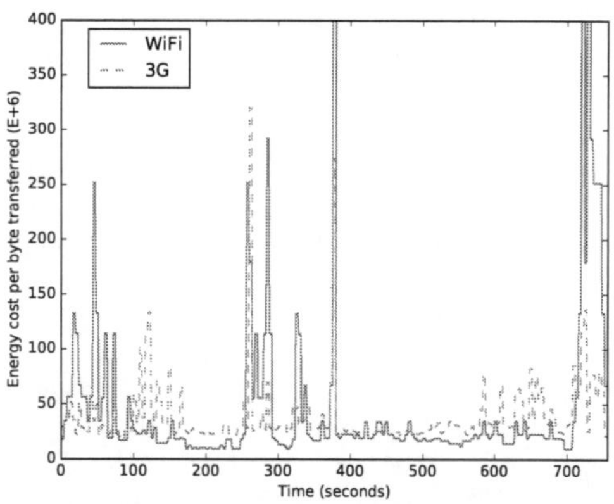

Figure 4. Energy cost per transferred byte for each network interface for a 12-minute long segment of a download process.

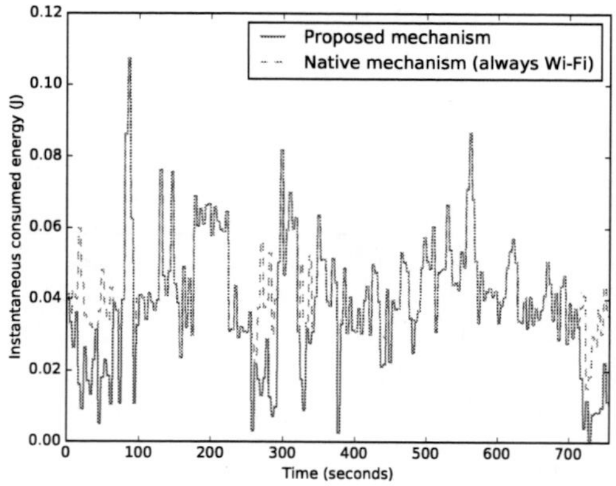

Figure 5. Comparison of the consumed instantaneous energy for both mechanisms for a 12-minute long segment of a download process.

To estimate the energy saving associated with the use of the proposed mechanism, we assume that the number of transferred bytes is constant, independent of which network interface is connected. The estimation of the consumed energy is obtained from (3). Figure 5 represents the comparison of the instantaneous energy consumption using the proposed mechanism and the Android native mechanism for the simulation dataset. We can see that, in certain moments of time, the proposed mechanism selects the 3G network interface, resulting in energy saving. Considering only these moments, the average energy saving is around 48%.

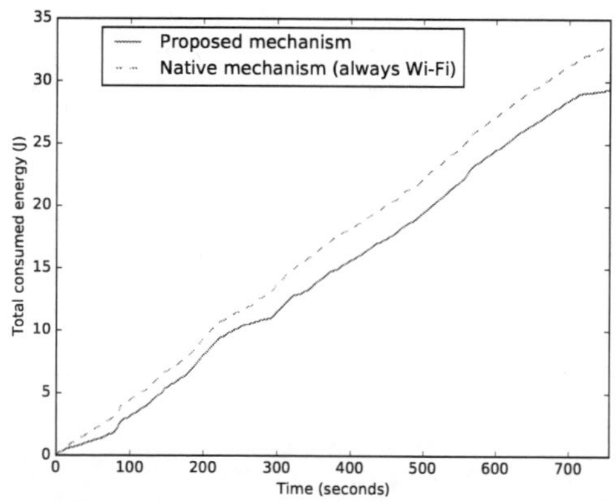

Figure 6. Comparison of the total consumed energy for both mechanisms for a 12-minute long segment of a download process.

Finally, we manage to analyze the total energy saving for the proposed mechanism. Figure 6 represents the total consumed energy by using the proposed and the Android native mechanisms. The estimated data for both mechanisms shows that our proposal generates an energy saving of approximately 11.2% on the scenario of variable network conditions. In addition, we believe that it is possible to reach even higher values of energy saving in more realistic scenarios, such as, for example, when the smartphone is placed in a poor Wi-Fi signal environment.

IV. Conclusion and Future Work

In this work, we proposed a dynamic wireless network interface-selection mechanism focused on minimizing the energy consumption of the mobile device, allowing an increase in battery life. For this, machine learning regression-based algorithms were used to predict the energy cost per transmitted byte for Wi-Fi and 3G network interfaces using field collected data. Numerical results showed that Random Forest and Multi-Layer Perceptron were the best regressors to estimate the energy cost per transferred byte for Wi-Fi and 3G network interfaces, respectively, among the investigated algorithms. On an 15-minutes long download simulation, our proposal presented around 48% of energy saving in situations where 3G had lower energy cost than Wi-Fi. For the whole simulation, the total energy saving was roughly 11.2%. Work is in progress to investigate the behavior of the proposed mechanism for other network scenarios, for example, in a streaming environment. In addition, we aim to find better models to estimate the energy cost for the network interfaces and to test a real implementation of the proposed method to validate the results obtained in this work.

Acknowledgment

This work was supported by the research cooperation project between Motorola Mobility (a Lenovo Company) and CIn-UFPE.

References

[1] Ericsson (2016), Ericsson Mobility Report. Available at https://www.ericsson.com/res/docs/2016/ericsson-mobility-report-2016.pdf [Access: 15 Jan 2017]

[2] R. Want, "When cell phones become computers," *IEEE Pervasive Comput.*, vol. 8, n. 2, pp. 2–5, 2009.

[3] E. Peltonen, E. Lagerspetz, P. Nurmi and S. Tarkoma, "Where has my battery gone?: A novel crowdsourced solution for characterizing energy consumption," *IEEE Pervasive Comput.*, vol. 15, n. 1, pp. 6–9, 2016.

[4] J. Kellokoski, J. Koskinen and T. Hamalainen, "Power consumption analysis of the always-best-connected user equipment," In Proc. of the *5th Int. Conf. on New Tech., Mobility and Security (NTMS)*, Istanbul, pp. 1–5, 2012.

[5] N. Ding et. al., "Characterizing and modeling the impact of wireless signal strength on smartphone battery drain," *ACM SIGMETRICS Perf. Eval. Rev.*, vol.41, n.1, pp. 29–40, 2013.

[6] 3GPP, "Feasibility study on 3GPP system to wireless local area network (WLAN) interworking," 3GPP, 2012.

[7] N. Abbas, S. Taleb, H. Hajj and Z. Dawy, "A learning-based approach for network selection in WLAN/3G heterogeneous network," In Proc. of the *3rd Int. Conf. on Commun. and Inform. Tech (ICCIT)*, Beirut, pp. 309–313, 2013.

[8] N. Abbas and J. J. Saade, "A fuzzy logic based approach for network selection in WLAN/3G heterogeneous network," In Proc. of the *2015 12th Annual IEEE Consumer Commun. and Networking Conf. (CCNC)*, Las Vegas - NV, pp. 631–636, 2015.

[9] Y. Lai, K. K. Chait and Y. Chen, "A utility-based intelligent network selection for 3G and WLAN heterogeneous networks," In Proc. of the *IET Int. Conf. on Wireless Commun. and Appl. (ICWCA 2012)*, Kuala Lumpur, pp. 1–6, 2012.

[10] B. Kim, Y. Cho and J. Hong, "AWNIS: Energy-efficient adaptive wireless network interface selection for industrial mobile devices," *IEEE Trans. Ind. Informat.*, vol. 10, n. 1, pp. 714–729, 2014.

[11] A. L. Buczak and E. Guven, "A survey of data mining and machine learning methods for cyber security intrusion detection," *IEEE Commun. Surveys Tuts.*, vol. 18, n. 2, pp. 1153–1176., 2016.

[12] N. Kolay and P. Erdogmus, "The classification of breast cancer with machine learning techniques," In Proc. of the *2016 Electric Electronics, Computer Science, Biomedical Engineerings Meeting (EBBT)*, Istanbul, pp. 1–4., 2016.

[13] M. Kuderer, S. Gulati and W. Burgard, "Learning driving styles for autonomous vehicles from demonstration," In Proc. of the *2015 IEEE Int. Conf. on Robotics and Automation (ICRA)*, Seattle, pp. 2641–2646, 2015.

[14] Motorola Moto G, Available at http://www.gsmarena.com/motorola_moto_g_dual_sim_(2nd_gen)-6648.php [Access: 25 Apr 2017]

[15] M. A. Hoque and S. Tarkoma, "Sudden drop in the battery level?: understanding smartphone state of charge anomaly," In Proc. of the *Workshop on Power-Aware Computing and Systems (HotPower'15)*. ACM, New York, NY, USA, pp. 26–30, 2015.

[16] J. Bornholt, T. Mytkowicz and K. S. McKinley, "The model is not enough: understanding energy consumption in mobile devices," In Proc. of the *2012 IEEE Hot Chips 24 Symp. (HCS)*, Cupertino, CA, pp. 1-3, 2012.

[17] Android API, Available at https://developer.android.com/guide/index.html [Access: 25 Apr 2017]

[18] I. Guyon, J. Weston, S. Barnhill and V. Vapnik, "Gene selection for cancer classification using support vector machines," *Machine Learning*, vol. 46, n. 1-3, pp. 389-422, 2002.

[19] M. Kuhn and K. Johnson, Applied Predictive Modeling. Springer: New York, 2013.

[20] T. Hastie, R. Tibshirani and M. Wainwright, "Statistical Learning with Sparsity: the lasso and generalizations. Chapman & Hall/CRC, 2015.

[21] L. Breiman, "Random Forests," *Machine Learning*, vol. 45, n. 1, pp. 5-32, 2001.

[22] C. Rasmussen and C. Williams, "Gaussian Processes for Machine Learning (Adaptive Computation and Machine Learning)," The MIT Press, 2005.

[23] R. Duda, P. Hart and D. Stork. "Pattern Classification (2nd Edition) Wiley-Interscience, 2000.

[24] A. Smola and B. Schlkopf, "A tutorial on support vector regression," *Statistics and Computing*, vol. 14, n. 3, pp. 199-222, 2004.

[25] F. Pedregosa et. al., "Scikit-learn: Machine Learning in Python," *J Mach Learn Res.*, vol. 12, pp. 2825-2830, 2011.

[26] P. Refaeilzadeh, L. Tang and H. Liu, "Cross-validation," Encyclopedia of Database Systems. Springer: Boston, 2009.

Mitigating Attacks in the Internet of Things with a Self-protecting Architecture

Ruan de A. C. Mello, Admilson de R. L. Ribeiro, Fernando M. de Almeida, Edward D. Moreno
Department of Computing
Federal University Sergipe UFS
São Cristóvão, Brazil
E-mails: ruanmello@gmail.com, admilson@ufs.br, fernando.m.al.91@gmail.com, edwdavid@gmail.com

Abstract—**Internet of Things (IoT) applications run in environments that have resource constraints and are unsecured. Due to the nature of their environment, IoT systems should be able to reason autonomously and take self-protecting decisions. Currently, an adequate architecture to incorporate self-protection in the IoT is not available. Thus, we design a new self-protecting architecture based on the MAPE-K (Monitor, Analyze, Plan, Execute and Knowledge) autonomic control loop that will run at the application layer so that developers can add several security services. In this paper, we address the impact caused by attacks (SinkHole, Selective Forward, Black Hole and Flooding) in relation to power consumption and interference in the operation of the network created from the Routing Protocol for Low Power and Lossy Networks (RPL) routing protocol.**

Keywords–Autonomic Systems; Self-protecting; IoT; MAPE-K loop; AIS.

I. INTRODUCTION

Recently, the integration of embedded systems, wireless networks and the Internet led to a new application type, namely Internet of Things (IoT) applications. A particular case of IoT applications is the participatory sensing application where people that live in communities and are dependent on each other for daily activities exchange information to reach their objectives [1]. Recommendations for a good restaurant, car mechanic, movie, phone plan and so on were and still are some things where community knowledge helps us in determining our actions.

IoT applications will have a great impact on people's life, but currently only a small number of such applications is available to our society. As the things are nodes of a network, individuals can control, locate, and monitor everyday objects remotely. For example, the use of wireless sensor technologies allows monitoring the health of people in real time, enabling brief diagnostics. The vital parameters of individuals such as blood pressure, temperature, and so on, are measured through sensor nodes that stay on the bodies of patients that continue to do their daily activities [2]. Many benefits can be provided by the IoT technologies in the health-care domain.

However, IoT applications run in environments that have resource constraints and are unsecured. The resources constraint of the IoT devices can lead to security breaches. For example, an attacker can try to maintain the IoT devices in operation all the time, with the intention to consume all their battery energy. This attack is a type of Denial of Service (DoS) attack and can have a great impact on the application availability without the possibility of control by users. Therefore, due to that environment, the security issue must be treated autonomously. That is, the self-protection property must be incorporated in the IoT systems [3].

However, the majority of security mechanisms in IoT is composed of protocols and algorithms that run at the physical layer or link layer of the protocol stack of the software system [4]. These mechanisms are adequate to protect against the problems relating to the confidentiality and the integrity, but in some cases they fail on considering the availability.

Considering the availability of applications, self-protection is the essential property that allows network nodes to communicate and react to attacks of hackers according to security policies defined by users [5]. Thus, IoT systems should be able to reason autonomously and make self-protecting decisions.

Therefore, in this context, we propose a self-protecting architecture for the Internet of Things based on the MAPE-K control loop [5] and the danger theory of the Artificial Intelligent System (AIS) [6]. To show the use of the architecture, we implement the execution phase describing the main attacks in the IoT and their impacts in relation to power consumption and interference in the operation of the network.

The remainder of this paper is organized into nine more sections. Section II presents the limitations of related works and highlights our contribution. Section III presents the autonomic loop MAPE-K. Section IV presents the Routing Protocol for Low Power and Lossy Networks. Section V gives a brief overview of the main attacks that occur in the IoT environment. Section VI outlines our architecture, considering the MAPE-K control loop and its phases are described. Section VII discusses how we implement the execution phase of our architecture. Section VIII presents the results obtained so far. Section IX concludes the paper and presents future works.

II. RELATED WORK

In the literature, there are several papers about computing security based on the AISs and autonomic computing. Kephart et al. [6] and White et al. [7] designed the first AISs in response to the first virus epidemics, when it was found out that the spreading of cure had to be faster that the contamination by viruses. After, SweetBair [8] used a more sophisticated technique to capture suspecting traffic and generate signatures of worms. As a variant of this pattern, Swimmer [9] and also Rawat and Saxena [10] presented an approach based on danger theory for attack detection in autonomic networks.

SVELTE [11], as the authors claim, is the first Intrusion Detector System (IDS) for the IoT. The work presented has a huge contribution to design an IDS with the characteristics of a network for IoT, considering the technologies used in the communications stack, such as IPv6 over Low power Wireless Personal Area Networks (6LoWPAN) and RPL routing protocol. However, its approach does not have autonomic characteristics for self protect the network from further attacks, only the determined attack on the network project level. Like the SVELT, the CAD [12] not only detects the attack, but also tries to mitigate the damage caused by the attacker. The CAD is directed to the wireless mesh network (WMN) and can differentiate between losses occurring in the normal events of a legitimate attack of the type Selective Forward.

The main limitation is that they are not well suited for the IoT environment. They only present some particular solutions that address a set of specific problems different of the IoT environment. Besides, they do not consider the possibility of development of new self-protecting services. Therefore, programmers are unable to decide which policies are more appropriate for their applications, considering still that the resolved policies of low-level protocols sometimes are not the most appropriate for all applications in the IoT.

Therefore, our solution advances previous solutions providing a new self-protecting architecture for the IoT and also the possibility to extend such architecture with new security services.

III. MAPE-K AUTONOMIC CONTROL LOOP

In March 2001, Paul Horn presented for the first time the MAPE-K Autonomic Control Loop at an IBM event. The MAPE-K Loop was presented as a reference model. Composed of five modules that can be seen in Figure 1, the MAPEK-K Loop is intended to distribute the tasks of each element of the autonomic computing [13]. The modules that build the MAPE-K Loop are, respectively, knowledge, monitoring, analysis, planning, and execution.

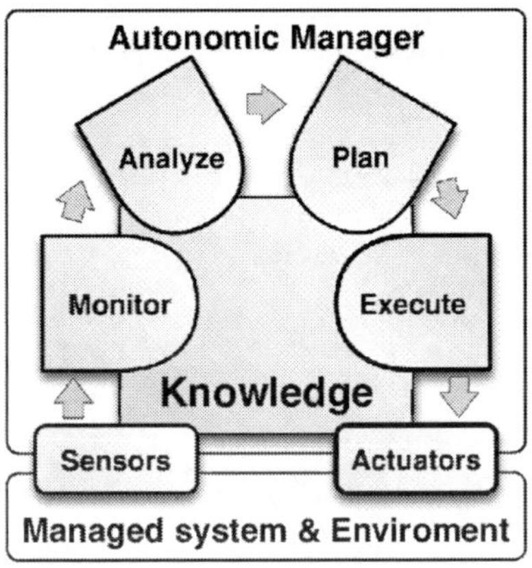

Figure 1. Mape-K Autonomic Control Loop [14].

- The Knowledge module is in charge of keeping relevant data in the memory to accelerate decision making.
- The Monitoring module uses sensors to collect data from the managed element, which could be a software or hardware resource, or an autonomic manager itself.
- The Analysis module provides mechanisms to interpret the collected data from the monitoring phase and predict future situations.
- The Planning module builds the necessary actions to achieve the goals.
- The Execution module uses effects to make changes on managed elements.

IV. ROUTING PROTOCOL FOR LOW POWER AND LOSSY NETWORKS

RPL is an IPv6 routing protocol for Low power and Lossy Networks (LLNs) that specifies how to build a Destination Oriented Directed Acyclic Graph (DODAG) using an objective function and a set of metrics and constraints to compute the best path [15].

The RPL differs from other routing protocols that operate in less-constrained environments. In LLNs, especially when the network is made of devices that must save energy, it is imperative to limit the control plane traffic in the network.

The graph built by RPL is a logical routing topology built over a physical network to meet a specific criteria and the network administrator may decide to have multiple routing topologies (graphs) active at the same time used to carry traffic with different set of requirements [15].

V. ATTACKS IN INTERNET OF THINGS

Most of threats in IoT environment attack the limited power of the sensors. The limited power of these devices exposes the network to many threats [16]. In this section, we will discuss some of the latest and more common attacks on the environment of the IoT and wireless sensor networks [17].

1) Selective forward: In a Selective Forward attack, the attacker node receives the transmission packets, but refuses to transmit some of them and drops those that it refused to transmit. The attacker must choose which packets to discard according to some standard such as size, destination or origin [12]. In this case, only the packets released by the attacker node can be freely transmitted.

2) Black Hole: In a Black Hole attack, the attacker node receives the transmission packets and drops all packets received, regardless of type, size, origin or destination [12].

3) Sinkhole: In a Sinkhole attack, the attacker tries to attract all the traffic from neighboring nodes [18]. So, practically, the attacker node listens to all data transmitted from neighboring nodes. Only this attack does not cause too much damage in the network, but together with another type of attack (Selective Forward or Black Hole), can become very powerful.

4) Flooding: In a Flooding attack, the attacker explores the vulnerabilities related to the depletion of the memory and the energy. One manner to take advantage of this vulnerability is when an opponent sends too many requests trying to connect to the victim, every request makes the victim allocate the resources in an attempt to maintain the connection [19]. Thus, to prevent the total resource depletion is necessary to limit the number of connections. However, this solution also prevents valid nodes to create a connection with the victim, causing problems such as queuing [19].

5) Hello Flood: In a HelloFlood attack, the attacker uses a device with a powerful signal to regularly send some messages; that way, the network is left in a state of confusion [17]. In order to find ad-hoc networks, many protocols use Hello Messages for discovering neighbor nodes and automatically create a network. With the Hello Flood attack, an attacker can use a device with high transmission power to convince every other node in the network that the attacker is its neighbor, but these nodes are far away from the attacker. In this case, the power consumption of sensors is significantly increased, because of protocols that depend on exchange information between neighbor nodes for topology maintenance or flow control [17].

Previously, we saw some of the most common attacks on IoT networks and, next, we analyzed the possible strategies to end or to mitigate the damage caused by them.

To stop the damages caused by attacks on a network, first it is necessary to detect these attacks, using an IDS. An IDS analyzes network activity and attempts to detect any unusual behavior that may affect the integrity of the network. Based on information provided by IDS, strategies are created to cope with the attacks. For example:

- To mitigate Sinkhole - If the geographical locations of the nodes of RPL DODAG are known, the effect of Sinkhole attacks can be mitigated by the use of flow control, making sure, that the messages are traveling to the correct destination. The RPL protocol also supports multiple instances DODAG offering alternative routes to the root DODAG [20].
- To mitigate Hello Flood - A simple solution to this attack, it is perform a bidirectional check for each message "HELLO" [21]. If there is no recognition, the path is assumed to be bad and a different route is chosen. If geographical locations of the nodes of RPL DODAG are known, all packets received from a node that is far beyond of the common network node transmission capacity can be dropped.
- To mitigate Selective Forward - An effective countermeasure against Selective Forward attacks is to ensure that the attacker cannot distinguish the different type of packets, forcing the attacker to send all or none packets [22].

Raza et al. [11] indicated that the most efficient and fastest way to stop the damage of routing attacks is to isolate the malicious node. Some forms to ignore the attacker node were studied. These forms are:

- The Black List: After identifying the nodes and finding the attackers, a list will be created and all the malicious nodes will be added in order to exclude them from the possible routes of traffic data. To ignore the attacker, a verification will be done against the Black List excluding all nodes found of the typical RPL DODAG that have a root and multiple nodes.
- The Gray List: After identifying the nodes and finding the attacker, a list will be created. The suspicious attacker node will be added to this list with the intention of excluding it from the possible routes of traffic data, for a predetermined time. After the end of the predetermined time the suspicious attacker node is deleted from the list. In this way, if there is any doubt about the identity of the attacker node, the node may re-join the network. To ignore the suspicious attacker nodes, when creating the routing, a verification will be done against the Gray List excluding all nodes found of the typical RPL DODAG that have a root and multiple nodes.
- The White List: As in the example of the Black List, a list will be created after identifying the nodes and finding the attacker node. But, this time, will be add into the White List only the valid nodes and all malicious nodes will be excluded. This way will have a verification stating which nodes are valid and must belong to a typical RPL DODAG with a root and several nodes.

VI. SELF-PROTECTION ARCHITECTURE

In Figure 2, we can see the self-protecting architecture for IoT proposed in this research. It consists of five modules (Monitoring, Analysis, Planning, Executing and Knowledge) and it is based on the MAPE-K autonomic control loop [13].

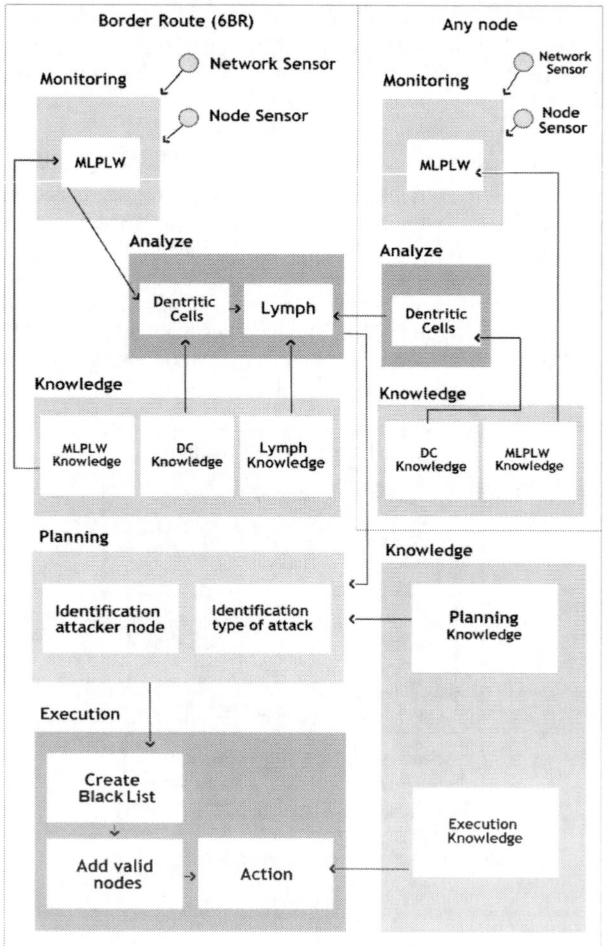

Figure 2. The Self-Protecting Architecture.

The monitoring and analysis modules are responsible, respectively, for collecting through the sensors, some information of the network that will be analyzed to measure the possibility of being associated with an attack. These two modules are present in the network nodes and in the border router (6BR).

The planning and execution modules will be responsible, respectively, for identifying the attacker, the type of attack and to mitigate the damage in the network. The information listed as relevant data for analysis, planning and execution is: type of transport protocol, type of application protocol, time of communication, number of messages sent, number of messages effectively sent and number of messages received.

The components of knowledge phase will be responsible for keeping all the knowledge acquired by the system. Knowledge about the planning and execution modules will be at 6BR. The information kept by the Knowledge Module will be used to facilitate and accelerate the discovery of the type of attack, the attacker node and the action to be taken to protect the network.

The complete design of this architecture can be found in Mello et al. [23]. The monitoring and analysis phases were implemented in [24]. Now, we describe how we implement the execution phase.

VII. Execution Phase

The component responsible for the execution phase should mitigate or stop the damage caused by the attacks occurred on the network. The type of attack and the identification of the attacker node will be the information that will influence in the choice of the predetermined action to mitigate or stop the damage in the network. These two important pieces of information will be provided by the Planning Phase. The reason to find out the attacker node is, trying to isolate as quickly as possible and create a new route, thus, avoiding further damage to the network. The type of attack will be among one of the two groups mentioned in Figure 3. According to the group selected there will be a specific action to solve the problem, because each type of attack causes different types of damage on the network.

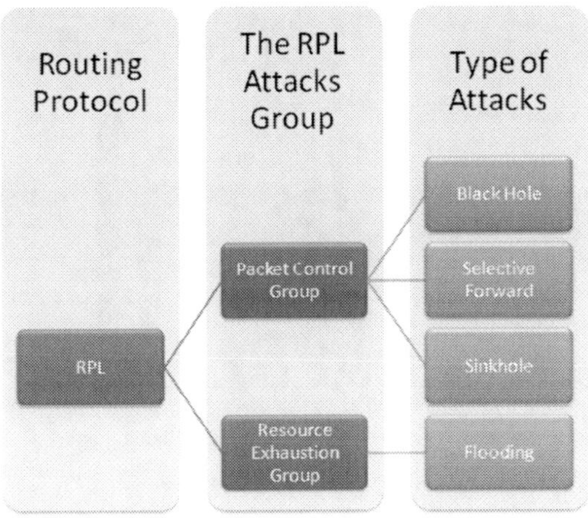

Figure 3. Taxonomy of RPL attacks

The first action to be taken by the components of the execution module, after the attack is detected, it is to ignore the malicious node. To perform this action it is important to identify the network nodes as legitimate or malicious. Raza et al. [11] say that it is necessary to be careful with the way of identifying nodes. If possible, it should be avoided the identification by IP address or MAC address, because they can be easily falsified. After making the identification of the nodes, some ways to ignore the attacker node were studied. Three ways to isolate the malicious node were analyzed before choosing the most convenient. The three ways are: Black List, Gray List and White List.

The way chosen was the Black List, because the maintenance of this list is simple. This way, all valid nodes will recalculate their rank in the RPL protocol (DODAG). To recalculate the rank of all valid nodes, it will be necessary to ignore the DODAG Information Object (DIO) of all nodes with higher rank than theirs and the DODAG Information Solicitation (DIS) and DIO of nodes that are present in the Black List. Thus, for a stranger node to join the network, it should be reported as safe and not be present in the Black List.

VIII. Results

It was possible to simulate the Flooding and Black Hole attacks (with SinkHole and Selective Forward variants). The simulations with and without the attacking node were performed in the Cooja, a simulator of the ContikiOS, following a DODAG topology in which there is a certain number of nodes and one of them will be the root.

We defined the number of nodes in the simulation and all used the same platform (Skymote). The routing protocol used was the RPL and the addressing protocol used was the IPV6.

It should also be noted that the simulation time should be long enough for the data collection to begin. In our simulation, we used a virtual time of 2 minutes. In the simulations, we used 11 nodes with a transmission rate of 50 meters and interference range of 100 meters. The network simulation was generated from the Cooja Simulator and can be seen in Figure 4.

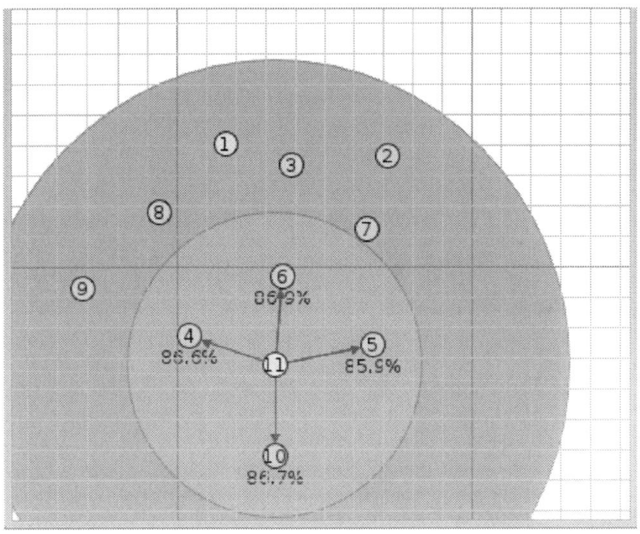

Figure 4. Network Simulation.

After running the simulation for 2 minutes (virtual), the Directed Acyclic Graph (DAGs) was generated by the Cooja Simulator looks as shown in Figure 5. The node with ID 1 is the root and the node with ID 11 seen in Figure 4 and Figure 5, at first, is a common valid node, thus enabling the simulation of the network without the presence of attacks. But to simulate the presence of the attacks on the network the node with ID 11 has been modified to act as the malicious node.

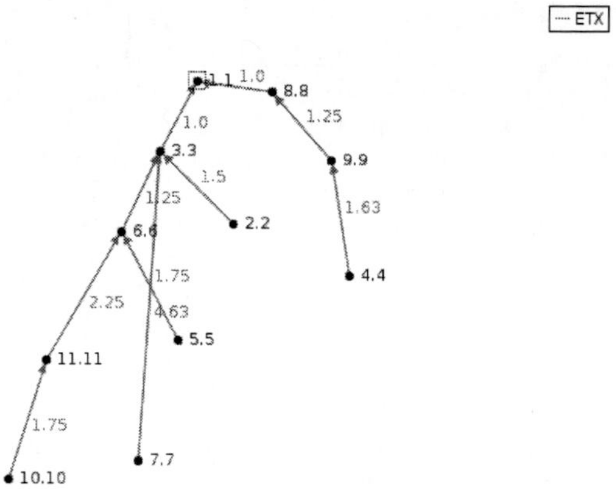

Figure 5. The Directed Acyclic Graph of the simulated network.

A. The simulation without attack

In this simulation, we do not have attacks and all nodes are valid. As can be easily seen in Figure 6, all nodes have the consumed power of less than 10%.

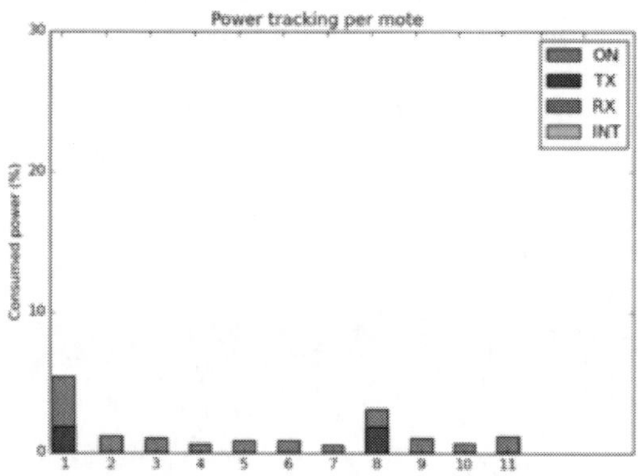

Figure 6. The Consumed Power without attack.

B. The simulation of the Black Hole attack

In this simulation the malicious node dropped all the collected data application messages instead of forwarding them. When using the Selective Forward variant in the simulation, only the received data plane messages of some nodes with IP specified by the attacker node were dropped. This way, it was easily observed a malfunction in the network in relation to packets delivery and packet integrity.

The Black Hole attack can also be enhanced if combined with a sinkhole attack. When simulating the Black Hole with the sinkhole variant, the DAG was changed. Some valid nodes (ID 4, 5 and 10) in the neighborhood of the malicious node (ID 11) have now set it as their parent. This way, the attack has become even more efficient, because it is listening and dropping a larger number of the received messages. The DAG changed can be seen in Figure 7 generated from the Cooja Simulator.

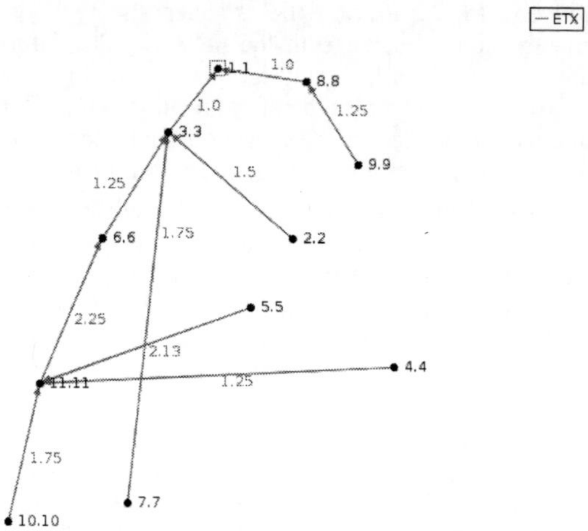

Figure 7. The DAG of the simulated network with Sinkhole attack.

C. The simulation of the Flooding attack

In this simulation the malicious node (Node with ID 11) impacts nodes with IDs 4, 5, 6 and 10 (Figure 4). It is very easy to see in Figure 8 that these nodes are particularly affected by the attack in terms of ON and RX times and the malicious node consumed a lot power with TX. So these nodes spend a lot of energy and memory, to read the requests sent by the malicious node. The power consumed by the attacker node and by the nodes affected by the attack is well over 10% but, the power consumed by other nodes remains below 10%.

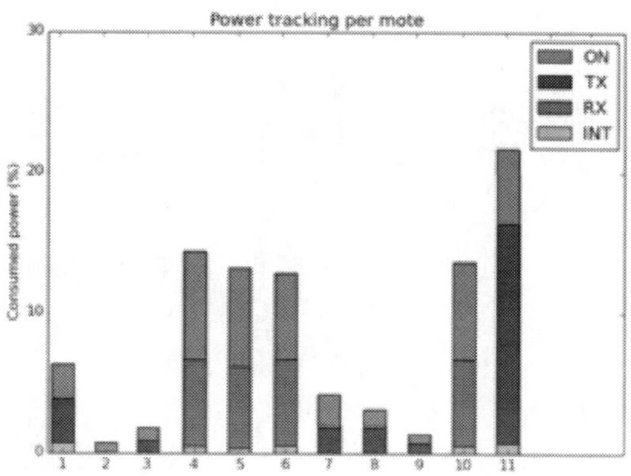

Figure 8. The Consumed Power with Flooding attack.

D. The simulation with our Architecture to isolate the attacker node

During the execution phase, our architecture is intended to isolate the attacker node so that it does not cause further damage to the network. When simulating the isolation of the attacker node, the DAG was changed and another node, besides the malicious node (ID 11) was also isolated.

The other node also isolated can be seen in Figure 9. This other node was the with ID 10. This occurred because the node with ID 10 was very far from the others.

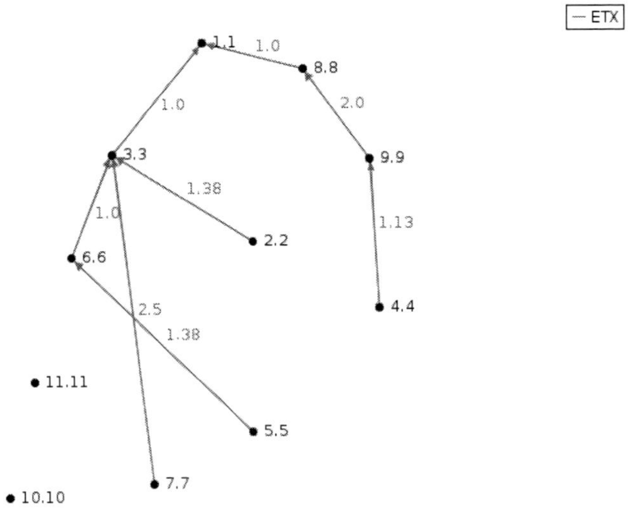

Figure 9. The DAG of the simulated network.

IX. CONCLUSION

In this paper, we have used the MAPE-K control loop to design a new self-protecting architecture for the IoT. With this architecture, it will be possible to incorporate security facilities in the IoT systems releasing the programmer to treat only the functional requirements. Besides, the user can extend the architecture developing new security services to handle specific attacks.

The research will help provide a self-protection mechanism for IoT networks, facilitate the detection and the classification of possible attacks on smart devices, mitigate the damage of the attacks suffered ensuring better performance and increasing the confidence of users when using devices connected to IoT network.

The Self-Protecting architecture deals with five different attacks (Sinkhole, Selective forward, Black Hole, Flooding and Hello Flood) bearing in mind the memory consumption and energy due to a lack of resource of the available devices in the IoT environment.

The performance of the system should be evaluated to verify if the Self-Protecting architecture has better results than related work. New attacks and new technologies will emerge, and then the work presented here may be extended to address those.

ACKNOWLEDGMENT

This work was supported by CAPES and FAPITEC/SE

REFERENCES

[1] D. INFSO, "Internet of things in 2020: Roadmap for the future," INFSO D, vol. 4, 2008.

[2] D. Niyato, E. Hossain, and S. Camorlinga, "Remote patient monitoring service using heterogeneous wireless access networks: architecture and optimization," IEEE Journal on Selected Areas in Communications, vol. 27, no. 4, 2009.

[3] O. Vermesan, P. Friess, and A. Furness, "The internet of things 2012: New horizons," IERC 3rd edition of cluster book, 2012.

[4] J.-P. Vasseur and A. Dunkels, Interconnecting smart objects with ip: The next internet. Morgan Kaufmann, 2010.

[5] M. R. Nami and M. Sharifi, "Autonomic computing: a new approach," in Modelling & Simulation, 2007. AMS'07. First Asia International Conference on. IEEE, 2007, pp. 352–357.

[6] J. Kephart, G. Sorkin, M. Swimmer, and S. White, "Blueprint for a computer immune system," in Artificial immune systems and their applications. Springer, 1999, pp. 242–261.

[7] S. R. White, M. Swimmer, E. J. Pring, W. C. Arnold, D. M. Chess, and J. F. Morar, "Anatomy of a commercial-grade immune system," IBM Research White Paper, 1999.

[8] G. Portokalidis and H. Bos, "Sweetbait: Zero-hour worm detection and containment using low-and high-interaction honeypots," Computer Networks, vol. 51, no. 5, 2007, pp. 1256–1274.

[9] M. Swimmer, "Using the danger model of immune systems for distributed defense in modern data networks," Computer Networks, vol. 51, no. 5, 2007, pp. 1315–1333.

[10] S. Rawat and A. Saxena, "Danger theory based syn flood attack detection in autonomic network," in Proceedings of the 2nd international conference on Security of information and networks. ACM, 2009, pp. 213–218.

[11] S. Raza, L. Wallgren, and T. Voigt, "Svelte: Real-time intrusion detection in the internet of things," Ad hoc networks, vol. 11, November 2013, pp. 2661–2674.

[12] D. M. Shila, Y. Cheng, and T. Anjali, "Mitigating selective forwarding attacks with a channel-aware approach in wmns," Wireless Communications, IEEE Transactions on, vol. 9, May 2010, pp. 1661–1675, doi:10.1109/TWC.2010.05.090700.

[13] J. O. Kephart and D. M. Chess, "The vision of autonomic computing," Computer, vol. 36, January 2003, pp. 41–50, doi:10.1109/MC.2003.1160055.

[14] D. Weyns, S. Malek, and J. Andersson, "Forms: a formal reference model for self-adaptation," in Proceedings of the 7th international conference on Autonomic computing. ACM, June 2010, pp. 205–214, doi:10.1145/1809049.1809078.

[15] T. Winter, "Rpl: Ipv6 routing protocol for low-power and lossy networks," 2012.

[16] L. Atzori, A. Iera, and G. Morabito, "The internet of things: A survey," Computer networks, vol. 54, October 2010, pp. 2787–2805, doi:10.1016/j.comnet.2010.05.010.

[17] D. Martins and H. Guyennet, "Wireless sensor network attacks and security mechanisms: A short survey," in Network-Based Information Systems (NBiS), 2010 13th International Conference on. IEEE, November 2010, pp. 313–320, doi:10.1109/NBiS.2010.11.

[18] P. Goyal, S. Batra, and A. Singh, "A literature review of security attack in mobile ad-hoc networks," International Journal of Computer Applications, vol. 9, November 2010, pp. 11–15.

[19] A. D. Wood and J. A. Stankovic, "Denial of service in sensor networks," Computer, vol. 35, December 2002, pp. 54–62, doi:10.1109/MC.2002.1039518.

[20] T. Heer, O. Garcia-Morchon, R. Hummen, S. L. Keoh, S. S. Kumar, and K. Wehrle, "Security challenges in the ip-based internet of things," Wireless Personal Communications, vol. 61, September 2011, pp. 527–542, doi:10.1007/s11277-011-0385-5.

[21] C. Karlof and D. Wagner, "Secure routing in wireless sensor networks: Attacks and countermeasures," Ad hoc networks, vol. 1, September 2003, pp. 293–315.

[22] L. Wallgren, S. Raza, and T. Voigt, "Routing attacks and countermeasures in the rpl-based internet of things," International Journal of Distributed Sensor Networks, vol. 2013, June 2013.

[23] R. de AC Mello, A. de RL Ribeiro, F. M. de Almeida, and E. D. Moreno, "An architecture for self-protection in internet of things," ICWMC 2016, 2016, p. 51.

[24] F. M. de Almeida, A. d. R. L. Ribeiro, and E. D. Moreno, "An architecture for self-healing in internet of things," UBICOMM 2015, 2015, p. 89.

Dynamic Lightpath Establishment Method Based on Maximum Spectrum Utilization for Elastic Optical Path Networks

Yuki Sato,
Tomotaka Kimura and Masahiro Muraguchi
Faculty of Engineering
Tokyo University of Science
Tokyo, Japan 125–8585
Email: {kimura,murag}@ee.kagu.tus.ac.jp

Kouji Hirata
Faculty of Engineering
Kansai University
Osaka, Japan 564–8680
Email: hirata@kansai-u.ac.jp

***Abstract*—In this paper, we propose a dynamic lightpath establish method for elastic optical path networks (EONs). EONs provide flexible frequency slot allocation and signal modulation. In EONs, a routing, modulation level, and spectrum allocation (RMLSA) problem is one of the most important technical issues. If routes, modulation formats, and frequency slots are appropriately determined for lightpaths, the spectrum efficiency is enhanced and the blocking probability of connection requests are reduced. To solve the RMLSA problem quickly and effectively, our proposed method focuses on the maximum spectrum utilization. The proposed method aims at smoothing the spectrum utilization of each link and alleviating the fragmentation of frequency slots by selecting routes, modulation formats, and frequency slots for new connections based on the maximum spectrum utilization. Through simulation experiments, we show that the proposed method effectively reduces the blocking probability of connection requests under the dynamic situations where connection requests dynamically are generated and released.**

Keywords–Dynamic Lightpath Establishment; Spectrum Allocation Method; Elastic Optical Path Networks.

I. INTRODUCTION

Recently, the traffic demands on the Internet have increased rapidly. To cope with this increase in traffic demands, optical path networks using wavelength division multiplexing (WDM) [1] have been implemented. In optical path networks, there is no bottleneck in the communication paths because optical signals are transmitted without optical-electrical-optical (OEO) conversion. Moreover, using WDM, many signals of different wavelengths are transmitted through a signal fiber in parallel. To realize optical path networks, a variety of technologies, such as device development, routing methods, and wavelength assignment methods have been studied [1].

Currently, optical path networks are implemented with *frequency grid* WDM systems that have discrete wavelength channels with bandwidth of 50 or 100 GHz. When a connection request arrives, the corresponding lightpath is established by allocating a wavelength channel to a path of the lightpath. The requested data is transmitted over the lightpath. In the optical path networks, even if the amount of bandwidth of a requested connection is small, a wavelength channel is allocated to the connection. because of the coarse spectrum allocation granularity. This coarse spectrum allocation causes low spectrum efficiency. To improve the spectrum efficiency, the elastic optical path networks (EONs) have been actively studied [2][3].

EONs provide flexible frequency spectrum allocation and signal modulation. The frequency spectrum is divided into narrow-band frequency grids called *frequency slots* (12.25 GHz or less) as shown in Figure 1. Furthermore, flexible modulation formats (e.g., BPSK, QPSK, and QAM) are used [4][5], unlike the traditional optical path networks that only use intensity modulation with a low transmission rate. Because of these flexible attributes, EONs are a promising technology for enhancing the use efficiency of the frequency spectrum.

We should consider a routing, modulation level, and spectrum allocation (RMLSA) problem to efficiently utilize the resources of EONs. A lightpath is established by an RMLSA algorithm that selects a route, a modulation format, and frequency slots for the lightpath. In general, RMLSA is categorized as static RMLSA [5][6][7] and dynamic RMLSA [8][9][10][11]. In static RMLSA, a traffic matrix that indicates the traffic volume between each sender and receiver pair is known in advance. Accordingly, routes, modulation formats, and frequency slots of lightpaths are determined by solving optimization problems or applying heuristic algorithms. On the other hand, in dynamic RMLSA, a traffic matrix is not available. Connection requests are stochastically generated and the lightpaths are dynamically established accordingly. The performance metric in EONs using dynamic RMLSA is typically the blocking probability of connection requests. When there are no spectrum resources along a requested connection, the connection request is blocked. This paper deals with dynamic RMLSA for designing EONs with low blocking probability.

In EONs, it is preferred that the frequency slots of each link is evenly used. If the frequency slots of a certain link is intensively used, the link becomes a bottleneck link. In this case, lightpaths cannot be established further through the link. Furthermore, the fragmentation of frequency slots degrades the performance of EONs because connection requests using many frequency slots are often blocked. To overcome this difficulty, in this paper, we propose an RMLSA method that focuses on the maximum spectrum utilization. The proposed method selects routes, modulation formats, and frequency slots for new connections based on the maximum spectrum utilization. By doing so, the proposed method aims at smoothing the spectrum utilization of each link and alleviating the fragmentation of frequency slots. The proposed method is expected to reduce the blocking probability of connection requests.

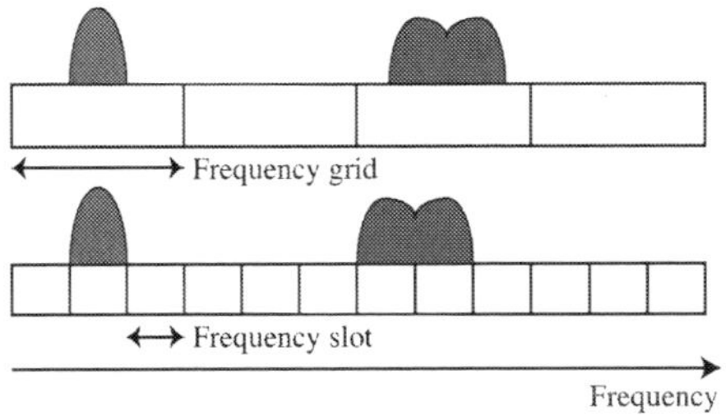

Figure 1. Frequency grids and slots.

The rest of this paper is organized as follows. In Section II, we explain EONs. Section III describes the proposed method. In Section IV, the performance of the proposed method is discussed with the results of the simulation experiments. Finally, we conclude this paper in Section V.

II. RMLSA IN ELASTIC OPTICAL PATH NETWORKS

Table I summarizes the symbols used in this paper. Graph $G = (V, E)$ represents an elastic optical network consisting of the set $\mathcal{V}$ of switching nodes and the set $\mathcal{E}$ of fiber links. Each link $e \in \mathcal{E}$ has N_{FS} frequency slots, which are labeled 1 to N_{FS} in ascending order from low frequency side, as shown in Figure 2. Mask $\boldsymbol{b}_e$ denotes the N_{FS}-bit bit-mask, and the ith element $\boldsymbol{b}_e[i]$ represents the utilization of the ith frequency slot on the link e. If $\boldsymbol{b}_e[i] = 1$, the ith frequency slot is currently used; otherwise, it is available for a new connection. As for the link A–B in the Figure 2, $\boldsymbol{b}_e = [0011111111100]$ immediately after the new connection uses the frequency slots. Guard bands are allocated to both ends of the frequency slots, and thus each connection needs the frequency slots used by guard bands.

Whenever a connection request arrives, the lightpath is established by an RMLSA method. In general, an RMLSA problem is divided to an RML problem and an SA problem. In the RML problem, a route (path) of the new connection is determined by a routing algorithm. An example of a routing algorithm is the K-shortest path algorithm [12], in which the first K shortest paths are maintained for each source-destination pair and the paths are selected in the order of the length. The modulation format of the connection is determined according to the transmission distance along the path selected by the routing algorithm. When the transmission distance is short, a multivalue modulation format (e.g., 8QAM or 16QAM) is adopted. In contrast, for long transmission distance, a low-value modulation format (e.g., BPSK or QPSK) is adopted to cope with the deterioration of communication quality.

In the SA problem, frequency slots are allocated to a path selected by an routing algorithm. When we allocate frequency slots, we should consider three constraints: spectrum continuity constraint, spectrum non-overlapping constraint, and spectrum contiguity constraint [11]. Let $\boldsymbol{a}$ denote the candidate spectrum allocation of a new connection along the path. Spectrum allocation $\boldsymbol{a}$ is represented by an N_{FS}-bit bit-mask, and the ith element $a[i] \in \{0, 1\}$ is a binary valuable. If $a[i] = 1$, the ith frequency slot is allocated to the path, otherwise, the ith frequency slot is not used for the path of the new connection. The SA problem determines the spectrum allocation $\boldsymbol{a}$ while satisfying the following three constraints.

TABLE I. SYMBOLS.

Symbol	Meaning
$\boldsymbol{a}$	N_{FS}-bit bit-mask. The spectrum allocation If the ith element $\boldsymbol{a}[i] = 1$, ith frequency slot on the link e is used, otherwise it is available.
$\boldsymbol{b}_e$	N_{FS}-bit bit-mask. If the ith element $\boldsymbol{b}_e[i] = 1$, ith frequency slot on the link e is used, otherwise it is available.
B_p	Number of frequency slots used by a connection along route p
C	Capacity of a frequency slot in case of 1-bit transmission per symbol
$\mathcal{E}$	Set of fiber links
G	Directed graph
K	Number of candidate routes
N_{FS}	Maximum number of frequency slots in each link
$\mathcal{V}$	Set of switching nodes
$\mathcal{P}_{s,d}$	Set of candidate routes between sender node s and receiver node d
R_p	Modulation format level on the route p
Z	Number of guard band slots
Λ	Volume of the traffic demand requested by a connection

- Spectrum continuity constraint – This constraint means that common frequency slots should be used all the links on the path, because this paper assumes that there is no spectrum converter in the network. Note that $a[i] = 1$ indicates that the ith frequency slots on all links along the path are allocated to the new connection.
- Spectrum non-overlapping constraint – The new connection should use available frequency slots that other connections do not use:

$$\sum_{i=1}^{N_{\mathrm{FS}}} a[i] \cdot b_e[i] = 0, \qquad \forall e \in p. \tag{1}$$

- Spectrum contiguity constraint – The frequency slots of the new connection should be successive.

$$\sum_{i=1}^{N_{\mathrm{FS}}} a[i] \cdot \mathrm{CRS}(\boldsymbol{a})[i] = \begin{cases} B_p - 1 & (B_p \in [1, N_{\mathrm{FS}} - 1]) \\ N_{\mathrm{FS}} & (B_p = N_{\mathrm{FS}}) \end{cases}, \tag{2}$$

  where $\mathrm{CRS}(\boldsymbol{a})$ indicates a N_{FS}-bit bit-mask that is the circular-right-shift of $\boldsymbol{a}$ by one bit.

If there exist no spectrum allocation satisfying with these constraints, the connection request is blocked.

The First-Fit method [9][10] is one of the simplest spectrum allocation methods. In the First-Fit method, the shortest path is first selected from candidate paths. If there exists a spectrum allocation satisfying with the constraints, the connection uses the frequency slots of the spectrum allocation along the path. When there are several spectrum allocations, the frequency slots with smallest indices are chosen. Otherwise, we select the second shortest path among the candidate paths, and then check whether feasible spectrum allocations satisfying the constraints exist. This procedure is repeated until a spectrum allocation is found or all the candidate paths have been checked.

We explain the spectrum allocation of the First-Fit method using an example where the frequency slots on a path are allocated as shown in Figure 3. When a connection that needs

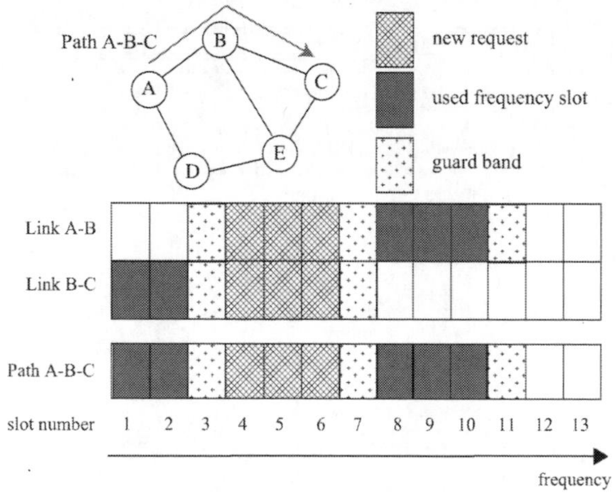

Figure 2. Frequency slots ($N_{\text{FS}} = 13$).

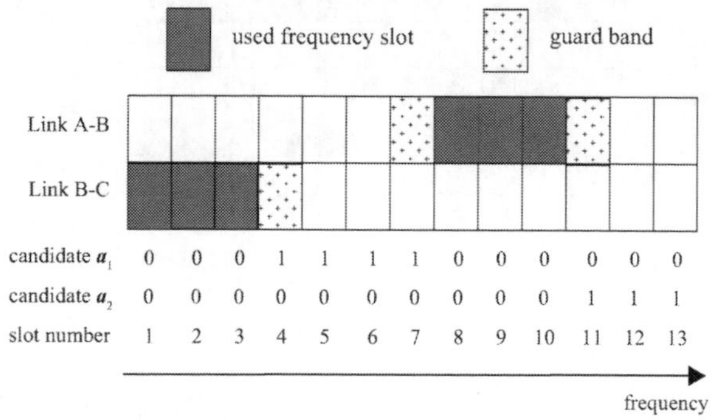

Figure 3. An example of spectrum allocations.

two frequency slots arrives, there are two feasible spectrum allocations, i.e., $\boldsymbol{a}_1$ and $\boldsymbol{a}_2$. The First-Fit method selects $\boldsymbol{a}_1$ because $\boldsymbol{a}_1$ includes frequency slots with smaller indices than $\boldsymbol{a}_2$. In the First-Fit method, the spectrum fragmentation frequently occurs, and thus the frequency slots can not be used efficiently.

III. Proposed Lightpath Establishment Method

The proposed method aims at reducing the blocking probability of the connection requests by efficiently using spectrum resources. In EONs, if the frequency slots of a certain link is intensively used, the link becomes a bottleneck link. In this case, lightpaths cannot be established further through the link. Furthermore, the fragmentation of frequency slots degrades the performance of EONs because connection requests using many frequency slots is often blocked. Therefore, in order to reduce the blocking probability of connection requests, the proposed method selects a route, a modulation format, and frequency slots for each connection while smoothing the spectrum utilization of each link and suppressing the generation of the fragmentation of frequency slots.

When a new connection request arrives, the proposed method selects a combination of a path, a modulation format, and frequency slots. The proposed method prepares K candidate paths $\mathcal{P}_{s,d}$ for each sender node s and receiver node d pair in advance. The path p of the connection is selected from among candidate paths $\mathcal{P}_{s,d}$ with feasible frequency slots. The modulation format is then determined based on the transmission distance of the path p. Finally, the frequency slots are allocated to the path p.

A. Candidate paths and modulation formats

In this paper, we prepare K candidate routes using a K-shortest path algorithm. For each sender and receiver pair (s, d), the procedure of K-shortest path algorithm is as follows. First, we calculate the shortest path p_1 between sender node s and receiver node d using Dijkstra's algorithm in the topology G, where the cost of each link is one. We adopt the path as a candidate path. $\mathcal{P}_{s,d} := \{p_1\}$. We then doubles the cost of the links $e \in p_1$. We find the shortest path p_2 on the resulting graph, and the path is adopted as a new candidate path. That is, $\mathcal{P}_{s,d}$ is updated as $\mathcal{P}_{s,d} := \mathcal{P}_{s,d} \cup \{p_2\}$. Next, we double the cost of the links $e \in p_2$. This procedure is repeated until K candidate routes are chosen and $\mathcal{P}_{s,d} = \{p_1, p_2, \ldots, p_K\}$ is constructed. Figure 4 shows an example of the K-shortest path algorithm ($K = 2$) on a toy topology. In the example, the candidate routes between sender node A and receiver node C $\mathcal{P}_{A,C}$ is obtained $\mathcal{P}_{A,C} = \{p_1, p_2\}$.

The modulation format of a new connection along each path is determined based on the transmission distance. Accordingly, the number of frequency slots used by the connection is given as follows. Let R_p denote the modulation format level on the route p, i.e., the capacity of the sub-carrier using a single bit per symbol (1 for BPSK, 2 for QPSK, and 3 for 8QAM). Moreover, C denotes the communication capacity of per frequency slot in the case of 1-bit transmission per symbol. We describe the calculation of the number of frequency slots when a connection requests traffic volume Λ. Let B_p denote the number of frequency slots used by a connection along path p. The value of B_p is given by:

$$B_p = \left\lceil \frac{\Lambda}{CR_p} \right\rceil + Z, \tag{3}$$

where Z indicates the number of frequency slots for a guard band.

B. Spectrum allocation

To avoid the fragmentation of frequency slots and smooth the spectrum utilization, our proposed method focuses on the maximum spectrum utilization. Let $f(p, \boldsymbol{a})$ denote the maximum spectrum utilization along path p when the spectrum allocation $\boldsymbol{a}$ is adopted on path p in a first-fit manner. Formally, $f(p, \boldsymbol{a})$ is given by:

$$f(p, \boldsymbol{a}) = \max_{i \in [1, N_{\text{FS}}]} \left\{ i \mid \sum_{e \in p} b_e[i] + a[i] \geq 1 \right\}. \tag{4}$$

Note that different paths have $\boldsymbol{a}$ of different sizes because the number B_p of frequency slots used by the paths is given by (3).

First, our proposed method calculates the maximum spectrum utilization $f(p, \boldsymbol{a})$ for each candidate route $p \in \mathcal{P}_{s,d}$, and then selects the path p and the frequency allocation $\boldsymbol{a}$ with

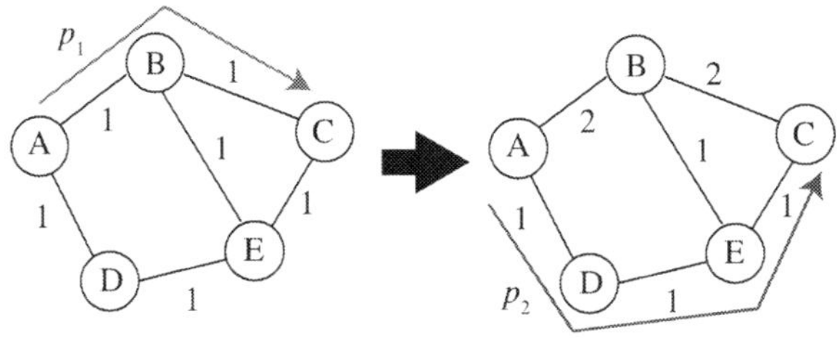

Figure 4. K-shortest path algorithm.

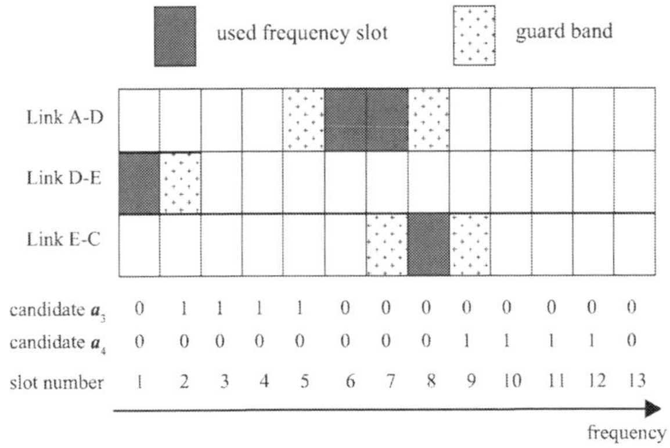

Figure 5. Path p_2 and its candidate spectrum allocations.

the minimum $f(p, \boldsymbol{a})$. In the proposed method, the frequency slots with large indices are reserved for future connections as much as possible, and thus the frequency slots used by established connections are squeezed into frequency slots with small indices, which helps to alleviate the fragmentation and smooth the frequency utilization.

C. Spectrum allocation example

We explain the spectrum allocation of our proposed method using an example where frequency slots on shortest path p_1 and second shortest path p_2 are used by the connections shown in Figs. 3 and 5, respectively. When a new connection that needs two frequency slots arrives, there are four feasible spectrum allocations $\boldsymbol{a}_1, \boldsymbol{a}_2, \boldsymbol{a}_3$, and $\boldsymbol{a}_4$. Our proposed method calculates the maximum index of used slots: $f(p_1, \boldsymbol{a}_1) = 11, f(p_1, \boldsymbol{a}_2) = 13, f(p_2, \boldsymbol{a}_3) = 9, f(p_2, \boldsymbol{a}_4) = 12$. $f(p_2, \boldsymbol{a}_3)$ is minimum, and thus our proposed method selects route p_2 and spectrum allocation $\boldsymbol{a}_3$.

IV. PERFORMANCE EVALUATION

A. Simulation Model

To evaluate the performance of the proposed method, we conduct simulation experiments with the network topology (24 nodes and 43 links) shown in Figure 6. For simplicity, we assume that the length of each link is the same, and thus the modulation format is determined in accordance with the hops between sender and receiver pairs. We adopt 8QAM for less than three hops, QPSK for three and four hops, and BPSK for more than four hops are adopted. Communication capacity C is set to be 2.5 Gbps, and Table II shows the transmission

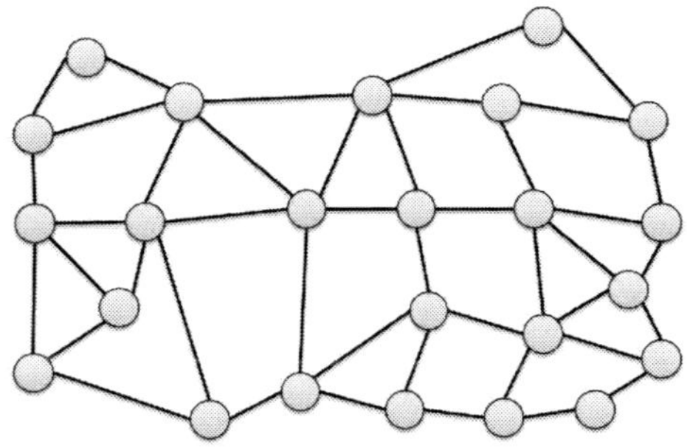

Figure 6. Network model.

TABLE II. TRANSMISSION CAPACITY PER SLOT.

Hops	Modulation Format	Capacity [Gbps/slot]
1, 2	8QAM	7.5
3, 4	QPSK	5.0
More than 4	BPSK	2.5

capacity per frequency slot. The number N_{FS} of frequency slots on each link is set to be 100, the guard-band width is one, and the number of candidate routes K is three.

The arrival of connection requests follows a Poisson process with the rate λ. The lifetime t_L of each connection request follows an exponential distribution with parameter μ or a log-normal distribution. The probability density function g of the log-normal distribution is given by:

$$g(t_L) = \frac{1}{\sqrt{2\pi}\sigma t_L} \exp\left(-\frac{(\log t_L - \xi)^2}{2\sigma^2}\right), \tag{5}$$

where σ and ξ are parameters satisfying $\mathrm{E}[t_L] = e^{\xi + \frac{\sigma^2}{2}}$. In the following, scenarios adopting the exponential distribution and the log-normal distribution are called the *exponential lifetime scenario* and the *log-normal lifetime scenario*, respectively. In the exponential lifetime scenario, $\mu = 10^{-4}$, and in the log-normal lifetime scenario, $\xi = 3.09$, $\sigma = 3.5$. By this setting, the mean lifetime of connections $\mathrm{E}[t_L]$ is same ($\mathrm{E}[t_L] = 10^4$) in both scenarios. Moreover, sender node and receiver node are randomly chosen from among the nodes in $\mathcal{V}$. The bandwidth requirement volume Λ of each connection is uniformly distributed between 1 and 10 Gbps.

We use two performance metrics: the blocking probability and the network utilization. The blocking probability of the connection requests is defined as follows:

$$\frac{\text{number of blocked connection requests}}{\text{total number of connection requests}}. \tag{6}$$

The network utilization is defined as follows:

$$\frac{\text{sum of spectrum utilization } \sum_{e \in \mathcal{E}} \mathrm{E}[u_e]}{\text{number of links } |\mathcal{E}|}, \tag{7}$$

where u_e indicates the spectrum utilization of link e, i.e., the number of used frequency slots divided by N_{FS}, and $\mathrm{E}[u_e]$ denotes the time average of the spectrum utilization of link e. For each setting, we collect 1,500,000 samples for calculating these performance metrics.

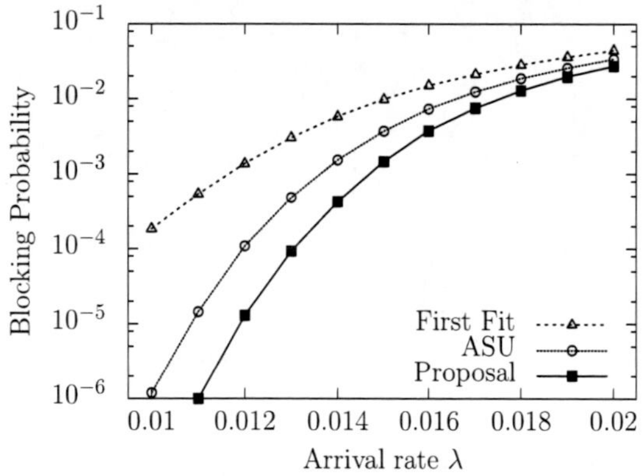

(a) the exponential lifetime scenario

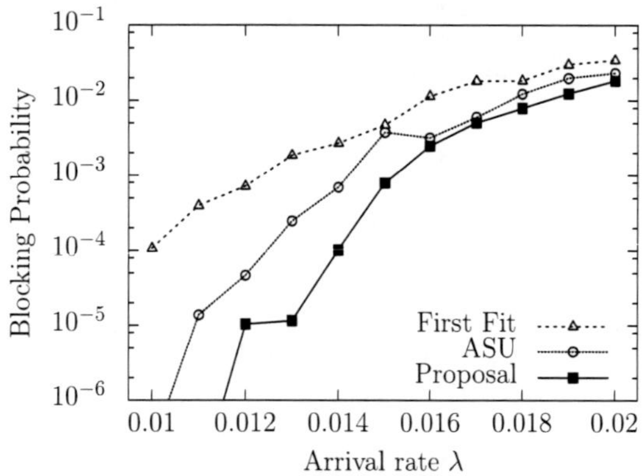

(b) the log-normal lifetime scenario

Figure 7. Blocking probability

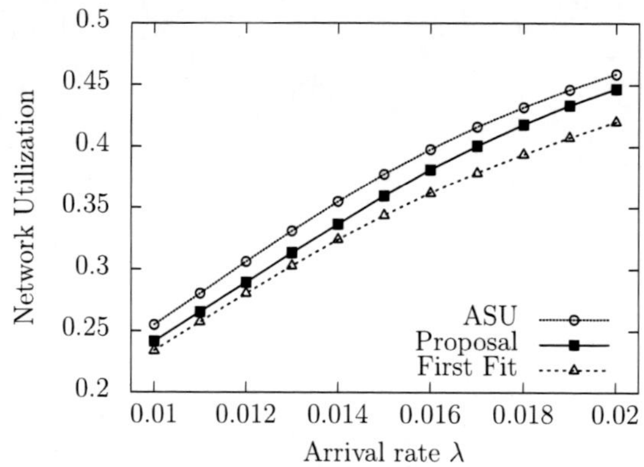

(a) the exponential lifetime scenario

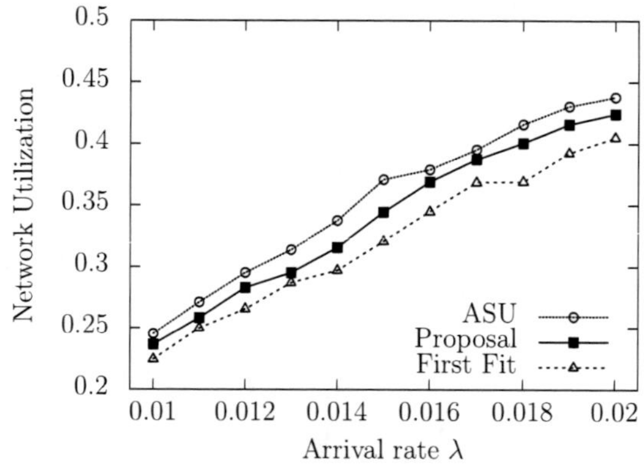

(b) the log-normal lifetime scenario

Figure 8. Network utilization

For the performance comparison, we show the results of the First-Fit and the average spectrum-utilization (ASU) methods. When a new connection request arrives, the ASU method calculates the average spectrum-utilization for each candidate route p, which is defined as the sum of the spectrum utilization among p ($\sum_{e \in p} u_e$) divided by the number of hops of route p ($|p|$). Next, the path with the minimum spectrum-utilization is selected, and if the feasible spectrum allocation exists along the path, the connection is assigned to the spectrum allocation. When there are some feasible spectrum allocations, the spectrum allocation with smalles indices is selected. When there is no feasible spectrum allocation along the path, the ASU method selects the second-minimum spectrum utilization path, and then checks whether a feasible spectrum allocation exists. This procedure is repeated until a feasible spectrum allocation is found. For the example in Figs. 3 and 5, the ASU method calculates the average spectrum-utilization for the candidate routes, which are 4/13 = 0.30 for path p_1 and {(4+2+3)/13}/3 = 0.23 for path p_2. Therefore, the route p_2 and feasible spectrum allocation $\boldsymbol{a}_3$ on the route p_2 are selected.

B. Results

Figure 7 shows the blocking probability as a function of the arrival rate λ. We observe that the blocking probability of our proposed method is smallest for any arrival rate λ. This result indicates that the maximum spectrum utilization is useful for alleviating the spectrum fragmentation. Moreover, in the log-normal lifetime scenario, connections with large lifetime occasionally arrive, which highly degrades the performance of the First-Fit method and the ASU method. In contrast, the proposed method works well even if those connections arrive.

Figure 8 shows the network utilization as a function of the arrival rate λ. The network utilization of the proposed scheme is larger than that of the First-Fit method. This result indicates that the free frequency slots are large and the frequency fragmentation frequently occurs in the First-Fit method. Moreover, the network utilization of the proposed method is smaller than that of the ASU method. Therefore, the ASU method wastes the frequency resources by allocating paths with large hops. Based on these results, we conclude that the proposed method effectively uses the frequency resources.

V. Conclusion

In this paper, we proposed a dynamic lightpath establishment method for EONs. Our proposed method focuses on the maximum spectrum utilization. By doing so, the proposed method aims at smoothing the spectrum utilization of each link and alleviating the fragmentation of frequency slots. Through simulation experiments, we showed that the proposed method effectively reduces the blocking probability of connection requests under the dynamic situations where connection requests dynamically are generated and released.

REFERENCES

[1] N. Charbonneau and V. M. Vokkarane, "A survey of advance reservation routing and wavelength assignment in wavelength-routed WDM networks," *IEEE Communications Surveys & Tutorials*, vol. 14, no. 4, pp. 1037–1064, 2012.

[2] B. C. Chatterjee, N. Sarma, and E. Oki, "Routing and spectrum allocation in elastic optical networks: A tutorial," *IEEE Communications Surveys & Tutorials*, vol. 17, no. 3, pp. 1776–1800, 2015.

[3] G. Zhang, M. D. Leenheer, A. Morea, and B. Mukherjee, "A survey on OFDM-based elastic core optical networking," *IEEE Communications Surveys & Tutorials*, vol. 15, no. 1, pp. 65–87, 2013.

[4] M. Jinno, H. Takara, B. Kozicki, Y. Tsukishima, Y. Sone, and S. Matsuoka, "Spectrum-efficient and scalable elastic optical path network: Architecture, benefits, and enabling technologies," *IEEE Communications Magazine*, vol. 47, no. 11, pp. 66–73, 2009.

[5] M. Jinno, B. Kozicki, H. Takara, A. Watanabe, Y. Sone, T. Tanaka, and A. Hirano, "Distance-adaptive spectrum resource allocation in spectrum-sliced elastic optical path network," *IEEE Communications Magazine*, vol. 48, no. 8, pp. 138–145, 2010.

[6] K. Christodoulopoulos, I. Tomkos, and E. A. Varvarigos, "Elastic bandwidth allocation in flexible OFDM-based optical networks," *Journal of Lightwave Technology*, vol. 29, no. 9, pp. 1354–1366, 2011.

[7] M. Takezaki and K. Hirata, "Static lightpath establishment method with multi-path routing in elastic optical networks," *Proc. of the 31st International Conference on Information Networking (ICOIN'17)*, pp. 109–111, 2017.

[8] K. Morita and K. Hirata, "Dynamic spectrum allocation method for reducing crosstalk in multi-core fiber networks," *Proc. of the 31st International Conference on Information Networking (ICOIN'17)*, pp. 686–688, 2017.

[9] A. Rosa, C. Cavdar, S. Carvalho, J. Costa, and L. Wosinska, "Spectrum allocation policy modeling for elastic optical networks," *Proc. of the 9th International Conference onHigh Capacity Optical Networks and Enabling Technologies (HONET'12)*, pp. 242–246, 2012.

[10] R. Wang and B. Mukherjee, "Spectrum management in heterogeneous bandwidth optical networks," *Optical Switching and Networking*, vol. 11, pp. 83–91, 2014.

[11] M. Zhang, C. You, and Z. Zhu, "On the parallelization of spectrum defragmentation reconfigurations in elastic optical networks," *IEEE/ACM Transactions on Networking*, vol. 24, no. 5, pp. 2819–2833, 2016.

[12] K. Bala, T. E. Stern, D. Simchi-Levi, and K. Bala, "Routing in a linear lightwave network," *IEEE/ACM Transactions on Networking*, vol. 3, no. 4, pp. 459–469, 1995.

Flexible Platform for Feeding Photonic Integrated Processors

Cátia Pinho[1,2], Francisco Rodrigues[1,2,3], Ana Tavares[1,2,3], George S. D. Gordon[4], Ali Shahpari[1,2], Mário Lima[1,2], Tim D. Wilkinson[4], António Teixeira[1,2]

[1] Instituto de Telecomunicações (IT), University of Aveiro, Portugal
[2] Department of Electronics, Telecommunications and Informatics (DETI), University of Aveiro, Portugal
[3] PICadvanced, Incubadora de Empresas, Universidade de Aveiro, Portugal
[4] Electrical Division, Engineering Department, University of Cambridge, 9, JJ Thomson Avenue, Cambridge, UK
e-mail: catiap@ua.pt, franciscoruivo@ua.pt, anamaia@ua.pt, gsdg2@cam.ac.uk, ali@ua.pt, mlima@ua.pt, tdw13@cam.ac.uk, teixeira@ua.pt

Abstract — **Enhanced Photonic Integrated Circuits (PIC) are required for the current demand of flexibility and reconfigurability in telecommunications networks. Thus, an extensive characterization and testing is necessary to provide an accurate prediction of the PIC performance. The use of Spatial Light Modulator (SLM) as a diffractive device to reconstruct images from Computer Generated Holograms (CGH) allows to modulate the wave form of a light beam. In this study, we proposed the use of the SLM technology as a flexible platform for feeding photonic integrated processors. Preliminary results were obtained, to produce a multiplexing/demultiplexing CGH to be applied into an optical chip for data compression based on Haar wavelet transform.**

Keywords - Photonic Integrated Circuits (PIC); Integrated Optics; Spatial Light Modulator (SLM); Computer Generated Holography (CGH).

I. Introduction

In the recent years, we have witnessed a huge increase in the data traffic which the traditional copper based electronic mediums fail to carry [1] [2]. The subsequent evolution in optical communications has led to the emergence of Photonic Integrated Circuits (PIC). PIC-based optical communication offers an efficient and cost-effective alternative to data transmission driving to a significant growth in the segment [1]. It is expected an annual growth rate of 25.2% during the estimate period of 2015 to 2022 [2]. Furthermore, PIC increasing demand can also be attributed to innovative applications in bio-photonics [1].

PIC can be characterized as a multiport device composed by an integrated system of optical elements embedded onto a single chip using a waveguide architecture [3]. The testing of optical components is more difficult than testing electrical components and for an accurate prediction of the PIC performance, an extensive characterization and testing is required [4]. Moreover, optical components testing is difficult and time-consuming, e.g., due to the tight 3D alignment tolerances for accurate coupling of light [4].

The SLM capability to dynamically reconfigure the light makes it an attractive technology to excite cores and/or modes [5], [6], as it allows the arbitrary addition or removal of channels by the software and it is anticipated that it can improve channel compensation. This feature can then be explored to feed/receive optical signal from the PIC.

SLM is an electrically programmable device that modulates light according to a spatial (pixel) pattern [7]. This device can control incident light in amplitude-only, phase-only or the combination phase-amplitude [7], [8]. However, common methods of hologram generation cannot arbitrarily modulate the amplitude and phase of a beam simultaneously [9], [10]. It is not then possible to simply address the inverse Fourier Transform of the desired pattern into the far-field and replicate the resulting distribution of amplitude and phase directly on the SLM [9]. Thus, it is necessary to apply optimization algorithms to calculate the best hologram possible within the constraints of the device [9].

The SLM based on nematic Liquid Crystal on Silicon (LCoS) technology is an electrically addressed reflection type phase-only spatial light modulator in which the liquid crystal is controlled by a direct and accurate voltage and can modulate the wave front of a light beam [8], [11]. It is used as a diffractive device to reconstruct images from Computer Generated Holography (CGH) [12]. This optical signal processing can be produced with different techniques, e.g., linear Fourier transform (i.e., linear phase mask) [13], Iterative Fourier Transform Algorithm (IFTA) [14], [15], Gerchberg-Saxton algorithm [16] and simulated annealing [17]. The use of a SLM as a diffractive device to reconstruct images from CGH allows to modulate the wave front of a light beam.

In this study, we proposed the use of the SLM technology as a flexible platform for feeding photonic integrated processors, i.e., to feed/receive optical signal from the PIC. Preliminary results were obtained, to produce an expected CGH to be applied into an optical chip for data compression based on Haar wavelet transform. The paper is organized in four sections. Section II describes the methodology applied. Subsection II-A presents the design of the PIC for data compression; subsection II-B presents the generation and optimization of the CGH; and subsection II-C presents the SLM setup. Section III and IV presents the obtained results and its discussion, respectively. Section V concludes the study and presents future work.

II. METHODOLOGY

The methodology is divided into three subsections: A) the design of the optical chip for data compression based in Haar wavelet transform; B) the algorithms used for the generation and optimization of the CGH; and C) the implementation of the SLM setup to acquire the CGH.

A. PIC for data compression based on Haar wavelet transform

The design of the new data compression chip based on Haar Transform (HT) is presented in Figure 1 [3].

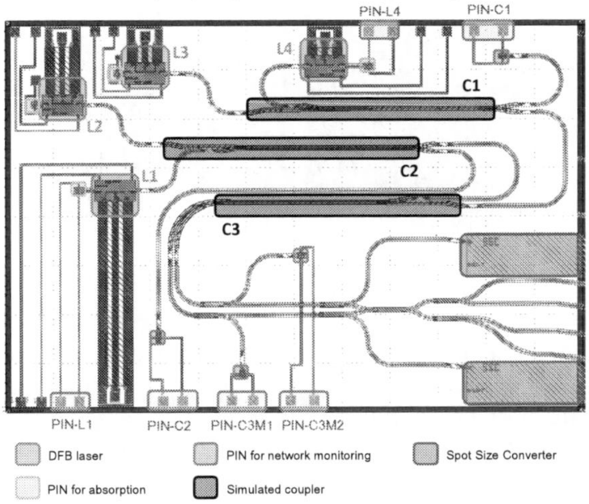

Figure 1. Design of an optical chip for data compression based on HT.

The chip is composed by four Distributed Feedback (DFB) lasers (L1-L4), three asymmetric couplers (C1-C3), six PIN photodiodes for network monitoring (PIN: L1, L4, C1, C2, C3M1, C3M2) two spot size converters, six multimode interferometers (MMI) 1x2 and one MMI 2x2.

The HT operations include Low-pass (L) and High-pass (H) filters applied over one dimension at a time. This filtering operation corresponds to the calculation of the average between two neighbors' pixels values (low-pass) or the difference between them (high-pass) [18]. The HT is implemented with a 3 asymmetric couplers (2x2) network, which reproduces the required operations, i.e., the average (sum) and the difference (subtraction) between the optical input pair [3]. The proposed asymmetric couplers were designed and simulated in the OptoDesigner from Phoenix Software [19].

The 2D HT can be decomposed in 4 sub-bands, LL, LH, HL and HH [18]. The LL gives the data compressed. In the chip these 4 sub-bands can be extrapolated from the 4 output waveguides (WG) at the end of the 3 asymmetric couplers network, see Figure 2. The measurements of the distance between the 4 WG at the end of the 3 asymmetric coupler network (represented as d1, d2 and d3 in Figure 2) have an order of magnitude of 200 μm. Measurements were performed with a Leica microscope (DM 750M; 1CC50 HD) and an objective of 20x (HI Plan EPI, 20x/0.40) [20].

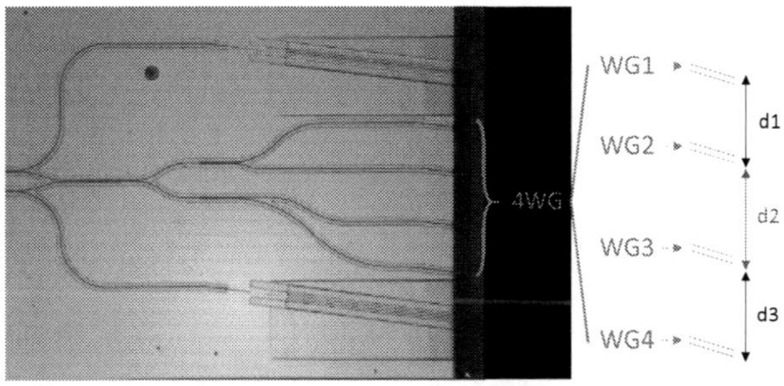

Figure 2. Measurements of the distance between the 4 waveguides (WG) at the end of the 3 asymmetric coupler network.

Further description of the design and characterization of the optical chip can be found in this study [3].

B. Generation of the CGH

The CGH produces a phase mask or diffractive optical element to apply to the SLM [13]. The information to be transformed (in the Fourier domain) is introduced into the optical system by the SLM, with a phase mask that is appropriate to the input function of interest [21]. The following calculus applied for the generation of the CGH were based in the Fourier optical principles presented in [21].

The CGH was obtained with a linear phase mask calculated in the frequency domain (1), where cx and cy are the horizontal and vertical tilt parameters, respectively; and fx and fy are the spatial frequency matrix arrays corresponding to the image to be generated in the X and Y axis, respectively.

$$Mask_{linear} = -2\pi(cx\,fx + cy\,fy) \qquad (1)$$

The mask transfer function to be sent to the SLM, is given by $H_{mask} = \angle(\exp(iMask_{linear}))$, ensuring that the phase values are set in the range of $[-\pi, \pi]$.

An estimation of the output signal is given by (2).

$$S_{out} = ifft(H(fft(S_{in}))) \qquad (2)$$

S_{in} describes the signal of the input beam (3), where $(x0, y0)$ provides the horizontal and vertical position and (wx, wy) the width and the height of the beam, respectively, see Figure 3.

$$S_{in} = \exp\left(-\left(2\frac{x - x0}{wx\,log(\sqrt{2})}\right)^2 - \left(2\frac{y - y0}{wy\,log(\sqrt{2})}\right)^2\right) \qquad (3)$$

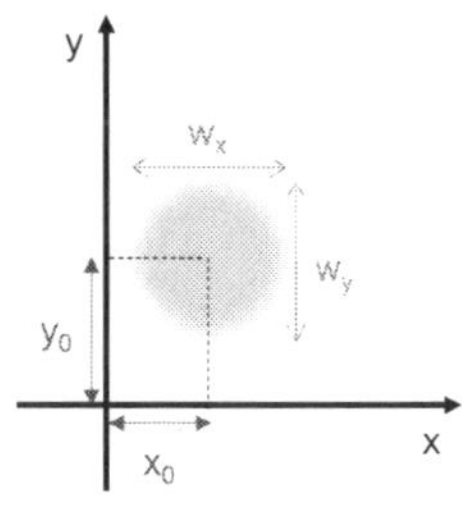

Figure 3. Diagram in Cartesian coordinate system describing the parameters $(x0, y0)$ and (wx, wy) used for the estimation of the Input beam S_{in}.

1) Optimization of the CGH

To obtain a hologram that replicates the output of the 4 WG of the optical chip (see Figure 2), the linear transformations in the Fourier domain presented in (4), (5) were applied.

$$H = \angle(e^{iH_1} + e^{iH_2} + e^{iH_3} + e^{iH_4}) \quad (4)$$

$$H_1 = \exp\left(i * \left(2\pi(cx_1 * fx + cy_1 * fy)\right)\right) \quad (5)$$

A phase-only SLM does not allow to simply address the inverse Fourier of the desired pattern into the far-field and replicate the resulting distribution of amplitude and phase directly on the SLM [9], thus it is challenging to spatially modulate the light with the expected resolution and accuracy.

To overcome this difficulty, an iterative algorithm to obtain the desired hologram with an error factor $\delta \leq 5\%$ was implemented. The main steps of the algorithm can be described as: i) generate a 1st linear phase mask to produce the expected initial field (I_{exp}), based on (4); ii) initially set the four values a_{1-4} to 1, from $H = \angle(a_1 e^{iH_1} + a_2 e^{iH_2} + a_3 e^{iH_3} + a_4 e^{iH_4})$; iii) acquire the hologram generated by SLM (I_{SLM}) with a camera and feed this data to the algorithm; iv) calculate the difference between the hologram generated and the initial field expected, defined as error factor: $\delta = abs(I_{SLM} - I_1) \leq 0.05$; iv) if the condition $\delta \leq 0.05$ is not satisfied repeat steps (ii-iv) by iteratively adjusting the values of a_{1-4} to compensate the error factor. The algorithm was developed in Matlab [22], which was able to control both SLM and camera hardware. The block diagram of the algorithm is presented in Figure 4.

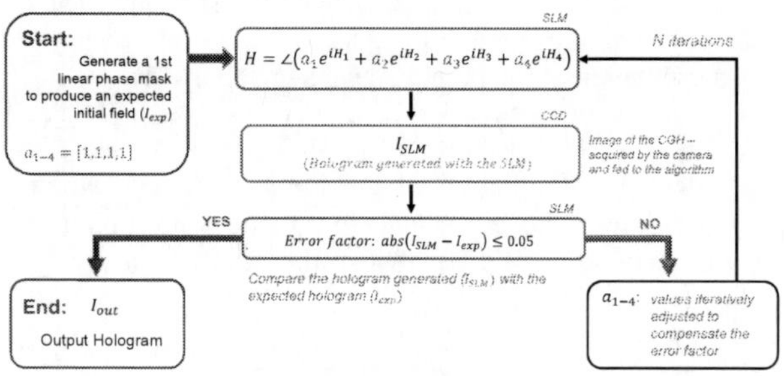

Figure 4. Block diagram of the algorithm applied for the optimization of the CGH.

The error factor (δ) reproduces the deviation of the generated hologram when compared with the expected output of the optical chip, i.e., the dimensions of the 4 WG.

C. Setup to generate the CGH

A reflective LCoS phase only SLM, model PLUTO-TELCO-012, with a wavelength range of 1400-1700 nm, an active area of 15.36 mm × 8.64 mm, a pixel pitch of 8.0 µm, a fill factor of 92% and reflectivity of 80% [8] was used to generate the hologram. The setup was composed by: a laser (1550nm wavelength); a polarization controller; two lenses (AC254-050-C-ML, AR coating 1050-1620nm) L1 and L2 with a focal length of 75mm and 250mm, respectively; a Near-Infrared (IR) (1460-1600nm) camera (sensing area: 6.4×4.8, resolution: 752×582, pixel size: 8.6×8.3) to capture the hologram produced; and a neutral density to avoid saturation in the camera acquisition, see Figure 5.

III. Results

The hologram was generated in 1st order of diffraction where the polarization was occurring.

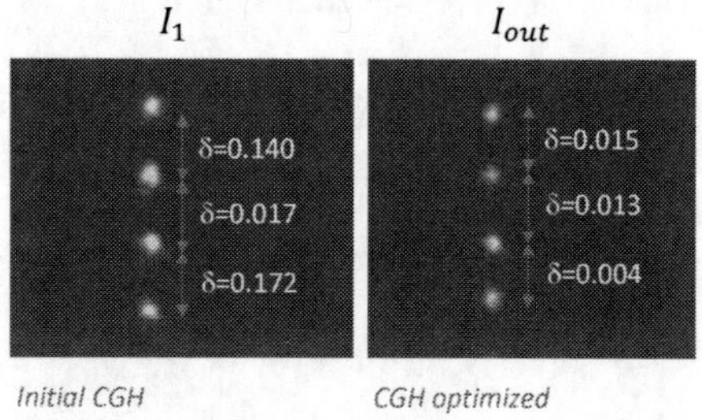

Figure 5. Hologram acquired by the IR camera, left: initial CGH; right: CGH optimized.

Figure 6 presents the holograms acquired by the IR camera, i.e., the initial hologram fed to the optimization algorithm with an obtained error factor $\delta \leq 17\%$ (left figure) and the final optimized CGH, with an error factor $\delta < 2\%$ (right figure).

IV. Discussion

A significant improvement in the generated hologram is achieved with CGH optimization, i.e., a reduction of the error factor (δ) by 15%. Nevertheless, optical artefacts associated with the diffraction of light were not completely eliminated, i.e., additional 2 spots (with less intensity) are generated. This diffraction artefact can cause a reduction of signal expected at the 4 output WG of the optical chip.

The phase mask that replicates the expected output of the optical chip can be used to multiplex/demultiplex the obtained result. Furthermore, a phase mask which addresses the HT operations can also be applied to invert the compression induced by the HT (optically implemented in the chip with the 3 asymmetric couplers network).

The use of the SLM will then allow to provide a proof of concept of the PIC operation.

V. Conclusion and Future Work

An extensive PIC characterization and testing is essential to provide an accurate prediction of its performance. To complement the PIC characterization process is proposed in this study a concept to use the SLM as a flexible platform for feeding photonic integrated processors. The capacity of the SLM to dynamically reconfigure light allows to feed and/or receive information to the PIC. This data can be used to provide a proof of concept of the operation performed by the optical chip, e.g., 2D HT. A first preliminary result was obtained, i.e., a phase mask that can be used to feed/receive

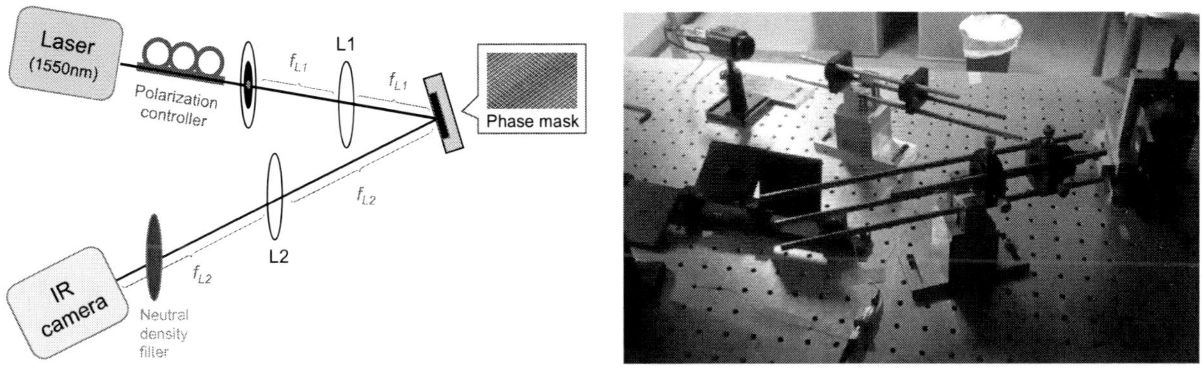

Figure 6. Left figure: Scheme of the hologram reconstruction system, using a laser of 1550nm, a polarization controller, lens L1, a LCoS-SLM, lens L2 and a IR camera. Right figure: Photography of the setup presented in the left figure.

the output of an optical chip for data compression based in the HT.

Further developments will be conducted to implement the HT in the phase mask applied to the SLM and tested with the optical chip, to quantitatively prove the proposed approach.

ACKNOWLEDGMENT

This work was supported by Fundação para a Ciência e a Tecnologia (FCT) under the project "COMPRESS- All-optical data compression" – PTDC/EEI-TEL/7163/2014 and the PhD scholarship PD/BD/105858/2014; and the QREN/COMPETE P2020 project "FutPON – Future Passive Optical Networks" – ref.3145. The authors acknowledge PICadvanced for its collaboration.

REFERENCES

[1] Grand View Research, "Photonic Integrated Circuit (IC) Market Size Report," 2016.

[2] Credence Research, "Photonic Integrated Circuits Market," 2016.

[3] C. Pinho et al., "Design and Characterization of an Optical Chip for Data Compression based on Haar Wavelet Transform," in OFC - Optical Networking and Communication Conference, 2017, p. Th2A.9.

[4] M. Smit et al., "An introduction to InP-based generic integration technology," Semicond. Sci. Technol., vol. 29, no. 8, p. 83001, 2014.

[5] J. Carpenter, S. Leon-saval, B. J. Eggleton, and J. Schröder, "Spatial Light Modulators for Sub-Systems and Characterization in SDM," in 2014 OptoElectronics and Communication Conference and Australian Conference on Optical Fibre Technology, 2014, no. July, pp. 23–24.

[6] H. J. Lee, H. S. Moon, S.-K. Choi, and H. S. Park, "Multi-core fiber interferometer using spatial light modulators for measurement of the inter-core group index differences," Opt. Express, vol. 23, no. 10, p. 12555, May 2015.

[7] Meadowlark Optics, "XY Spatial Light Modulator," 2015. [Online]. Available: http://www.meadowlark.com/xy-spatial-light-modulator-p-119#.VfLwdhFVhHx. [Accessed: 01-Aug-2016].

[8] Holoeye, "Spatial Light Modulators," Holoeye Photonics AG, 2013. [Online]. Available: http://holoeye.com/spatial-light-modulators/. [Accessed: 01-Aug-2016].

[9] J. Carpenter, "Holographic Mode Division Multiplexing in ptical Fibres," University of Cambridge, 2012.

[10] G. Lazarev, A. Hermerschmidt, and S. Kr, "LCOS Spatial Light Modulators : Trends and Applications," Opt. Imaging Metrol. Adv. Technol., pp. 1–29, 2012.

[11] Hamamatsu, "Phase spatial light modulator LCOS-SLM," in Handbook LCOS-SLM, 2012, pp. 1–14.

[12] M. Kovachev et al., "Reconstruction of Computer Generated Holograms by Spatial Light Modulators," Multimedia Content Representation, Classification and Security, vol. 4105. Springer Berlin Heidelberg, pp. 706–713, 2006.

[13] C. Pinho, A. Shahpari, I. Alimi, M. Lima, and A. Teixeira, "Optical transforms and CGH for SDM systems," in 2016 18th International Conference on Transparent Optical Networks (ICTON), 2016, pp. 1–4.

[14] Y. Torii, L. Balladares-Ocana, and J. Martinez-Castro, "An Iterative Fourier Transform Algorithm for digital hologram generation using phase-only information and its implementation in a fixed-point digital signal processor," Optik (Stuttg)., vol. 124, no. 22, pp. 5416–5421, 2013.

[15] O. Ripoll, V. Kettunen, and H. P. Herzig, "Review of iterative Fourier-transform algorithms for beam shaping applications," Opt. Eng., vol. 43, no. 11, pp. 2549–2556, 2004.

[16] R. Gerchberg, W. O. Saxton, B. R. W. Gerchberg, and W. O. Saxton, "A Practical Algorithm for the Determination of Phase from Image and Diffraction Plane Pictures," Optik (Stuttg)., vol. 35, no. 2, pp. 237–246, 1972.

[17] J. Carpenter and T. D. Wilkinson, "Graphics processing unit–accelerated holography by simulated annealing," Opt. Eng., vol. 49, no. 9, pp. 95801–7, 2010.

[18] G. Parca, P. Teixeira, and A. Teixeira, "All-optical image processing and compression based on Haar wavelet transform," Appl. Opt., vol. 52, no. 12, pp. 2932–2939, 2013.

[19] Phoenix Software, "OptoDesigner 5 - The ultimate Photonic Chip Design environment," 2016. [Online]. Available: http://www.phoenixbv.com/product.php?submenu=dfa&subsubmenu=3&prdgrpID=3. [Accessed: 12-Sep-2016].

[20] Leica Microsystems, "Leica Application Suite," Http://Www.Leica-Microsystems.Com/, 2015. [Online]. Available: http://www.leica-microsystems.com/products/microscope-software/life-sciences/las-easy-and-efficient/. [Accessed: 04-Sep-2016].

[21] J. W. Goodman, Introduction to Fourier Optics, 2nd ed., McGraw-Hill Series in Electrical and Computer Engineering, 1996.

[22] The MathWorks, "MATLAB - The language of technical computing," 2015.

New QoT-Aware Rerouting Algorithms in WDM All-Optical Networks

Naama Amdouni[1,2] and Taoufik Aguili[1]

[1]Université de Tunis El Manar, École Nationale d'Ingénieurs de Tunis, Laboratoire de Systèmes de Communications, 1002, Tunis, Tunisie;
[2]Université de Jendouba, Institut Supérieur de l'Informatique du Kef, 7100, Le Kef, Tunisie;
Email: naama.amdouni@gmail.com, taoufik.aguili@enit.rnu.tn

Abstract—**The wavelength continuity constraint and the wavelength integrity constraint imposed by Wavelength-Division Multiplexing (WDM) all-optical networks have been, for a long time, the main constraints to be considered when solving the Routing and Wavelength Assignment (RWA) problem in such networks. However, in addition to the two aforementioned constraints, a third constraint cannot be neglected anymore. This constraint is related to the lightpaths' Quality of Transmission (QoT), which might become potentially unacceptable when the optical signal propagates through long distances. Indeed, in WDM all-optical networks, no signal regeneration at intermediate nodes is allowed which induces some impairments in the transmission signal. Since these impairments continue to degrade the signal quality as it progresses toward its destination, the received Bit Error Rate (BER) at the destination node might become unacceptably high. This result might lead to inefficient utilization of network resources resulting in higher rejection ratios. This is especially severe when dynamic lightpath demands are considered. In this paper, we propose to use rerouting as a solution to improve the network throughput. We investigate and compare three different rerouting categories, namely, passive rerouting, active rerouting and hybrid rerouting. To the best of our knowledge, this is the first attempt to use active and hybrid rerouting for optimizing WDM all-optical network throughput with transmission impairments consideration. Multiple simulation studies have been carried out on different network topologies to evaluate and compare the performance of the proposed algorithms.**

Keywords–WDM all-optical networks; passive, active and hybrid rerouting; Wavelength continuity constraint; Quality of Transmission (QoT); Service disruption period.

I. Introduction

WDM [1] optical networks are promising candidates that are expected to satisfy the continually evolving requirements for higher bandwidth services. Nowadays, 40 and 100 Gbps connections are used thanks to WDM all-optical networks, also known as WDM transparent optical networks, in which the signals remain in the optical domain. In such a network, data traffic is transported from one node to another in the form of optical pulses carried over an end-to-end optical path, called lightpath. A lightpath, generally spanning several fiber-links, is established by allocating the same wavelength on all the fiber links it traverses. This requirement is referred to as the wavelength continuity constraint. Also, two lightpaths sharing the same fiber must be identified by different wavelengths. This requirement is called wavelength integrity constraint. The problem of establishing lightpaths with the objective of optimizing the utilization of network resources is known as the Routing and Wavelength Assignment (RWA) problem [2]. Many surveys have been carried out to investigate the RWA problem assuming an ideal optical medium [2]. But such a perfect optical transmission could never be achieved in a realistic WDM network where fibers and non ideal components induce multiple transmission impairments which affect significantly the quality of transmission. Indeed, to ensure the feasibility of proposed algorithms, in addition to the two aforementioned constraints, a third constraint cannot be ignored anymore. This constraint is related to the lightpaths' QoT, which might become potentially unacceptable when the optical signal propagates over long distances without electrical regeneration.

Taking into account physical layer impairments, wavelength continuity constraint and wavelength integrity constraint when solving the RWA problem leads to inefficient utilization of network resources and results in higher rejection ratios. Traffic rerouting is a viable and cost effective solution to improve the network throughput conditioned by the aforementioned constraints. There are two ways to rearrange an existing lightpath. One is wavelength rerouting (WRR), which keeps the original path of the lightpath to be rerouted but reassigns a different wavelength to the fiber links along the path. Another is lightpath rerouting (LRR), which consists of finding a new path with possibly another wavelength to replace the old path. A comprehensive survey of rerouting techniques can be found in [3]. Transmission of the existing lightpaths to be rerouted must be temporarily shut-down to protect data from being lost or misrouted. This period is referred to as the service disruption period. It has been demonstrated in [4] that WRR induces a service disruption period shorter than that induced by LRR. Traffic rerouting can be divided into three categories with respect to the timestamp of initiating the rerouting procedure. The first is passive rerouting, which initiates the rerouting procedure when an incoming lightpath demand is about to be rejected due to lack of resources. It aims at rearranging a certain number of existing lightpaths to free a wavelength-continuous route for the incoming lightpath demand. The second category is active rerouting, also called intentional rerouting, which reroutes dynamically existing lightpaths to a more suitable physical path according to some predefined criteria, without affecting other lightpaths, so as to achieve a better rejection ratio performance. The third category is hybrid rerouting which combines passive rerouting and active rerouting. In this paper, the main objective consists in applying active and hybrid rerouting to maximize the number of established lightpath demands satisfying the required QoT for a given physical network topology with a fixed number of wavelengths per fiber-links and minimize the incurred service disruption period. Lightpath demands are assumed to be with random arrivals and departures and referred to as Random Lightpath Demands (RLDs). Four main physical layer impairment effects are considered as dominating factors that affect signal quality, namely Chromatic Dispersion (CD), Polarization Mode Dispersion (PMD), Optical Signal to Noise Ratio (OSNR) and Nonlinear Phase Shift (ϕ_{NL}).

The remainder of this paper is organized as follows. In Section II, we briefly describe the investigated problem and present related works. In Section III, the QoT computation as well as the four QoT parameters considered in this paper are presented. In Section IV, we present in details our proposed QoT-aware rerouting algorithms. Performance results are presented and analyzed in Section V. Finally, Section VI concludes the paper.

II. Description of the Investigated Problem and Related Work

Taking into account the impact of physical layer impairments when solving the RWA problem in order to make the proposed RWA algorithms more effective has been, recently, extensively investigated in the literature [5]. Impairments can be classified into linear and non-linear effects [5]. Linear effects are independent of signal power and affect wavelengths individually. Amplifier Spontaneous Emission (ASE), PMD, and CD investigated in [5][6][7], are generally considered as the predominant factors inducing signal degradation when evaluating network performance in low-speed transmission systems. However, in high-speed optical networks non-linear impairments as well as linear ones become more prominent and could not be ignored anymore. Self-Phase Modulation (SPM), considered in [8], and Four Wave Mixing (FWM) investigated in [9], are some of the important non-linear impairments affecting transmitted signal quality. Taking into account physical layer impairments should lead to lower network performance especially in terms of rejection ratio. That is why, we propose here to use traffic rerouting to alleviate the effect of considering these impairments.

The traffic rerouting concept has been applied to WDM all-optical networks to alleviate only the impact of the wavelength continuity constraint. Different rerouting techniques have been proposed so far in the literature [3]. But, they assumed perfect physical layer conditions. To the best of our knowledge, the first attempt to use rerouting as a solution to maximize the number of established RLDs satisfying the required QoT is found in our studies presented in [10][11][12], where passive lightpath and/or wavelength rerouting was considered. In this paper, we investigate active and hybrid rerouting to alleviate the transmission impairments consideration effect and minimize the incurred service disruption period. The performances of our QoT-aware rerouting algorithms are evaluated and compared to those of our impairment-aware passive lightpath rerouting algorithm previously published in [10] through illustrative numerical examples.

III. Quality of Transmission Computation

In WDM all-optical networks, the QoT is generally evaluated in terms of BER. Generally, the required value of BER in optical networks is varying between 10^{-9} and 10^{-12}. Determining the BER value instantaneously may be sometimes very difficult. That is why another factor called Q-factor is used to estimate the QoT in the network.Equation (1) shows the relationship between $Q-$factor and BER.

$$BER = \frac{1}{2} erfc\left(\frac{Q}{\sqrt{2}}\right) \tag{1}$$

To provide a qualitative description of the QoT in the network, the Q-factor is estimated by combining four linear and nonlinear effects. The effects considered in this study are respectively: CD, PMD, SNR and ϕ_{NL}. In the following subsections, we discuss the aforementioned four main quality of transmission parameters and estimate the associated Q-factor based on the models proposed in [5].

A. Chromatic Dispersion

The disparity in propagation velocity causes an optical pulse broadening in the time domain. This phenomenon is called CD. The CD's power penalty is given by (2) [5].

$$EOP_{DC} = 10log\left(\sqrt{1 + (DL\frac{\sigma_\lambda}{\sigma_0})}\right) \tag{2}$$

where σ_0 is the pulse width, σ_λ is the spectral width, L is the fiber-link length and D represents the dispersion parameter characterizing the single mode fiber (SMF) used in the transmission system.

B. Polarization Mode Dispersion

Different propagation velocities cause pulse broadening in the frequency domain called PMD. The PMD's power penalty is evaluated according to (3), where T_B is the bit time.

$$EOP_{PMD}=5.1\left(\frac{\left(\sum_{f\in links}\left(\left(\sum_{f\in spans}(PMD_{span}(f))^2\right)^{\frac{1}{2}}(f)\right)^2\right)^{\frac{1}{2}}}{T_B}\right)^2 \tag{3}$$

C. Optical Signal to Noise Ratio

The amplification site, used to compensate fiber absorption losses, consists of Erbium-doped fiber amplifier (EDFA) and a section of compensating dispersion fiber (DCF) [5]. Optical amplifiers affect transmitted signal quality by their own component of noise known as ASE. The OSNR, which represents the ratio of the average signal power to the average noise power, is the parameter used to evaluate the degradation due to ASE noise. The OSNR computed along a fiber-line composed of M amplifier stages is obtained according to the following equation [5]:

$$\frac{1}{OSNR} = \sum_{1\leq i\leq M}\left(\frac{1}{\frac{P_s}{P_{ASE}}}\right) = \sum_{1\leq i\leq M}\left(\frac{NF_{stage}h\nu\Delta f_i}{P_s}\right) \tag{4}$$

where NF_{stage} is the noise figure of the stage, h is Plank's constant, ν is the optical frequency and Δf represents the bandwidth that measures the NF.

D. Nonlinear Phase Shift ϕ_{NL}

Enhancing the intensity of the optical signal propagating through the fiber raises the fiber nonlinearities which create a nonlinear phase shift ϕ_{NL} computed according to Equation 5 [5]:

$$\phi_{NL} = \frac{n_2 \omega_0 P_{in}}{c A_{eff}} \left(\frac{1 - e^{\alpha L}}{\alpha} \right) \tag{5}$$

where α is the attenuation parameter, n_2 represents the cladding index, A_{eff} is the area of cross-section of the fiber core and ω_0 and c are respectively the frequency and the light velocity.

E. Q-factor Estimation

The Q-factor considering the four impairment parameters described above is estimated according to the following expression:

$$Q = \left(\sqrt{\frac{OSNR \Delta f_{opt} EXTP}{EOP_{DC} EOP_{\phi_{NL}} \Delta f_{elect}}} \right) \frac{1}{EOP_{PMD}} \tag{6}$$

where Δf_{opt} is the optical bandwidth, Δf_{elect} is the electrical bandwidth and $EXTP$ is the extinction ratio which represents the ratio between the "one" level and the "zero" level.

IV. THE PROPOSED ALGORITHMS

In this section, we describe our QoT-aware rerouting algorithms called the *QoT-Aware Active Rerouting* algorithm and the *QoT-Aware Hybrid Rerouting* algorithm and referred to as the *QoT-AAR* and the *QoT-AHR* algorithms, respectively. Our proposed algorithms aim to optimize the network throughput in WDM all-optical networks with QoT consideration and minimize the incurred service disruption period. Both algorithms use the same routing and active rerouting procedures. They consider the RLDs sequentially, that is demand by demand at their arrival dates and compute for each RLD a suitable path-free wavelength that meets the required QoT without considering any rerouting. Also, both algorithms execute an active rerouting procedure when an established RLD leaves the network. Already established lightpaths that can be set up on a new vacant shorter path are selected to be rerouted by the active rerouting procedure in order to improve the network resources utilization efficiency. The main difference between the two proposed algorithms is that the QoT-AHR algorithm launches a passive wavelength rerouting procedure to hopefully free a wavelength-continuous route with an acceptable QoT to accommodate an incoming RLD which will otherwise be blocked by the routing procedure. On the other hand, the QoT-AAR algorithm rejects any RLD failed to be set up by the routing procedure.

Our proposed algorithms differ from the previously published ones in the following aspects: First, when solving the RWA problem, they explicitly take into account the physical impairments imposed by the optical layer. However, rerouting algorithms previously presented in the literature did not consider any transmission impairments. Second, our algorithms do not construct any auxiliary graph with crossover edges to determine the set of existing lightpaths that should be rerouted. Also, they do not use a random search algorithm to compute the RWA for lightpath requests. We hope, therefore, that our algorithms are less Central Processing Unit (CPU) intensive than rerouting algorithms previously presented in the literature.

In the following subsections, first we define some notations. Then, we detail the routing and rerouting procedures, respectively.

A. Notations

- $\Lambda = \{\lambda_1, \lambda_2, ..., \lambda_W\}$ is the set of available wavelengths on each fiber link. W denotes the number of available wavelengths per fiber link. We assume that all the network links have the same number of available wavelengths.
- The ith RLD, is defined by a $5-$tuple $(s_i, d_i, \pi_i, \alpha_i, \beta_i)$. s_i and d_i are the source and the destination nodes of the lightpath demand, respectively; π_i is the number of requested lightpaths. For the sake of simplicity, we assume here that $\pi = 1$. α_i and β_i are the setup and teardown times of the lightpath demand, respectively.
- $P_{i,k}$, $1 \leq i \leq D$ (D the total number of RLDs), $1 \leq k \leq K$, represents the kth alternate shortest path connecting node s_i to node d_i. We use the hop count as the link metric and compute beforehand K-alternate (loop-free) shortest paths for each source-destination pair (if as many paths exist, otherwise we only consider the available ones).
- $C_{i,k,w}$ is the cost of using wavelength λ_w on $P_{i,k}$. The cost function is determined as follows:
  $C_{i,k,w} =$
  $\begin{cases} \varepsilon, & if\ \lambda_w\ is\ path-free\ on\ P_{i,k} \\ +\infty, & if \lambda_w\ is\ already\ used \end{cases}$
  ε is a tiny positive value corresponding to the hop count on $P_{i,k}$.

B. The routing procedure

The routing procedure uses the Quality Path Selection Algorithm (QPSA) described in [5]. To establish an incoming RLD, the QPSA considers the K-alternate shortest paths (computed offline) in turn according to their number of hops. It looks for the first path-free wavelength with a Q-factor higher than the fixed threshold, $Q_{threshold}$. The Q-factor associated with each couple (path, wavelength) is estimated according to the expression given by (6). The RLD is hence established on the first met suitable path among its K-alternate shortest paths if such path exists.Otherwise, we distinguish two cases: the QoT-AAR algorithm rejects the RLD definitively, or, the QoT-AHR algorithm executes a passive wavelength rerouting procedure.

C. The active rerouting procedure

Both algorithms execute the active rerouting procedure every time an established RLD leaves the network. The active procedure first computes ϕ_i^t, the set of existing RLDs that should be rerouted when the ith RLD leaves the network at time t knowing that the rerouting of an existing RLD is allowed once during its life period in order to avoid the rerouting of an active RLD multiple times as the RLDs departure times may be very close. By doing so, we reduce the number of RLDs to be rerouted and consequently the overall service disruption period. Once ϕ_i^t is computed two cases may happen:

- $\phi_i^t = \emptyset$: None of the existing RLDs satisfy the preceding constraints. No rerouting is to be executed.
- $\phi_i^t \neq \emptyset$: Each RLD in ϕ_i^t is hence rerouted to a vacant shorter path using the routing procedure described in Subsection IV-B. The costs of the new path's edges used by the rerouted RLD are updated to $+\infty$ and to 1 the costs of the released path's edges.

D. The passive rerouting procedure of the QoT-AHR algorithm

The QoT-AHR algorithm launches the passive rerouting procedure whenever the routing procedure fails to satisfy an incoming RLD. It aims at freeing a wavelength-continuous route that meets the required QoT as follows:
For each shortest path k, $1 \leq k \leq K$, associated to the incoming RLD numbered i and for each wavelength λ_w, $1 \leq w \leq W$, we determine the set of RLDs that should be rerouted $\phi_{i,k,w}$ to set up the incoming RLD numbered i. We then compute the corresponding rerouting cost $RC_{k,w} = |\phi_{i,k,w}|$. After that we compute RC^{min} the minimum rerouting cost to satisfy the new RLD on $P_{i,k^{min}}$. If RC^{min} is finite, the kth-alternate shortest path and the wth wavelength that requires a minimum number of already established RLDs to be rerouted is hence selected. Let ϕ^{min} denote the corresponding set of RLDs to be rerouted. Two cases may happen: all the RLDs in ϕ^{min} can be rerouted by only changing the used wavelength whilst keeping the same physical path. In this case, the incoming RLD is serviced using $P_{i,k^{min}}$ on wavelength $\lambda_{w^{min}}$. $C_{i,k^{min},w^{min}}$ is updated to $+\infty$. We also update the costs of the new paths used by the rerouted RLDs to $+\infty$ and to 1 the cost of the released paths. The second case that may happen is that $P_{i,k^{min}}$ using $\lambda_{w^{min}}$ cannot be freed because one or several RLDs cannot be rerouted. In that case, we update $RC_{k^{min},w^{min}}$ to $+\infty$ and compute again the minimum cost. If RC^{min} is infinite, the incoming RLD is rejected definitively.

V. Simulations results

In order to evaluate the performance of the QoT-aware rerouting algorithms presented in the previous section, we carried out multiple simulation experiments on the $15-$node Pacific Bell network topology and the $16-$node Cost Core network topology, respectively. We assume that 43 wavelengths are available on each fiber-link of the network ($W = 43$). Also, $5-$alternate shortest paths ($K = 5$) are computed for each possible source-destination pair in the network. We assume that RLDs arrive at the network randomly according to a Poisson process with common arrival rate per node r and once accepted, will hold the circuits for exponentially distributed times with mean holding time equal to 10 much larger than the network-wide propagation delay and the connection set-up delay. The source and destination nodes of the RLDs are drawn according to a random uniform distribution in the intervals $[1, 15]$ and $[1, 16]$ for the $15-$node network and the $16-$node network, respectively. The required value of the $Q-$factor is chosen equal to 6 which corresponds to a BER of 10^{-9}.

We generate 25 test-scenarios, that is, 25 different traffic matrices, run algorithms for each scenario, and compute mean values. The QoT-aware rerouting algorithms performances are measured in terms of average rejection ratio and average ratio of rerouted RLDs. The average rejection ratio is defined as the ratio of the average number of rejected RLDs to the total number of RLDs arriving at the network. The average ratio of rerouted RLDs is computed as the average number of rerouted RLDs divided by the total number of RLDs arriving at the network. In the following, we only provide the curves obtained with the $15-$node network as those obtained with the $16-$node network present the same tendency.

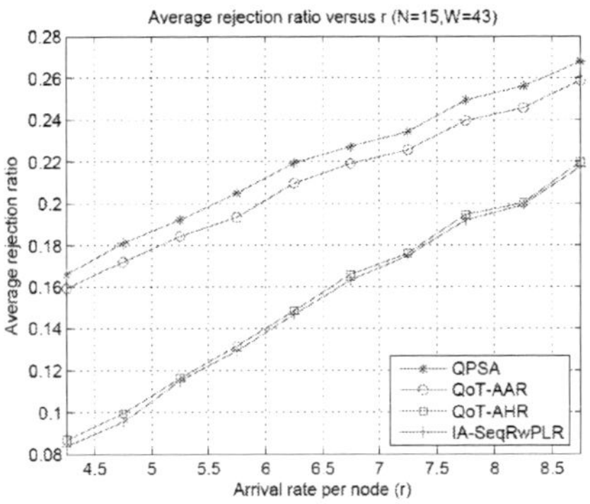

Figure 1. Average rejection ratio versus r.

In the following, we propose to compare the average rejection ratios, computed by our proposed QoT-aware rerouting algorithms to those computed by the Quality Path Selection Algorithm (QPSA) described in [5] which computes the RWA for RLDs sequentially taking into account QoT requirements and our Impairment-Aware Sequential Routing with Passive Lightpath Rerouting (IA-SeqRwPLR) algorithm described in [10]. The IA-SeqRwPLR algorithm considers the RLDs sequentially and computes for each RLD a suitable path and a suitable path-free wavelength that meet the minimum QoT requirement. The rerouting procedure is launched whenever the routing procedure fails in setting up the considered RLD. The rerouting procedure aims at freeing a path-free wavelengths that meets the required QoT by rerouting a minimum number of already established RLDs either by only changing the used wavelength whilst keeping the same physical path or by changing the physical path and then possibly the used wavelength.

In Figure 1, we draw the average rejection ratios computed by the four algorithms described above for various arrival rates per node, r. From Figure 1, one may deduce three main conclusions.

- The average rejection ratios increase with r due to the limited number of available resources with acceptable Q-factor. Thanks to rerouting (be it passive, active or hybrid), the average rejection ratio is improved. On the average, the rejection ratio is reduced up to: 8.58% (respectively 6.55% for the 16-node network) with the IA-SeqRwPLR algorithm, 8.16% (respectively 6.12% for the 16-node network) with the QoT-AHR algorithm and 1.5% (respectively 1.3% for the 16-node network) with the QoT-AAR algorithm.
- The IA-SeqRwPLR and the QoT-AHR algorithms outperform the QOT-AAR algorithm, outlining a significant improvement in term of average rejection ratio. In fact, the QOT-AAR algorithm has the worst rejection ratio performance because it is so difficult, for a given established RLD, to find a new shorter

physical path satisfying the required QoT among its K shortest paths. Also, imposing that an established RLD can be rerouted on new physical path only once during its life period results in decreasing the number of rerouted RLDs and hence the network resources consumption reduction becomes limited.

- Unexpectedly the IA-SeqRwPLR algorithm has a rejection ratio that is slightly lower than that computed by the QoT-AHR algorithm despite the fact that the QoT-AHR algorithm applies both active and passive rerouting procedures. This is mainly due to the fact that when applying passive rerouting procedure LRR rerouting is not allowed which causes the failure of the passive wavelength rerouting procedure to free a wavelength-continuous route to set up an incoming RLD. Also, the active procedure does not provide an impressive network resources consumption reduction as discussed above.

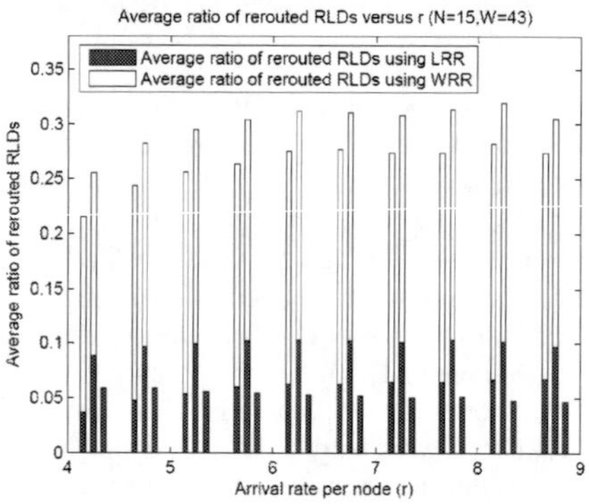

Figure 2. Average ratio of rerouted RLDs versus r.

In Figure 2, each group of three bars shows the average ratio of rerouted RLDs computed using the IA-SeqRwPLR, the QoT-AHR and the QoT-AAR algorithms respectively with respect to r. The height of the blue bar indicates the average ratio of rerouted RLDs using LRR whereas the height of the white one shows the average ratio of rerouted RLDs using WRR.

We notice, obviously, that the IA-SeqRwPLR and the QoT-AHR algorithms require more RLDs to be rerouted when r increases. In fact, when r increases, the probability that an incoming RLD be rejected is higher and hence, more existing RLDs have to be rerouted to set up the new RLD and consequently the number of RLDs to reroute increases. Under high traffic load, the average number of rerouted RLDs reaches an upper bound corresponding to the network saturation. Unlike those algorithms, the average ratio of RLDs to be rerouted by the QoT-AAR algorithm decreases when r increases. Indeed, when the network reaches its saturation regime, it becomes difficult to reroute an active lightpath to a shorter path satisfying the required QoT.

We also notice that the average ratios of rerouted RLDs by the IA-SeqRwPLR and the QoT-AHR algorithms using LRR are much lower than the average ratios of rerouted RLDs using WRR. This should, hopefully, lead to short service disruption period.

VI. Conclusion and Future Work

In this paper, we have investigated the RWA problem with signal-quality constraint for dynamic traffic in WDM all-optical networks. Our proposed RWA algorithms apply active or hybrid rerouting to alleviate the inefficiency brought by the wavelength continuity and the QoT requirement constraints. Obtained results show that passive and hybrid rerouting work much better than active rerouting. Passive lightpath rerouting is an efficient way to improve the rejection ratio performance with a short service disruption period. Our forthcoming studies will consider more physical layer impairment effects to make the proposed algorithms more effective.

References

[1] N. Naas and H. Mouftah, "Towards realistic planning of WDM transport network", Proc. 2005 7th International Conference Transparent Optical Networks, pp. 54-57, 2005.

[2] H. Zang, J.P. Jue, and B. Mukherjee, "A review of routing and wavelength assignment approaches for wavelength-routed WDM networks," Optical Networks Magazine, vol. 1, no. 1, pp. 47-60, 2000.

[3] E. W. M. Wong, A. K. M. Chan, and T. S. P. Yum, "A taxonomy of rerouting in circuit switched networks," IEEE Communications Magazine, vol. 37, no. 11, pp. 116-122, 1999.

[4] K. C. Lee and V. O. K. Li, "A wavelength rerouting algorithm in wide-area all-optical networks," IEEE/OSA Journal of Lightwave Technology, vol. 14, no. 6, pp. 1218-1229, 1996.

[5] M. Bakri, M. Kouba, M. Menif, and I.Ouerda, "Static lightpath establishment with transmission impairments consideration in WDM all-optical networks," Proc. the 7th International Workshop on Design of Reliable Communication Networks, pp. 251-258, 2009.

[6] R. Sabella, E. Iannone, M. Listanti, M. Berdusco, and S. Binetti, "Impact of transmission performance on path routing in all-optical transport network," IEEE/OSA Journal of Lightwave Technology. vol. 16, no. 11, pp. 1965- 1972, 1998.

[7] B. Ramamurthy,D. Datta, H. Feng, J. Heritage, and B. Mukherjee, "Impact of transmission impairments on the teletraffic performance of wavelength-routed optical networks," IEEE/OSA Journal of Lightwave Technology, vol. 17 no. 10, pp. 1713-1723, 1999.

[8] I. Cerutti, A. Fumagalli, and M. J. Potasek, "Effects of chromatic dispersion and self-phase Modulation in multihop multirate WDM rings," IEEE Photonics Technology Letters, vol. 14, no. 3, pp. 411-413, 2002.

[9] I. E. Fonseca, M. R. N. Ribeiro, and H. Waldman, "Differentiated optical QoS under a low complexity FWM-aware wavelength assignment algorithm," Proc. the Optical Network Design and Modeling Conference, pp. 431-438, 2005.

[10] N. Amdouni, M. Koubàa, and T. Aguili, "A Novel lightpath rerouting algorithm for dynamic traffic with transmission impairments consideration in WDM all-optical networks," Proc. IEEE International Conference on Computer Systems and Industrial Informatics (ICCSII12), pp. 1-6, 2012.

[11] N. Amdouni, M. Kouba, and T. Aguili, "On the impact of lightpath rerouting on connection provisioning with transmission impairments in WDM all-optical Networks," Journal of Emerging Trends in Computing and Information Sciences, vol.4, pp. 76-84, 2013.

[12] N. Amdouni and T. Aguili, "A new wavelength rerouting scheme with short service disruption period for dynamic traffic in WDM transparent optical networks with physical layer impairments consideration," in press. 2016 7th International Conference on Sciences of Electronics, Technologies of Information and Telecommunications (SETIT), pp. 1-4, 2016.

Performance Improvement of AMBE 3600 bps Vocoder with Improved FEC

Ali Ekşim and Hasan Yetik
Center of Research for Advanced Technologies of
Informatics and Information Security
(TUBITAK-BILGEM) Turkey
e-mail: {ali.eksim, hasan.yetik}@tubitak.gov.tr

***Abstract*—Efficiency and performance of the heavily used electronic devices in the field are always open for debate. As the technology advances, efficiency and performance of the electronic devices increase. Digital communication systems are also getting their share of this development trend. Digital communication systems, such as Digital Private Mobile Radio, Digital Mobile Radio/MotoTRBO, Association of Public-Safety Communications Officials-International Project 25 and Icom-Kenwood NEXEDGE use half rate Advanced Multi-Band Excitation (AMBE) 3600 bps vocoder to provide clean and intelligible voice communication service. Although this half rate vocoder incorporates Forward Error Correction (FEC) coding to protect voice frames, its error correction performance does not meet today's standards. To improve the FEC performance of the vocoder, in this work, we assess the FEC portion of the vocoder and propose a better performing FEC scheme. The proposed 2/3 rate convolutional code with vocoder frame length reduction provides a 4.41 dB coding gain in the high signal-to-noise region compared to AMBE FEC while preserving audio quality. Since all works are conducted around the vocoder section, improvements can be easily implemented in existing digital communication systems and standards.**

Keywords- Digital mobile radio; forward error correction; perceptual evaluation of speech quality; punctured convolutional coding; speech codec; vocoder.

I. INTRODUCTION

From small sites to huge organizations, mobile communication systems have evolved from analog to digital in order to keep up with the fast pace of the modern world. Since digital radios provide better sound quality and extensive data services compared to their analog counterparts, they are commonly used in areas where people need wireless communication. There is a large number of digital radio systems, which are already available, such as Digital Private Mobile Radio (dPMR) [1], Digital Mobile Radio (DMR) [2]-[3], NXDN [4], APCO P25 [5], digital smart technologies for amateurs (D-Star) [6], etc. All digital radios incorporate at least one type of vocoder to provide voice services over digital communication channel. There is a vast number of speech coders currently available. Advanced Multi-Band Excitation Speech Codec (AMBE) [1]-[2] is one of them and it is used in many communication systems. AMBE half rate 3600 bps vocoder is used in the following digital radio systems: dPMR, DMR/MotoTRBO, APCO P25 and NXDN [1]-[6]. AMBE 3600 bps vocoder consists of 1150 bps Forward Error Correction (FEC) and 2450 bps vocoder data.

AMBE speech codec is a type of speech compression technique. It consists of encoder and decoder. It can encode samples of voice data to a compressed stream and can generate synthesized voice output bits from the compressed bit stream [7].

In theory, digital radios outperform their analog counterparts in terms of voice quality. We do not always have ideal conditions and also we do not always have high Signal-to-Noise Ratio (SNR) value. Due to attenuation and distortions in the communication channel, the overall Bit Error Rate (BER) performance of the digital radio degrades hence lowers the voice quality. Even though every 49 data bits of vocoder are accompanied by 23 FEC bits, the AMBE vocoder FEC cannot perform well. For this reason, limited communication range and bad audio quality can happen in noisy environments. To enhance the voice quality without modifying digital communication standards and protocols, the AMBE vocoder FEC should be improved. AMBE vocoder is an independent system which is realized in an isolated integrated circuit (IC) or a software library.

To improve the FEC performance of the AMBE vocoder, a better FEC can be employed. In [8], the authors show that replacing the AMBE forward error correction scheme with a combination of block code and 5/6 rate Punctured Convolutional Code (PCC) provides 3.35 dB additional gain in the high SNR region. But, we can further increase the coding gain using solely convolutional codes, hence increasing the audio quality and the communication range. Although Turbo codes provide more coding gain than convolutional codes, they are not suitable for short block size such as 49 bits [9] [10]. In addition, it is widely known that Low Density Parity Check codes work better when large block sizes are utilized [11]. Because we are dealing with a small block size, convolutional codes are selected in the proposed FEC scheme. In this work, we proposed and present an improved FEC which outperforms the AMBE standard and the FEC scheme proposed in [8].

In the following section, existing FEC schemes are described. In Section 3, the proposed FEC scheme is explained. In Section 4, the performance analysis is presented. In Section 5, the results of the paper and the conclusion are explained. In the last section, the future work is given.

II. EXISTING FEC SCHEMES

AMBE 3600 bps vocoder is a very low-rate speech coder used for voice transmission. Due to the high compression ratio every bit of information in the compressed speech data stream has low or high importance, but not zero. Compressed audio is more vulnerable to bit errors compared to the sampled audio. Depending on which parameter bits are exposed to bit error, they either distort or impair the synthesized voice. So, vocoder frames must be protected very well to prevent audio loss in those digital radios using speech codecs like AMBE 3600 bps half rate speech coder.

FEC is a largely researched and advanced technique to detect and correct errors in data frames. Different error correction codes can recover different number of bits. If the data is received with a greater number of errors than that the employed FEC can recover, the decoder cannot reconstruct the received data correctly. In those conditions, catastrophic errors occur while reconstructing data frames. In an environment where BER is very low, the AMBE vocoder performs well and provides good voice quality at 3600 bps [7]. However, when the BER values are very high, the AMBE vocoder cannot correct the received vocoder frame errors, hence cannot reconstruct the audio. To make the AMBE vocoder more noise resistant, a better FEC scheme should be implemented.

One of the most commonly used vocoders, the half rate AMBE 3600 bps speech coder, is composed of 2450 bps voice and 1150 bps FEC data. By standard, AMBE coded voice is sent in 20 ms voice packets. Each voice frame is composed of 49 voice data bits and 23 FEC bits. The FEC used in the AMBE 3600 bps vocoder incorporates one extended Golay (24,12) code and one Golay (23,12) code. There is also data dependent scrambler and modulation key parameter involved in the FEC scheme. Standard FEC implementation is employed to protect the most sensitive 24 bits while the remaining bits are left unprotected [5]. Block diagrams of the AMBE 3600 bps FEC encoder and decoder are given in Figure 1 and Figure 2, respectively.

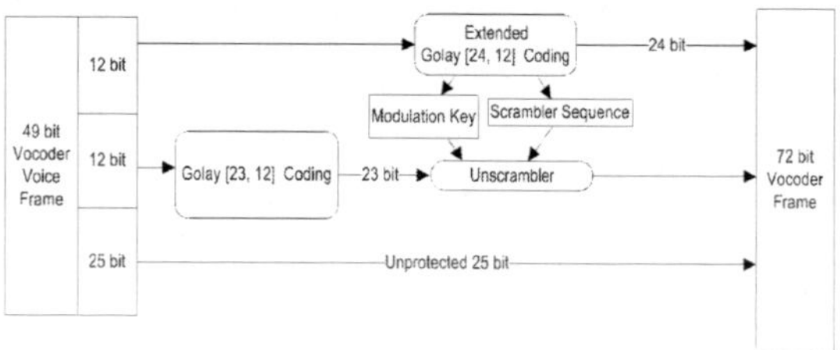

Figure 1. 3600 bps AMBE's vocoder FEC encoder scheme

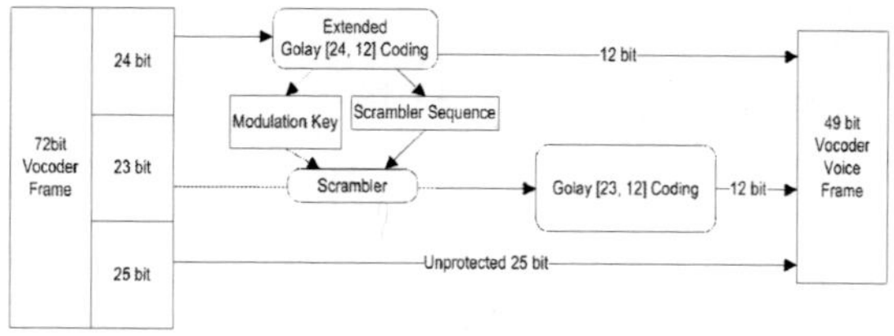

Figure 2. 3600 bps AMBE`s vocoder FEC decoder scheme.

As seen in Figure 1 and Figure 2, AMBE FEC scheme uses modulation key and data dependent scrambler derived from the first Golay code while encoding or decoding the second Golay code. If an irrecoverable error occurs in the first Golay code, the modulation key and the descrambler sequence cannot be calculated correctly. Wrong modulation key and descrambling sequence create more errors and escalade the overall erroneous bit count. Due to the high number of bit errors, irrecoverable frames cannot be decoded and discarded. Hence, the voice quality falls catastrophically and the received speech cannot be synthesized at all due to high BER. This chain reaction becomes self-inflicted destruction for the vocoder frames. In such situations, the AMBE vocoder offers comforting silence or frame repetition in the place of irrecoverable frames.

By standard, AMBE 3600 bps speech coder does not protect the whole voice frame from errors. Although less error sensitive or less significant vocoder parameter bits have less impact on synthesized voice quality, their effect is non-zero. All the bits in compressed speech have either a major or a minor effect on the overall synthesized voice quality. For a communication channel where the BER value is lower than P_b=10^{-5}, there is no noticeable change in voice quality and intelligibility. In contrast, when the BER value is higher than P_b=10^{-5}, the synthesized voice quality degrades and impairs intelligibility.

In order to improve the voice quality of the AMBE 3600 bps vocoder by making the vocoder more immune to errors, vocoder frames should have better protection than what AMBE provides. To enhance FEC performance, Golay (23,12) code along with 5/6 rate convolution code FEC scheme was implemented in the AMBE 3600 bps vocoder [8]. Hybrid FEC encoder and decoder block diagrams of the referenced work are given in Figure 3 and Figure 4, respectively.

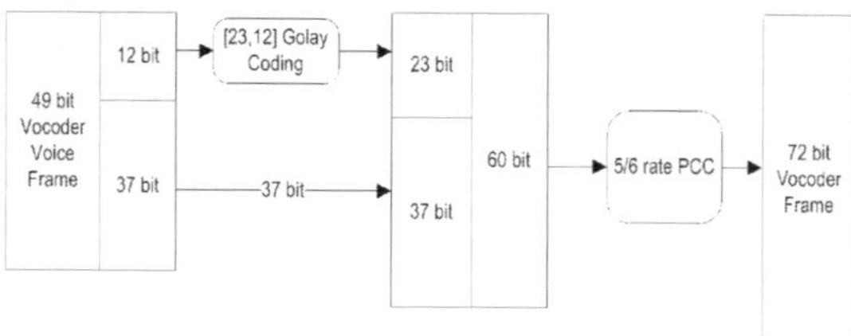

Figure 3. Hybrid FEC encoder block diagram for vocoder in [8].

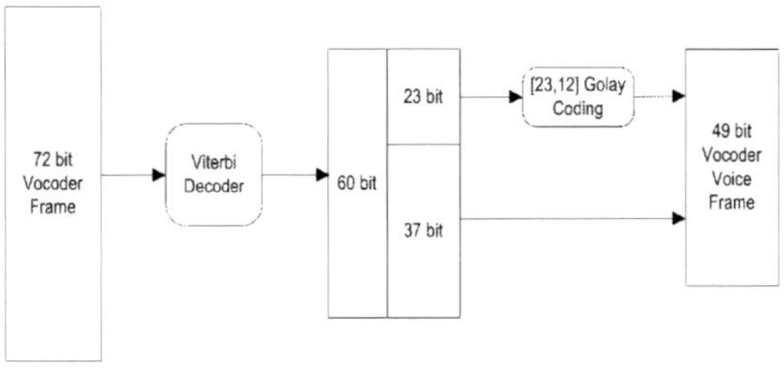

Figure 4. Hybrid FEC decoder block diagram for vocoder in [8].

In the given work, Golay (23,12) code adds additional 11 bits to 49 bits and makes 60 bits of data. After 5/6 rate convolutional code is applied, the frame becomes 72 bits. The referenced work incorporates block and convolutional codes in sequence to avoid making any modification to the AMBE vocoder frame while improving the FEC performance and synthesized audio quality.

III. PROPOSED FEC SCHEME

For further improvement on the AMBE FEC performance, instead of using solely block codes or using block and convolutional codes in sequence, utilizing purely convolutional code yields increased coding gain. To utilize a better convolutional code than in [8], the number of FEC bits in vocoder frame should be increased by 1 bit. As given above, the AMBE standard produces 23 FEC bits for every 49 vocoder data bits. In digital radio systems where vocoders and compressed data are used extensively, bit stealing is common practice to reduce data length to optimize the FEC or transmitted data rate [13] [14]. In order to steal 1 bit from vocoder voice frame data, more than 100 hours (over 19 million voice frames) of AMBE 3600 bps coded records have been analyzed in terms of individual bit probabilities in the vocoder voice frame. Bit probabilities in vocoder voice frame are given in Figure 5.

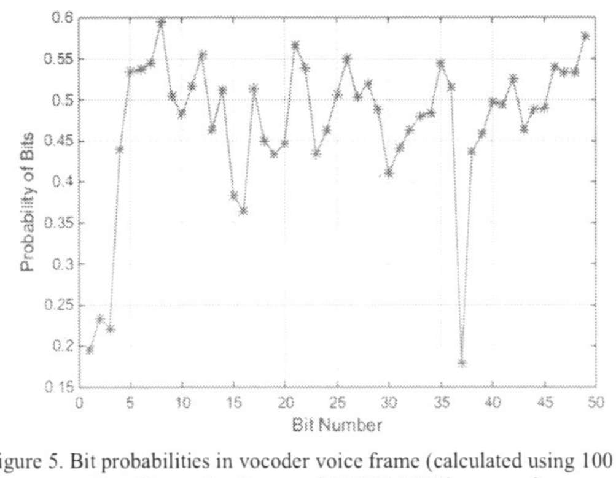

Figure 5. Bit probabilities in vocoder voice frame (calculated using 100 hours, over 19 million voice frames of AMBE 3600 bps record).

As seen in Figure 5, 37th bit in voice frame is zero with a 82.104% probability. Additionally, 37th bit is one of the less sensitive bits in AMBE 3600 bps voice frame and represents the least significant bit of 5-bit gain value [7]. Having said that, we decided to discard the 37th bit in vocoder frames prior to encoding, and add 37th bit back to the frame with zero value after decoding. After bit stealing was taken into account, a vast number of vocoder voice frames were processed and their voice quality was assessed by using the perceptual evaluation of speech quality (PESQ) method. PESQ is an objective method for speech quality assessment of narrow-band telephone networks and speech codecs developed by the International Telecommunication Union (ITU) [15] [16]. Results of the PESQ tests showed that the stolen bit has very low impact on voice quality and intelligibility hence, its effect is negligible. PESQ test results for randomly selected synthesized speech files are shown in Table 1.

TABLE 1. MEAN OPINION SCORES OF RANDOMLY SELECTED AND SYNTHESIZED SPEECH FILES AFTER PROPOSED BIT STEALING PROCEDURE APPLIED

	Raw MOS	MOS LQO
File 1	4.392	4.480
File 2	4.416	4.496
File 3	4.434	4.508
File 4	4.353	4.453
File 5	4.419	4.498

After bit stealing, 48 bit long vocoder voice frame became suitable for 2/3 rate PCC. The proposed PCC can obtain a 1/2 rate convolutional code with constraint length 12 and the generator polynomial [6765 4627] [17]. The block diagrams of the proposed FEC encoder and decoder are given in Figure 6 and Figure 7, respectively.

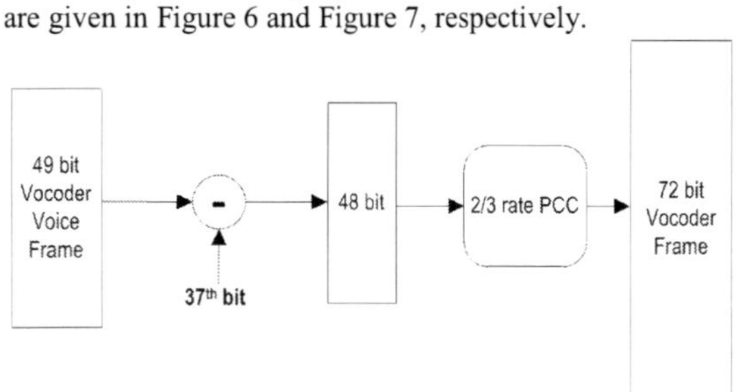

Figure 6. Block diagram of proposed 2/3 convolutional FEC encoder for vocoder.

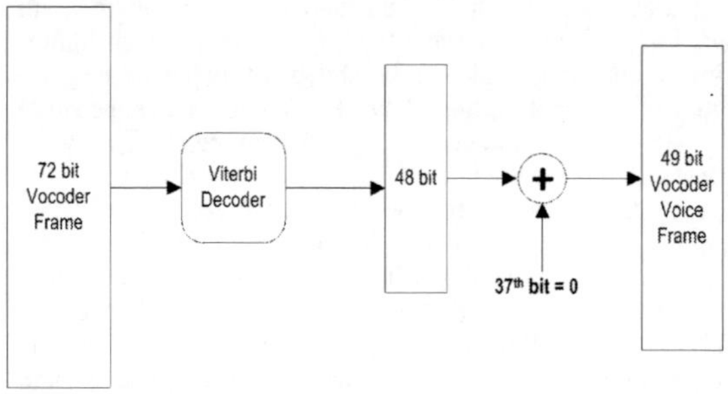

Figure 7. Block diagram of proposed 2/3 convolutional FEC decoder for vocoder.

IV. PERFORMANCE ANALYSIS

The bit error probabilities of the proposed FEC scheme are evaluated for four-level frequency-shift keying (4-FSK) modulation by Monte Carlo simulations. In the simulations, additive white Gaussian noise (AWGN) channel is employed. For comparison, the BER curves of uncoded 4-FSK, AMBE standard, Golay codes, hybrid Golay and 5/6 rate PCC FEC and the proposed 2/3 rate PCC FEC are also included in Figure 8.

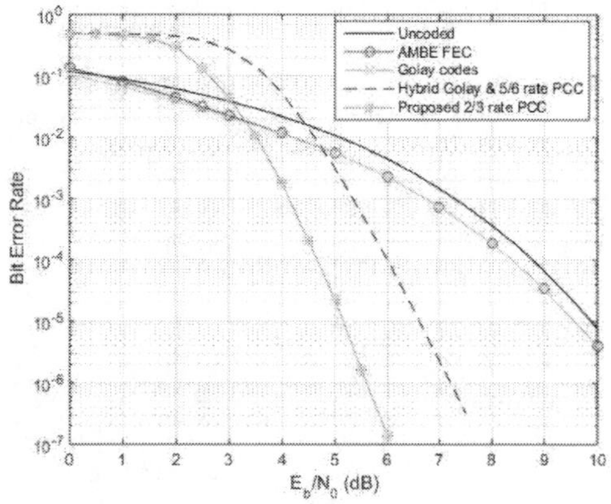

Figure 8. BER performance of uncoded, AMBE FEC, Golay (23,12) codes (AMBE FEC without scrambler), hybrid Golay (23,12) and 5/6 rate PCC and proposed 2/3 rate PCC.

Compared to uncoded 4-FSK, the AMBE FEC scheme provides an E_b/N_0 advantage of approximately 0.31 dB for a BER value of $P_b=10^{-5}$. The hybrid Golay and 5/6 rate PCC FEC scheme [8] provides an E_b/N_0 advantage of approximately 3.35 dB with respect to the AMBE FEC scheme. Relative to the hybrid Golay and 5/6 rate PCC FEC scheme, the proposed 2/3 rate punctured convolutional code FEC scheme provides an E_b/N_0 advantage of approximately 1.06 dB. Moreover, 2/3 rate punctured convolutional code FEC achieves 4.41 dB coding gain with respect to the AMBE FEC. Also, it can be clearly seen that the Golay code without data dependent scrambler (cyan curve), which is performance of Golay (24,12) and Golay (23,12) codes in sequence, is better than the AMBE FEC due to the high number of bit errors caused by the scrambler in low E_b/N_0 values.

V. CONCLUSION

For any of the digital radio systems listed in the introduction section, the received vocoder frames are conveyed to DVSI's AMBE 3000 vocoder IC or vocoder software library within the radio central processing unit or digital signal processing without any interpretation or processing. Since voice frames are protected only by vocoder FEC, it is easy to change vocoder FEC to obtain more coding gain without modifying the air interface protocols used in radios. In this work, bit stealing enabled us to use 2/3 rate PCC inside the AMBE 3600 bps vocoder while preserving audio quality, as shown in the PESQ test results. Audio quality measurements are given in terms of mean opinion score and obtained using PESQ method. With the help of 2/3 rate PCC, we obtained 1.51 dB and 4.41 dB coding gain compared to the study in [8] and AMBE 3600 bps FEC respectively. Increased coding gain provides increased voice quality and procures higher communication link quality in noisy environments. Increased coding gain may also help to extend battery consumption in battery powered radio. By utilizing the proposed FEC, we need less transmission power to achieve the same performance and communication range than that available with the present FEC.

VI. FUTURE WORK

For further improvement on AMBE FEC performance, unequal error protection techniques can be utilized to obtain more coding gain or increased voice quality. For future work, unequal error protection schemes will be evaluated and applied in order to enhance voice quality or coding gain.

REFERENCES

[1] dPMR Association. dPMR Product Class Interoperability Classification Guide. [Online]. Available from: http://www.dpmr-mou.org/downloads/dPMR-Product-Class-Marking-0v8.pdf retrieved: September, 2016.

[2] DMR Association. Benefits and Features of DMR. [Online]. Available from: www.dmrassociation.org/downloads/documents/DMR-Association-White-Paper_Benefits-and-Features-of-DMR_160512.pdf retrieved: July, 2016.

[3] Tait Radio Communication. Technologies and Standards for Mobile Radio Communications Networks. [Online]. Available from: http://utilities.taitradio.com/__data/assets/pdf_file/0005/39461/tait_technologycomparison_whitepaper_eng.pdf retrieved: September, 2016.

[4] NXDN Technical Specifications, NXDN TS 1-D V1.3, November, 2011.

[5] APCO Project 25 Half-Rate Vocoder, TIA-102.BABA, 2009.

[6] Digital Voice Systems, Inc. AMBE-3003 Vocoder Chip. [Online]. Available from: http://www.dvsinc.com/products/a3003.htm

[7] J. C. Hardwick, "Half-rate Vocoder", U.S. Patent 8 359 197 B2, Jan. 22, 2013.

[8] A. Eksim and H. Yetik, "Voice Quality Enhancement for ETSI Digital Mobile Radio Standard Using Improved FEC Scheme," to appear in Proceedings of the 40th International Conference on Telecommunications and Signal Processing, Barcelona, Spain, July 5-7, 2017

[9] C. Berrou, A. Glavieux and P. Thitimasjshima, "Near Shannon limit error-correcting coding and decoding: turbo codes", IEEE International Conf. Commun., pp. 1064-1070, 1993.

[10] C. Berrou, "The ten-year-old turbo codes are entering into service", IEEE Communication Magazine, vol. 41, no. 8, pp. 110-116, Aug. 2003.

[11] M. G. Luby, M. Mitzenmacher, M. A. Shokrollahi, and D. A. Spielman, "Improved Low-Density Parity-Check Codes Using Irregular Graphs", IEEE Trans. Information Theory, vol. 47, no. 2, pp. 585-598, Feb. 2001.

[12] M. K. Simon, S. M. Hinedi, and W. C. Lindsey, "Digital Communication Techniques: Signal Design and Detection," Englewood Cliffs, New Jersey: Prentice-Hall, 1995.

[13] K. Kondo and T. Suzuki, "Method and System for Transmitting Variable Rate Speech Signal", U.S. Patent 4 903 301, Feb. 20, 1990.

[14] D. Karakos and A. Papamarcou, "A relationship between quantization and watermarking rates in the presence of additive Gaussian attacks," in IEEE Transactions on Information Theory, vol. 49, no. 8, pp. 1970-1982, Aug. 2003.

[15] ITU-T Recommendation P.800, Methods for subjective determination of transmission quality, Geneva, 1996.

[16] ITU-T Recommendation P.862, Perceptual evaluation of speech quality (PESQ), an objective method for end-to-end speech quality assessment of narrowband telephone networks and speech codecs, Geneva, 2001.

[17] P. Lee, "Further Results on Rate 1/N Convolutional Code Constructions with Minimum Required SNR Criterion," in IEEE Transactions on Communications, vol. 34, no. 4, pp. 395-399, Apr 1986.

Accuracy of Power Prediction Models in ZigBee Sensor Networks Applied in Grass Environment

Teles de Sales Bezerra,
José Anderson Rodrigues de Souza,
Reinaldo Cézar de Morais Gomes

Federal University of Campina Grande, Brazil
Emails: {teles, joseanderson}@copin.ufcg.edu.br,
reinaldo@computacao.ufcg.edu.br

Erlandson de Sales Bezerra

State University of Paraíba, Brazil

Email: erlandson.angra@gmail.com

Saulo Aislan da Silva Eleutério,
Anderson Fabiano Batista
Ferreira da Costa
and Jerônimo Silva Rocha

Federal Institute of Education, Science
and Technology of Paraíba, Brazil
Emails: sauloaislan20@gmail.com,
anderson@ifpb.edu.br and
jeronimorocha@gmail.com

Abstract—**Wireless Sensor Networks (WSNs) have become an area of great interest due to their usage in a wide range of applications. A preliminary study concerning the viability of a WSN introduced in the environment is recommended, considering that this type of network is applied with several variables that influence the operation of the network. Those variables directly affect the network performance metrics such as the Received Signal Strength Indicator (RSSI). The present paper provides a study about the application of a WSN on a specific environment to practice sports, in which the RSSI metric was used to study the link quality. The study uses several power prediction models, and the results were compared with real measurements in order to identify the best prediction model in this particular environment.**

Keywords–Wireless Sensor; RSSI; Sports environment; Real measurements.

I. Introduction

Wireless Sensor Networks (WSNs) have became a very interesting research topic in the last few years. The recent advances in microelectromechanical systems technologies, wireless communications, and digital electronics have enabled the development of low-cost sensor nodes, that are capable of communicating with each other over short distances. Small nodes consist of a few components: a radio part for spreading data, a sensor part for sensing environment phenomena, a processing unit and a power supply. The potential application of wireless technologies has also been recognized by the Institute of Electrical and Electronics Engineers (IEEE), which set up a standardization group 802.15.4 for designing a new physical layer for low-data rate communications combined with positioning capabilities [1].

WSNs came into the spotlight during the past years due to the advances in wireless communications, such as new information technologies and electronic attributes developed for those technologies [2]. It is even possible to affirm that WSNs are a quite promising technology of this generation since they have a great utility because of their implementation in industrial control systems. Other advantages to be mentioned are their low cost and multi-functional sensors that perform surveillance functions and day-to-day activities control.

It is because of their versatility that WSNs have generated increasing interest in the past few years [3]. In the last two decades, surveys indicate that the wireless systems will be capable of extending even more the application fields. There are applications such as in health care, home automation and automation in general. A relevant topic observed while researching wireless systems, was the characterization of how the radio signals range varies according to indoor and outdoor environments because of the conditions on some ambient factors, that can immediately make a transmission harder to be done, due to interferences [4].

The main goal of this research is to perform a study in addition to the works presented by [5] and [6], in which the authors conducted a performance analysis of ZigBee devices in each environment. This work uses the same space so that, from the results presented in [5] and [6] the performances can be compared with power prediction models, and, thus, estimate the accuracy of the proposed model. This application has importance because of the existence of different places, such as for sporting events, which makes necessary the use of resources to provide improvements, such as water, in environments where this type of WSN is widely used.

This paper is organized as follows: Section II shows fundamental concepts in ZigBee and RSSI. Section III shows the related works and Section IV shows the importance of power prediction in networks. In Section V the mechanisms of Radio Frequency (RF) Propagation are shown. Section VI shows the Propagation Models used in this paper. In Section VII the Statistical Methods used to analyze the measurements are explored. Section VIII shows the Methodology of Experiments and finally, Section IX shows the results and conclusion about this work.

II. ZigBee Technology and RSSI

The ZigBee technology is an option to supply a space in WSN's network architecture. This technology has advantages compared of other communications protocols, such as Wi-Fi [7] and Bluetooth [8]. ZigBee technology has a protocol which supports mesh, star and tree networks, creating more than one path possible between transmitter and receiver.

Thus, an information packet that can not be transmitted through one path can find another path that may deliver it. This works in a similar way with the routing table which is created by a router, making possible the delivery of a packet.

ZigBee operates in three frequency bands: 868 MHz in Europe, 915 MHz in the USA and 2.4 GHz in the rest of the world. It bases on IEEE's 802.15.4 protocol to implement the Physical (PHY) and Media Access Control (MAC) layers from the OSI model. Other layers are defined by *ZigBee Alliance* [9]. In many applications, and in the ZigBee Technology the performance is measured by the RSSI metric.

Received Signal Strength Indicator (RSSI) is used as a measurement system to estimate the transmission quality between two nodes based on their relative distance. RSSI is implemented under IEEE 802.11 Standard [10]. This method uses relative distance to estimate the transmitted signal quality by comparing the received signal with probability distributions and location measurements based on the statistic analysis method [11]. On RSSI, its importance is due to the severity of fading effects on wireless communications, causing their existence to directly affect the performance of wireless communications systems [6], [12], [13], [14]. Most 802.11 radio modules support RSSI, which means it is possible to calculate received power to each received packet. The power or energy of a signal travelling between two nodes is a signal parameter that contains information related to the distance between those nodes. This parameter can be used together with path-loss and shadowing model for distance estimation [1].

III. Related Works

Various papers have been published with the purpose of investigating the effects on the propagation of radio signals in the *ZigBee* devices. Jafer et al. [15] have investigated the effects caused by external factors on the RF signals. Specifically, they have analysed the RF activity outdoors for 24 hours in order to investigate the influence of time on the RSSI measurements and therefore to estimate the difference between day and night measurements. The effects of the communication were aleatory and erratic because people might have been passing through the area. The effects of internal factors on RSSI measurements have also been analyzed, such as the effect of polarization antenna between the transmitter and the receiver [16], or the effect of the conception of hardware devices [17]. Pellegrini et al. [18] perform a RF propagation analysis using collected RSSI values.

IV. Importance of Propagation Prediction

Before implementing the designs and confirming the planning of wireless communication systems, accurate propagation characteristics of the environment should be noted. Propagation prediction usually provides two types of parameters corresponding to the large-scale path loss and small-scale fading statistics. The path loss information is vital to determine the coverage of a base-station (BS) placement and also in optimizing it. The small-scale parameters usually provide statistical information on local field variations and this, in turn, leads to the calculation of important parameters that helps improve receiver (Rx) designs and combat the multipath fading. Without propagation predictions, these parameter estimations can only be obtained by field measurements which are time consuming and expensive [19].

V. Radio Frequency Propagation

With the increasing capacity of mobile communications, the size of a cell is becoming continuously smaller: from macrocell to microcell, and then to picocell. The service for environments includes both outdoor and indoor areas.

When propagation is considered in an outdoor environment, three different areas catch our attention: urban, suburban, and rural areas. In those cases, the terrain profile of the particular area needs to be considered. The terrain profile may vary from a simple, curved Earth to a highly mountainous region. The presence of trees, buildings, moving cars, and other obstacles must also be taken into account. The direct path, reflections from the ground and buildings, and diffraction from the comers and buildings' rooftops are the main contributors to the total field generated at a receiver, due to radio-wave propagation.

Reflection, diffraction, and scattering are the three basic propagation mechanisms that impact propagation in mobile communication systems [20] which will be briefly explained below.

A. Reflection

Reflection occurs when a propagating electromagnetic wave impinges upon an object that has very large dimensions compared to the wavelength of the propagating wave. It occurs from the surface of the ground, from walls, and from furniture. And when it does, the wave may also be partially refracted.

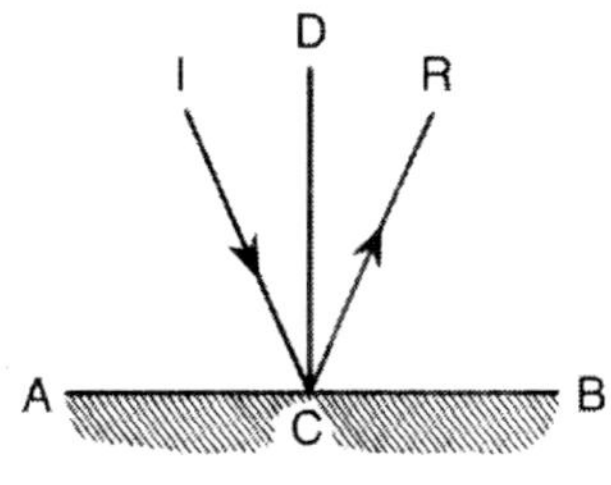

Figure 1. Reflection.

The coefficients of reflection and refraction are functions of the material properties of the medium, and generally depend on the wave polarization, the angle of incidence, and the frequency of the propagating wave [20]. These effects are shown in Fig. 1.

B. Diffraction

Diffraction occurs when the radio path between the transmitter and receiver is obstructed by a surface that has sharp edges, (Fig. 2).

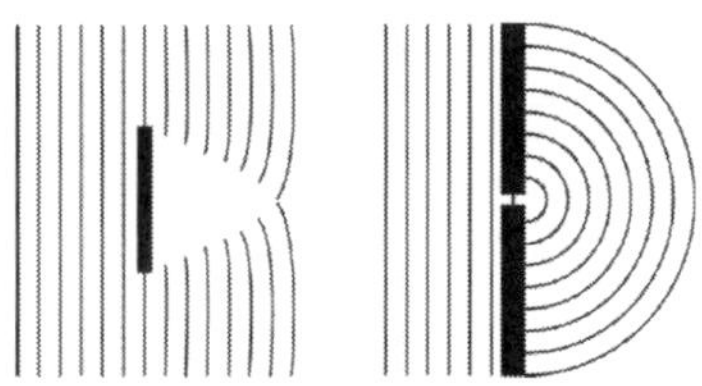

Figure 2. Diffraction.

The waves produced by the obstructing surface are present throughout space and even behind the obstacle, giving rise to the bending of waves around the obstacle, even when a line of sight (LOS) path does not exist between the transmitter and receiver. At high frequencies, diffraction - like reflection - depends on the geometry of the object, as well as on the amplitude, phase, and polarization of the incident wave at the point of diffraction [20]. These effects are shown in Fig. 2.

C. Scattering

Scattering occurs when the medium through which the wave propagates, consists in objects with dimensions that are small compared to the wavelength, and also where the volume number of obstacles per unit is large. Scattered waves are produced by rough surfaces, small objects, or by other irregularities in the channel.

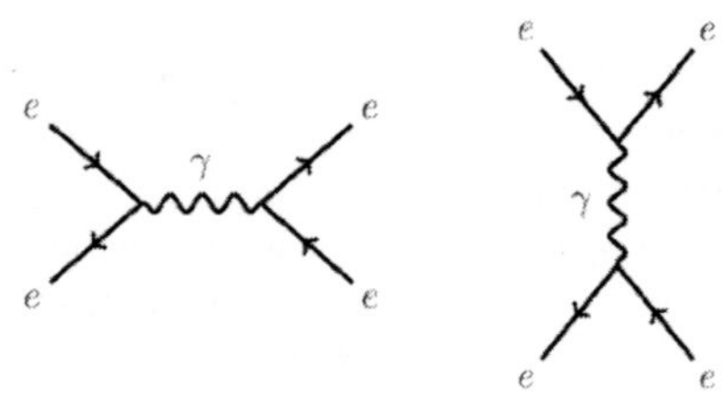

Figure 3. Scattering.

In practice, foliage, street signs, lampposts, and stairs within buildings can induce scattering in mobile-communication systems. A sound recognition on the physical details of the objects can be used to accurately predict the scattered signal strength [20]. These effects are shown in Fig. 3.

VI. Propagation Models

Propagation models are fundamental tools for designing and deploying any wireless communication system including WSNs. The models are closely related to the system working environment and characteristics. In general, propagation models are methods and algorithms used to predict the signal strength level along with the description of the signal level variability. Its main purpose is to predict the distortion and attenuation of the RF signal that will reach the receiver [21].

Currently there are many mathematical models with the purpose of predicting the average strength of the wireless signal transmission between two network devices. These models are useful in estimating the radio area of coverage of a transmitter and they are called propagation models, featuring the signal strength when there is a separation between transmitter and receiver. The PL_{dB} represents the losses of the model, **d** represents the distance, **f** represents the frequency, and the λ is a wavelength and all losses from these models are given in **dBm**.

A. Free Space Model

This model determines the power at the receiver in meters of transmitting power, the gain of the antennas and the distance between sender and receiver. They are not contemplated in the model losses that may occur, due to the propagation environment and the coverage area of an antenna that could be irregular. The satellite communication, as there is line of sight between transmitter and receiver, can be used as propagation model. The attenuation (path loss) for the Free Space model is defined by equation (1).

$$PL_{dB} = -10 * log(\frac{G_t * G_r * \lambda^2}{(4 * \Pi)^2 * d^2}) \quad (1)$$

Where G_t and G_r represents the transmitter gain and receiver gain.

B. Log-Distance Model

Defined in [22] and [23], Log-Distance model considers that the average received power decreases logarithmically with distance from the transmitter. This model is characterized by the (2) equation.

$$PL_{dB} = PL(d_0) + 10 * n * log(\frac{d}{d_0}) \quad (2)$$

Table I shows the values for the coefficients (n).

TABLE I. N EXPONENTS.

Environment	Path loss exponent (n)
Free space	2
Urban area	2.7 to 3.5
Shadowed urban	3 to 5
Obstructed in building	4 to 6

C. Shadowing Adapted Model

Adapted models are implemented from the classic models by adjusting (adaptation) their coefficients relation to field measurement by the minimum mean square error technique. The main advantage of this approach is the fact that it "encapsulates" some model input parameters, thus avoiding problems related to bad dimensioning, which can lead to considerable errors of prediction. It is defined in [24] by equation (3).

$$PL_{dB} = -10 * \beta * log(d) + 9 \quad (3)$$

Where β is a path loss exponent of the environment.

D. Tewari, Swarup and Roy Model

This model is defined in [25]. This model was developed based on measurements performed in the forest of India, which resembles in some attributes, the Amazon rainforest [25], and it is defined by equation (4).

$$\begin{aligned} PL_{dB} = 88 + 20 * log(f_{MHz}) + 40 * log(d_{Km}) - \\ 20 * log[H_t(m) * H_r(m)] + L_f(dB) \end{aligned} \quad (4)$$

Where H_t represents transmitter height, H_r represents receiver height and L_f represents environmental losses defined in [25].

E. Weissberger Model

For empirical models, it was found that the model developed by Weissberger estimate the excess of attenuation produced by vegetation, which is a model of interest when providing for the existence of foliage, and to make prediction for small stretches [26]. The loss model is given by equations (5) and (6).

Case $d \leq 14m$:

$$PL_{dB} = 0.45 * f^{0.284} * d \quad (5)$$

Case $14m \leq d \leq 400m$:

$$PL_{dB} = 0.45 * f^{0.284} * d^{0.588} \quad (6)$$

Where d represents distance and f represents frequency.

F. ITU-R Model

The International Telecommunication Union Recommendations (ITU-R) Model, defined in [27], is given by equation (7).

$$PL_{dB} = 0.2 * f^{0.3} * d^{0.6} \quad (7)$$

G. COST 235 Model

Defined by [28], this model is given by equations (8) and (9).

$$PL_{dB} = 15.6 * f^{-0.009} * d^{0.26} - With\ leaf \quad (8)$$

$$PL_{dB} = 15.6 * f^{-0.2} * d^{0.5} - Without\ leaf \quad (9)$$

H. RIM Model

RIM (Radio Irregularity Model) is a model developed purposefully for wireless sensor networks. In isotropic models of radio coverage, the received power is obtained by equation (10).

$$P_r = P_t - PL + F \quad (10)$$

Where P_r represents received power, P_t represents transmitted power, PL represents the path losses and F represents component of fading. This model is defined by [29] and as the literature already mentions, the radio coverage is not a perfect circle in real environments [23], neither it resembles a circle. The RIM model is based on this irregularity. To symbolize the irregularity of the radio coverage model, the parameter DOI (Degree of Irregularity), was introduced in the RIM model. Fig. 4 shows this irregularity of behavior in the propagation.

It is possible to observe that the bigger by the image irregularity of the radio coverage is, the higher the DOI value parameter. The description of the DOI calculation irregularity is given by equation (11).

$$PR = PE - (PL_{DOI} * K_i) + F, \quad (11)$$

where:

- PL_{DOI} = *Path Loss* with DOI adjustment;
- F = Component of *fading*.
- K_i = Coefficient representing the difference in losses *path loss* in different directions, where $K_i = 1, case(i = 0)$, i.e., the angle being the angle 0 is analyzed, in reference to line of sight;
- i = Coefficient of i-nth degree.

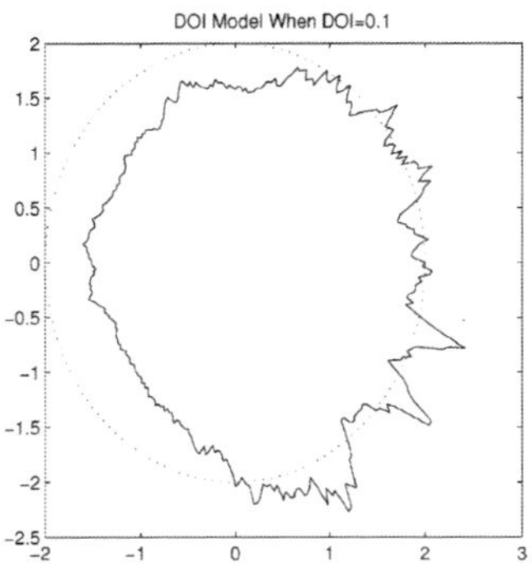

Figure 4. Irregularity coefficient in the radio coverage.

VII. USED STATISTICAL METHODS

The results obtained have undergone a process of statistical analysis for validating data. Such reliability is based on the methods that follow.

A. Mean Square Error (MSE)

In practical terms, the Mean Square Error (MSE) equals the sum of the variance and tendentiousness square estimator. An estimator is used to deduce the value of an unknown parameter in the statistical model. The estimating of MSE is expressed by (12).

$$MSE = \frac{\sum_{t=1}^{n} e_t^2}{n}, \quad (12)$$

where:

- e_t: error caused by the difference between sample and predicted value;
- n: number of periods.

B. Mean Absolute Percentage Error (MAPE)

The average absolute percentage error calculation estimates how exact is the actual value with the estimated one, in percentage. Such a connection is expressed by (13).

$$MAPE = \frac{\sum_{t=1}^{n} \left| \frac{(A_t - P_t)}{A_t} * 100 \right|}{n}, \quad (13)$$

where:

- A_t: real value in t period;
- P_t: prediction in t period.

VIII. Methodology of Experiments

The methodology adopted during the assembly from a RSSI measurer and subsequent measurements with it were made under the following step's schedule.

- First Step: The used device had a direct-access terminal on a specific pin to read the RSSI. A PWM (Pulse Width Modulation) modulated signal was read in the pin. This signal was treated as an analogical output but it is, as a matter of fact, a digital output that generates an alternating signal (*low* and *high* digital levels), where the data is codified in how long the pin's output stands on a digital level.

- Second Step: Compatibility tests were performed between the used Arduino Uno R3 platform and the XBee modules and basic trigger circuits with the modules, in order to verify whether there was correct communication maintenance between the devices. At this stage, the prototypes were assembled in assembly boards. Other electronic components were also added to the project, such as a 16×2 LCD (Liquid Crystal Display) display for showing the reading values, and components responsible for maintaining and feeding the display, among other devices.

- Third Step: At this stage, the source-code executed by the prototype was written. The source-code development used an open-source programming framework for microcontrollers, called *Wiring*, that includes several on-the-box applications allowing an easy development of various input-output operations. That is one of the reasons whereby it is the standard development language for Arduino projects. The analogical pin (the one who provides the RSSI value) was read through the *pulseInt()* function, made for occasions like this one. This function reads a *high* or *low* pulse on the pin and then returns to its duration in milliseconds. Thus, it measures the PWM pulses length.

Figure 5. Receiving device standing on the ground, during first measurement.

The code executed by the micro-controller responsible for the reading function can be found in the following code, and Fig. 5 shows the prototype.

```
int dur = pulseInt (A1,LOW,200);
float val = analogRead(A1);
int rssi=(dur+50)*(-1);
```

- Fourth Step: The measurements were made on an outdoor sports field, Fig. 6. The transmitter was fixed and the receiver was taken to increasingly longer distances from the transmitter. Two tests were made: on the first, both devices were on ground level. Starting with one meter distance, the transmitter's signal strength on the receiver was measured. The distance was increased up to the point where there was no connection. This test was performed on a sunny day, in the afternoon, with low wind, temperatures between 28 and 31 Celsius degrees, and air humidity at 65%.

Figure 6. Place of measurements.

- Fifth Step: At this stage we did the analyzes of samples collected from the comparison variables of the models used and the real measurements.

IX. Results and Conclusions

From the conclusion of the data analysis, which was the last stage of the work methodology, we obtained satisfactory results that were expected for the work proposed. Fig. 7 shows the curve obtained from the real RSSI values versus power prediction curves for each propagation model.

The calculations of Mean Square Error (MSE) and Mean Absolute Percentual Error (MAPE) were used as statistical methods to measure the approximation of the actual measurement with the proposed models. The results are described in Table II.

TABLE II. TABLE OF RESULTS.

Model	MSE	MAPE
Log-Distance n =2	218.810050	17.019827
Log-Distance n=3	399.298599	24.947916
Log-Distance n=4	1319.050187	45.931788
Log-Distance Shadowing	67.151034	9.985123
Free Space (Friis)	184.344305	19.477650
RIM-DOI	252.340084	16.715468
Weissberger d<14	**44.966762**	6.869068
Weissberger d>14	395.457018	22.606341
Tewari, Swarup e Roy	1855.379165	57.330225
ITU-R	635.934654	30.098993
COST 235 With leaf	144.596843	**5.358066**
COST 235 Without leaf	550.381070	27.301250

The deployment of a WSN in sports environment requires the study of signal propagation in order to find the best way of positioning sensor nodes, and the power of prediction of RSSI values is very important to building this network. This work contributes to the deployment of WSNs in the region of the Campina Grande - Paraíba in order to optimize the usage of resources, such as water and electricity, considering that those sports environments require a lot of water.

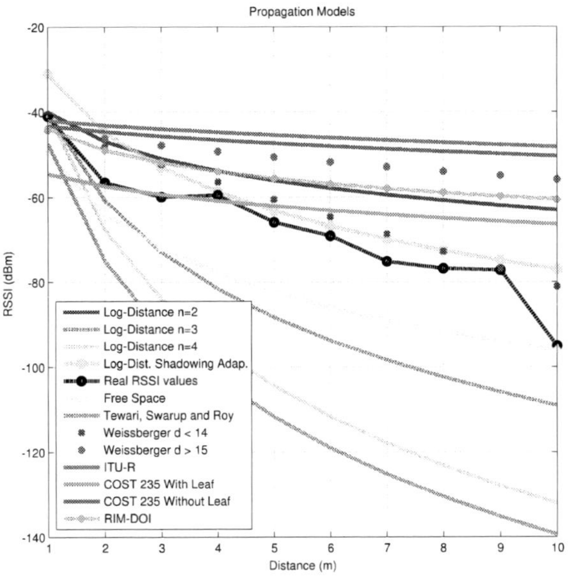

Figure 7. Used Models and Real RSSI Values.

From the analysis of the propagation models to power prediction, we conclude that the Weissberger Model $d < 14$ and COST 235 with leaf are the best way to model the power prediction in that area, but other models also had good results. The major contribution to the research was the use of a technology, such as ZigBee, applied to the monitoring of sports practicing areas. That was the main objective of this research, which was effectively reached.

The requirement of the experiments stands in the verification of the viability of applying ZigBee in that specific type of environment, since to our knowledge, was not done in literature so far. In addition, it was possible to perform an experiment to test the effectiveness of an external RSSI meter, which can be used visually and externally.

For this work, we chose to study only the transmission range of the sensors in sports environments. In future work, we intend to study the impact of climate on those measurements, arranging the schedules for data collection on different days with different climate and temperatures.

ACKNOWLEDGEMENT

The authors thank: IEEE Student Branch - Campina Grande, Federal Institute of Education, Science and Technology of Paraíba, LaBee Laboratory and National Council for Scientific and Technological Development (CNPq).

REFERENCES

[1] M. Malajner, K. Benkic, P. Planinsic, and Z. Cucej, "The accuracy of propagation models for distance measurement between wsn nodes," in Systems, Signals and Image Processing, 2009. IWSSIP 2009. 16th International Conference on. IEEE, 2009, pp. 1–4.

[2] F. Yahaya, Y. Yussoff, R. Rahman, and N. Abidin, "Performance analysis of wireless sensor network," in 5th International Colloquium on Signal Processing Its Applications, 2009. CSPA 2009, March 2009, pp. 400–405.

[3] I. Akyildiz, W. Su, Y. Sankarasubramaniam, and E. Cayirci, "A survey on sensor networks," IEEE Communications Magazine, vol. 40, no. 8, Aug 2002, pp. 102–114.

[4] R. Pellegrini, S. Persia, D. Volponi, and G. Marcone, "RF propagation analysis for ZigBee sensor network using RSSI measurements," in 2nd International Conference on Wireless Communication, Vehicular Technology, Information Theory and Aerospace Electronic Systems Technology (Wireless VITAE), 2011, Feb 2011, pp. 1–5.

[5] T. Bezerra, S. Silva, E. Silva, M. Sousa, and M. Cavalcante, "Performance evaluation of zigbee transmissions on the grass environment," in UBICOMM 2014, The Eighth International Conference on Mobile Ubiquitous Computing, Systems, Services and Technologies, 2014, pp. 287–290.

[6] T. Bezerra, S. Silva, J. Souza, E. Silva, and M. Sousa, "Análise de desempenho em redes de sensores sem fio a partir de um medidor de rssi aplicada ao monitoramento de Áreas de preservação ambiental e ambientes para prática desportiva," in XXI Congr. Intl. de Ingenieria Electronica, Electrica y Computacion INTERCON 2014, 2014, pp. 209–214.

[7] IEEE Std 802.15.1 IEEE Standard for Information technology-Telecommunications and information exchange between systems- Local and metropolitan area networks- Specific requirements Part 15.1: Wireless Medium Access Control (MAC) and Physical Layer (PHY) Specifications for WirelessPersonal Area Networks (WPANs). IEEE Std. 802.15.1.

[8] "IEEE standard for information technology - telecommunications and information exchange between systems - local and metropolitan area networks specific requirements part 15.4: Wireless medium access control (MAC) and physical layer (PHY) specifications for low-rate wireless personal area networks (LR-WPANs)," IEEE Std 802.15.4, 2003, pp. 1–670.

[9] ZigBee Alliance, retrieved: May, 2017. [Online]. Available: http://www.zigbee.org

[10] K. Benkic, M. Malajner, P. Planinsic, and Z. Cucej, "Using rssi value for distance estimation in wireless sensor networks based on zigbee," in Systems, Signals and Image Processing, 2008. IWSSIP 2008. 15th International Conference on. IEEE, 2008, pp. 303–306.

[11] C. Park, D. Park, J. Park, Y. Lee, and Y. An, "Localization algorithm design and implementation to utilization rssi and aoa of zigbee," in Future Information Technology - FutureTech, 2010 5th International Conference on. IEEE, 2010, pp. 1–4.

[12] N. W. Lo, D. D. Falconer, and A. U. Sheikh, "Adaptive equalization for a multipath fading environment with interference and noise," in Vehicular Technology Conference, 1994 IEEE 44th. IEEE, 1994, pp. 252–256.

[13] J.-L. Chu and J.-F. Kiang, "Multipath effects on beacon performances," in Networking, Sensing and Control, 2004 IEEE International Conference on, vol. 1. IEEE, 2004, pp. 635–638.

[14] R.-H. Wu, Y.-H. Lee, H.-W. Tseng, Y.-G. Jan, and M.-H. Chuang, "Study of characteristics of rssi signal," in Industrial Technology, 2008. ICIT 2008. IEEE International Conference on. IEEE, 2008, pp. 1–3.

[15] E. Jafer, B. O'Flynn, C. O'Mathuna, and R. Spinar, "A study of the rf characteristics for wireless sensor deployment in building environment," in Sensor Technologies and Applications, 2009. SENSORCOMM'09. Third International Conference on. IEEE, 2009, pp. 206–211.

[16] M. Barralet, X. Huang, and D. Sharma, "Effects of antenna polarization on rssi based location identification," in Advanced Communication Technology, 2009. ICACT 2009. 11th International Conference on, vol. 1. IEEE, 2009, pp. 260–265.

[17] J. Hightower, C. Vakili, G. Borriello, and R. Want, "Design and calibration of the spoton ad-hoc location sensing system," unpublished, August, 2001.

[18] R. M. Pellegrini, S. Persia, D. Volponi, and G. Marcone, "Rf propagation analysis for zigbee sensor network using rssi measurements," in Wireless Communication, Vehicular Technology, Information Theory and Aerospace & Electronic Systems Technology (Wireless VITAE), 2011 2nd International Conference on. IEEE, 2011, pp. 1–5.

[19] M. F. Iskander and Z. Yun, "Propagation prediction models for wireless communication systems," Microwave Theory and Techniques, IEEE Transactions on, vol. 50, no. 3, 2002, pp. 662–673.

[20] T. K. Sarkar, Z. Ji, K. Kim, A. Medouri, and M. Salazar-Palma, "A survey of various propagation models for mobile communication," Antennas and Propagation Magazine, IEEE, vol. 45, no. 3, 2003, pp. 51–82.

[21] T. Stoyanova, F. Kerasiotis, A. Prayati, and G. Papadopoulos, "A practical rf propagation model for wireless network sensors," in Sensor Technologies and Applications, 2009. SENSORCOMM'09. Third International Conference on. IEEE, 2009, pp. 194–199.

[22] T. S. Rappaport, Wireless Communications: Principles and Practices. Pearson Prentice Hall, 2009.

[23] R. M. P. Jacinto, "Modelação da propagação numa rede de sensores sem fios," Master degree dissertation, Lisbon New University, Science and Technology Faculty publisher, Portugal, vol. 1, no. 1, 2012.

[24] A. Fanimokun and J. Frolik, "Effects of natural propagation environments on wireless sensor network coverage area," in System Theory, 2003. Proceedings of the 35th Southeastern Symposium on. IEEE, 2003, pp. 16–20.

[25] R. Tewari, S. Swarup, and M. Roy, "Radio wave propagation through rain forests of india," Antennas and Propagation, IEEE Transactions on, vol. 38, no. 4, 1990, pp. 433–449.

[26] T. C. Braga, "Monitorização ambiental em espaços florestais com rede de sensores sem fios," PHD Thesis, U. Madeira, Madeira University publisher, Portugal, vol. 1, no. 1, 2010.

[27] R. ITU-R, "P. 1238-7," Propagation data and prediction methods for the planning of indoor radio communication systems and radio local area networks in the frequency range, vol. 900, 2012.

[28] A. Nordbotten, "Cost 235: Radiowave propagation effects on next generation fixed-services telecommunication systems," Telektronikk, vol. 92, 1996, pp. 128–130.

[29] G. Zhou, T. He, S. Krishnamurthy, and J. A. Stankovic, "Models and solutions for radio irregularity in wireless sensor networks," ACM Transactions on Sensor Networks (TOSN), vol. 2, no. 2, 2006, pp. 221–262.

A Proposal for a New OFDM Wireless System using a CAZAC Equalization Scheme

Ryota Ishioka, Tomotaka Kimura and Masahiro Muraguchi

Faculty of Engineering, Tokyo University of Science, Tokyo, Japan
Email: 4316609@ed.tus.ac.jp, {kimura, murag}@ee.kagu.tus.ac.jp

***Abstract*—It is well known that one of the most serious drawbacks of the orthogonal frequency division multiplexing (OFDM) scheme in wireless applications is its high peak-to-average power ratio (PAPR), which decreases the efficiency of power amplifiers (PAs) and increases transmitter power consumption. We propose a constant amplitude zero auto-correlation (CAZAC) equalization scheme, which is a robust way of overcoming the PAPR problems with the OFDM scheme. The CAZAC equalization scheme makes the PAPR of multilevel quadrature amplitude modulation (M-QAM) OFDM signals into the PAPR of M-QAM single-carrier signals. This paper proposes a new wireless system that introduces the CAZAC equalization scheme. CAZAC improves the estimated power-added efficiency of the PAs for a 16-QAM OFDM system with 52 subcarriers from 10 to 30% because it reduces the PAPR of 5 dB while the system imposes no penalties on the bit error rate (BER). The paper also provides theoretical analysis of CAZAC equalization and information on spectral control and the efficiency of BER under fading environments.**

Keywords–OFDM; CAZAC sequence; Zadoff-Chu sequence; PAPR reduction.

I. INTRODUCTION

Orthogonal frequency division multiplex (OFDM) systems that attain high speeds and high capacity have recently been attracting attention in wireless applications, e.g., wireless local area networks (WLANs), third generation partnership project long-term evolution (3GPP LTE), and the digital video broadcasting-terrestrial (DVB-T) standard [1] [2].

However, the main drawback of OFDM is its high Peak-to-Average Power Ratio (PAPR), which decreases the efficiency of the power amplifiers (PAs) and increases transmitter power consumption [3] [4]. Therefore, a number of techniques have been proposed to reduce the PAPR [3]. Well-known techniques are clipping-and-filtering, partial transmit sequence (PTS), and selected mapping (SLM). Clipping-and-filtering limits the peak amplitude of the transmission signal. However, non-linear distortion causes BER to degrade. PTS partitions input data into disjoint sub-blocks. Moreover, each sub-block are weighted by a phase factor.

This technique chooses the phase factor to minimize the PAPR of combined signals. SLM generates multiple candidate data blocks. All data blocks represent the same information. Although PTS and SLM can be expected to create a certain reduction in PAPR, both techniques need side information in the receiver, which decreases spectral efficiency. The most practical solution to improving PAPR is to introduce single carrier frequency division multiplexing access (SC-FDMA). The 3GPP LTE system adopts SC-FDMA for uplink multiple access systems [2] [5]. However, SC-FDMA has not been considered to be suitable for next-generation high-speed communications.

A new PAPR reduction technique with constant amplitude zero auto-correlation (CAZAC) equalization was recently proposed [6] [7]. This technique multiplies frequency domain OFDM symbols and CAZAC sequences to reduce the PAPR of OFDM signals. However, this technique needs to use all subcarriers in the frequency domain, which violates the spectrum mask defined by the IEEE 802.11 a/g standard. Since this is not an easy problem to solve, CAZAC equalization was used for visible light communications that did not need to take spectral management into consideration.

This paper proposes a new wireless communication system with the Zadoff-Chu sequence scheme, which is one of the most well known CAZAC schemes. The M-QAM OFDM signal acts as if it were an M-QAM single-carrier signal in the system by introducing the Zadoff-Chu sequence scheme as the CAZAC scheme. Therefore, CAZAC improves the estimated power-added efficiency of PAs from 10 to 30% for a 16-QAM OFDM system with 52 subcarriers because it reduces the PAPR of 5 dB while the system imposes no penalties on BER. This paper also provides a theoretical analysis of Zadoff-Chu sequence equalization and information on spectral control and BER under fading environments.

This paper is organized as follows. Section II analyze the CAZAC-OFDM system and consider applying CAZAC-OFDM to wireless communication. Section III presents the effect of CAZAC-OFDM in wireless communication. Finally, conclusions are drawn in Section IV.

II. PROPOSED SYSTEM

A. OFDM system

The frequency domain symbol, $\boldsymbol{X} = [X_0, X_1, ..., X_{N-1}]^T$ in OFDM systems is modulated by N-size Inverse Fast Fourier Transform (IFFT), which converts the frequency domain to the time domain. The discrete-time OFDM signal with N subcarriers is represented as

$$x_n = \sum_{k=0}^{N-1} X_k e^{j2\pi kn/N}, \qquad (1)$$

where $j = \sqrt{-1}$ and n are the discrete time indices. However, receiver acquires frequency domain symbol Y by applying

FFT to received signal y.

$$
\begin{aligned}
Y_k &= \frac{1}{N}\sum_{n=0}^{N-1} y_n e^{-j2\pi kn/N} \\
&= \frac{1}{N}\sum_{n=0}^{N-1} \{x_n + \sigma^2\} e^{-j2\pi kn/N}, \qquad (2)
\end{aligned}
$$

where σ^2 is noise power.

The PAPR of the OFDM signal (1) can be expressed as:

$$
\mathrm{PAPR} = \frac{\max |x_n|^2}{\mathrm{E}[|x_n|^2]}, \qquad (3)
$$

where $\mathrm{E}[\cdot]$ is the expectation operator. PAPR is an index that represents the amplitude fluctuation of the OFDM signal for each frame. We can see from Eq. (2) that the OFDM signal is composed of a plurality of subcarrier signals, which causes an increase in amplitude fluctuations. A high PAPR signal requires the power amplifier to operate at a large input-back-off (IBO) due to the corresponding value of the PAPR to amplify the transmission signal without distortion. Increasing the IBO generally greatly decreases the efficiency of PA.

B. CAZAC-OFDM

CAZAC sequences involve constant amplitude and provide excellent cross-correlation properties. Therefore, CAZAC sequences are used in wireless communication systems such as channel estimation and time synchronization. The Zadoff-Chu sequence is one of these CAZAC sequences. The Zadoff-Chu sequence, $\{c_k\}$, is represented as:

$$
c_k = \begin{cases} e^{j\pi k^2/L} & (L \text{ is even}) \\ e^{j\pi k(k+1)/L} & (L \text{ is odd}) \end{cases}, \qquad (4)
$$

where L is the length of the CAZAC sequence and k = 0,1,...,$N^2 - 1$ denotes the sequence index. CAZAC sequences are generated by cyclic shift of the original CAZAC sequence. The periodic cross-correlation function, ρ, is defined as:

$$
\begin{aligned}
\rho(m) &= \sum_{n=1}^{L-1} c_n c^*_{(c-m) \bmod L} \\
&= \begin{cases} L & (m = 0) \\ 0 & (m \neq 0) \end{cases}, \qquad (5)
\end{aligned}
$$

where m represents integer variable. In this paper, we choose $L = N^2$ in this paper, where CAZAC $N \times N$ precoding matrix $\boldsymbol{M}$ is represented as:

$$
\boldsymbol{M} = \begin{bmatrix} c_0 & c_1 & \cdots & c_{N-1} \\ c_N & c_{N+1} & \cdots & c_{2N-1} \\ \vdots & \vdots & \ddots & \vdots \\ c_{(N-1)N} & c_{(N-1)N+1} & \cdots & c_{N^2-1} \end{bmatrix}. \qquad (6)
$$

Frequency domain symbol $\boldsymbol{X}' = [X'_0, X'_1, ..., X'_{N-1}]$ in CAZAC-OFDM is represented as:

$$
\boldsymbol{X}' = \boldsymbol{M}\boldsymbol{X}. \qquad (7)
$$

Therefore, the CAZAC-OFDM time signal is represented as:

$$
x'_n = \sum_{k=0}^{N-1} X'_k e^{j2\pi kn/N}. \qquad (8)
$$

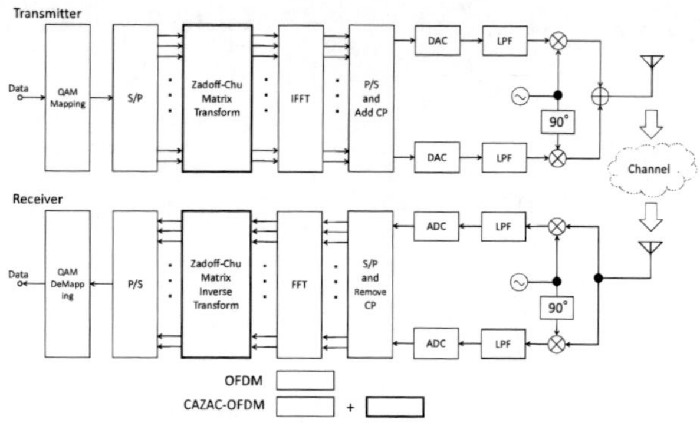

Figure 1. Proposed CAZAC-OFDM system

All sub-carriers in a CAZAC-OFDM system include data symbols. This system cannot include null sub-carriers. Therefore, the spectrum of the proposed system does not satisfy the spectrum mask.

The Zadoff-Chu sequences in Eq. (5) have periodic cross-correlation performance. Therefore the original frequency domain symbol, X, can be demodulated by using complex conjugate $\boldsymbol{M}^H$.

$$
\boldsymbol{M}\boldsymbol{M}^H\boldsymbol{X} = N\boldsymbol{X}. \qquad (9)
$$

Figure 1 shows the configuration for a transmitter and receiver in the CAZAC-OFDM system, which applies CAZAC precoding matrix $\boldsymbol{M}$ to the mapping data after serial-parallel conversion.

C. Analysis of CAZAC OFDM

We clarify why the PAPR of CAZAC-OFDM was the same as the PAPR of mapped data signals such as 16 QAM. Frequency domain symbol $\boldsymbol{X}'$ is represented as:

$$
\begin{aligned}
\boldsymbol{X}' &= \boldsymbol{M}^T\boldsymbol{X} \\
&= \begin{bmatrix} c_0X_0 + c_1X_1 + \cdots + c_{N-1}X_{N-1} \\ c_NX_0 + c_{N+1}X_1 + \cdots + c_{2N-1}X_{N-1} \\ \vdots \\ c_{(N-1)N}X_0 + \cdots + c_{N^2-1}X_{N-1} \end{bmatrix} \qquad (10)
\end{aligned}
$$

We assumed that $L = N^2$ was even in the following since the OFDM system uses FFT, which rapidly computes the discrete Fourier transform (DFT) with input data having a length with a power of two. Therefore, we propose that baseband OFDM signal x_n can be represented as:

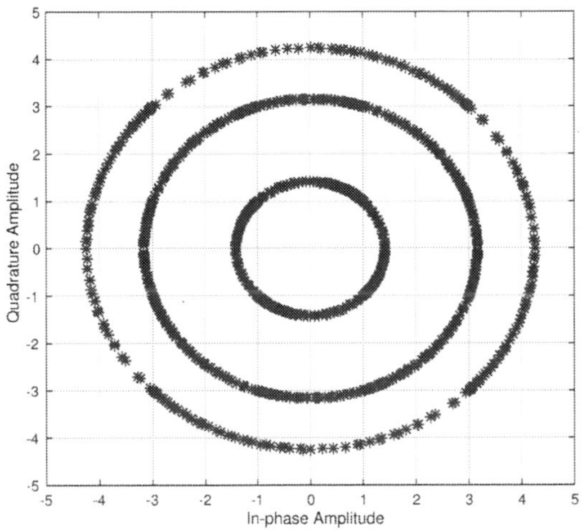

Figure 2. Constellation diagram in time signal which is equalized by CAZAC sequence

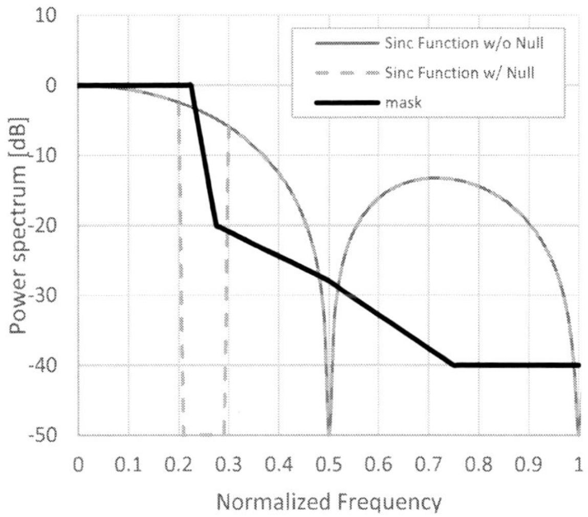

Figure 3. Power spectrum of sinc function with and without Null sub-carriers

$$
\begin{aligned}
x_n &= \sum_{k=0}^{N-1}\left\{\sum_{l=0}^{N-1} c_{l+kN}X_l\right\} e^{j2\pi kn/N} \\
&= \sum_{k=0}^{N-1}\left\{\sum_{l=0}^{N-1} e^{j\pi(l+kN)^2/L}X_l\right\} e^{j2\pi kn/N} \\
&= \sum_{l=0}^{N-1} e^{j\pi l^2/N^2}\left\{\sum_{k=0}^{N-1} e^{j2\pi k(l+n)/N}e^{j2\pi k^2}\right\} X_l \\
&= \sum_{l=0}^{N-1} e^{j\pi l^2/N^2}\left\{\sum_{k=0}^{N-1}\left\{-e^{j2\pi(l+n)/N}\right\}^k\right\} X_l . \quad (11)
\end{aligned}
$$

Equation (11) can be transformed as:

$$
\sum_{k=0}^{N-1}\left\{-e^{j2\pi(l+n)/N}\right\}^k = \begin{cases} N & (-e^{j2\pi(l+n)/N}=1) \\ 0 & (-e^{j2\pi(l+n)/N}\neq 1) \end{cases} . \quad (12)
$$

In this case, if $-e^{j2\pi(l+n)/N} = 1$, then $2(l+n)/N$ is odd. From $0 \leq l \leq N-1$ and $0 \leq n \leq N-1$, l and n correspond one to one. Therefore, when Eq. (12) $= N$, l is represented as:

$$
l = (N/2 - n) \bmod N. \quad (13)
$$

Therefore, x_n is represented as:

$$
x_n = N \cdot c_{(N/2-n) \bmod N} \cdot X_{(N/2-n) \bmod N}. \quad (14)
$$

The signal at time n in Eq. (11) is obtained by rotating the symbol of X_m. Therefore, the time signal of the proposed system looks like a single-carrier signal. Figure 2 plots the baseband signal on the complex plane. We applied 16 QAM as constellation mapping to the frequency domain symbol in this case. The PAPR of a single-carrier signal is generally lower than that of a multi-carrier signal.

The proposed system firstly applies FFT to input signal $\boldsymbol{Y}$ on the receiver side to obtain for get symbol $\boldsymbol{Y}$ in the frequency domain. The proposed system then multiplies the received signal $\boldsymbol{Y}$ and the inverse matrix, $\{\boldsymbol{M}^T\}^H$.

$$
\begin{aligned}
\boldsymbol{Y'} &= \{\boldsymbol{M^T}\}^{\boldsymbol{H}}\boldsymbol{Y} \\
&= \{\boldsymbol{M^T}\}^{\boldsymbol{H}}\{\boldsymbol{M^T X}+\boldsymbol{G}\} \\
&= N \cdot \boldsymbol{X} + \overline{\boldsymbol{M}}\boldsymbol{G}, \quad (15)
\end{aligned}
$$

where $\boldsymbol{G}$ is the noise added to each subcarrier and $\overline{\boldsymbol{M}}$ is the conjugate of the matrix $\boldsymbol{M}$. All elements of the matrix $\boldsymbol{M}$ are complex number on the unit circle. In addition, all elements of the matrix $\overline{\boldsymbol{M}}$ are also complex number on the unit circle. Therefore, noise is dispersed for all sub-carriers. As a result, the proposed system is robust against noise including only specific frequency components such as frequency selective fading.

D. Proposed system

The frequency domain symbol of CAZAC-OFDM in Eq. (10) includes data sub-carriers in all sub-carriers. Figure 3 plots the difference between the spectrum with and without null sub-carriers. If the IEEE 802.11 specifications are taken into consideration, the normalized frequency can be multiplied by 40 MHz. The filtering normalized frequency in Fig. 3, which is smaller than 0.25, degrades BER. It is necessary, on the other hand, to reduce the power spectrum by 20 dB between the normalized frequencies of 0.225 and 0.275 according to the specifications of the spectrum mask. Therefore, it is not possible for filtering to satisfy the spectrum mask.

We solved this problem in this research by decreasing the symbol rate. Moreover, data sub-carriers were allocated to all sub-carriers without using null sub-carriers. Therefore, the proposed system did not decrease the data rate despite the decreasing symbol rate.

III. Performance Evaluation

We conducted simulation experiments with the matrix laboratory MATLAB/Simulink to evaluate the performance

TABLE I. SIMULATION SPECIFICATION.

Modulation	OFDM	CAZAC-OFDM
Mapping	16QAM	16QAM
Bandwidth	20 MHz	16 MHz
Symbol time	4 μ sec	5 μ sec
Data rate	48 Mbps	48 Mbps
Carrier frequency	100 MHz	100 MHz
Number of data subcarriers	48	60
FFT size	64	64

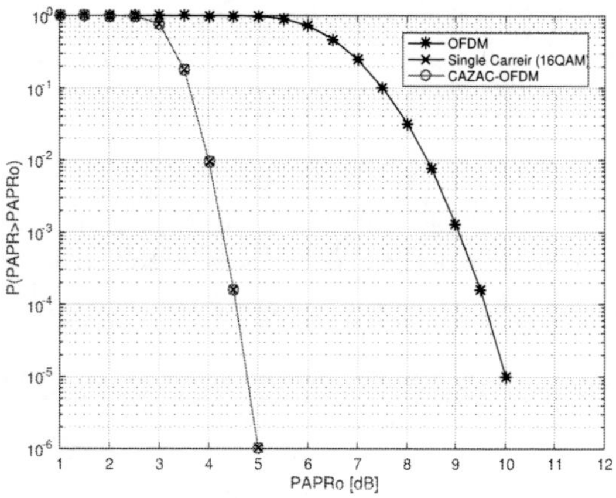

Figure 4. CCDF performance

of the proposed system. Table I summarizes the simulation setting. We will now present the simulation results of OFDM and single-carrier (16 QAM) systems to enable a comparison of performance.

We first considered the complementary cumulative distribution function (CCDF) of PAPR to evaluate the performance of PAPR, which is the probability that PAPR will be higher than a certain PAPR value $PAPR_0$, i.e., $\Pr(PAPR > PAPR_0)$. Figure 4 plots the CCDF of PAPR using the proposed system as well as the OFDM and single-carrier systems. We found that the PAPR of the proposed system was almost equal to that of the single-carrier system. Moreover, the PAPR of the proposed system was improved by 5.8 dB at the CCDF of 10^{-3} compared with the OFDM system. This PAPR reduction resulted from CAZAC equalization. The CAZAC equalization in Fig. 2, converted the amplitude of the OFDM signal to the amplitude of the mapped data such as 16 QAM, which improved PAPR.

We next examined the bit error rate (BER) of the proposed system. We considered three channels: additive white Gaussian noise (AWGN), AWGN & frequency selective fading channels, and Rayleigh fading. A specific frequency (101 MHz) was highly attenuated, as plotted in Fig. 5 in the AWGN & frequency selective fading channels, in addition to AWGN.

Figure 6 plots the BER of the proposed system and the OFDM system under AWGN and the AWGN & frequency selective fading channels. The results indicate that the proposed system does not degrade BER. The signal power of specific sub-carriers is highly attenuated in the OFDM system, and thus BER is large even when the noise power is low. In contrast, the BER of the proposed system is small because the influence

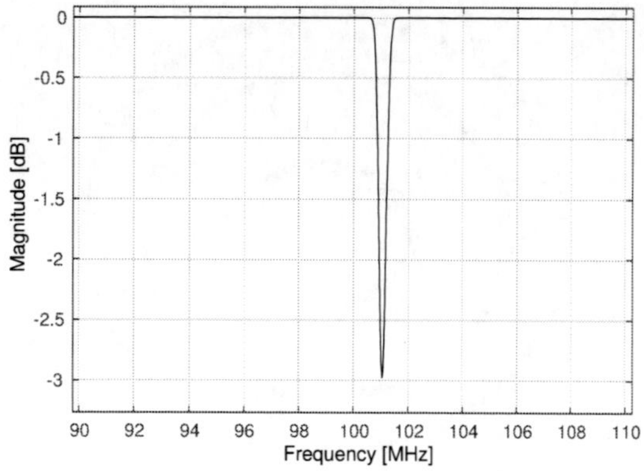

Figure 5. Frequency selective fading model

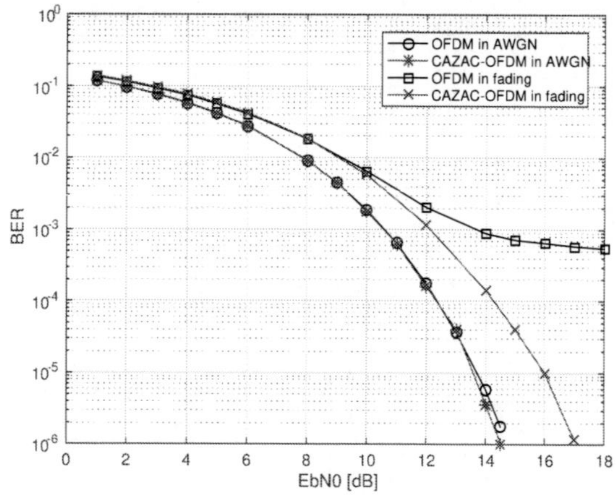

Figure 6. BER versus EbN0 under AWGN and frequency selective fading environments

of fading is spread to all sub-carriers. This indicates that the proposed system has excellent capabilities to resist frequency selective fading.

Figure 7 plots the BER of the proposed and the OFDM systems under AWGN and Rayleigh fading channels. We found that the BER of the proposed system was comparable to that of the OFDM system in both channels. Therefore, CAZAC equalization did not affect the multi-path fading compensation of OFDM.

Finally, we show the spectrum of the proposed system in Fig. 8. By decreasing the symbol rate, the spectrum of the proposed system satisfies the spectrum mask standardized by IEEE 802.11 specification [1]. Therefore, the proposed scheme can be applied to wireless communication systems such as Wi-Fi and LTE.

IV. Conclusion

We proposed a new OFDM wireless system using the CAZAC scheme, which made the PAPR of the M-QAM OFDM signal into the PAPR of an M-QAM single-carrier signal. We found the performance of the system was the

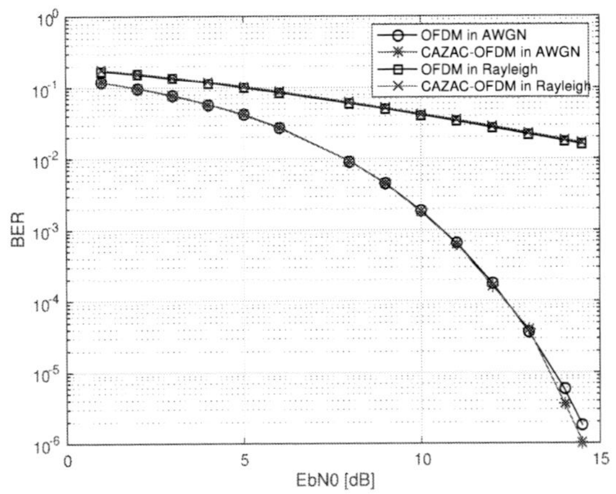

Figure 7. BER versus EbN0 under AWGN and Rayleigh fading environments

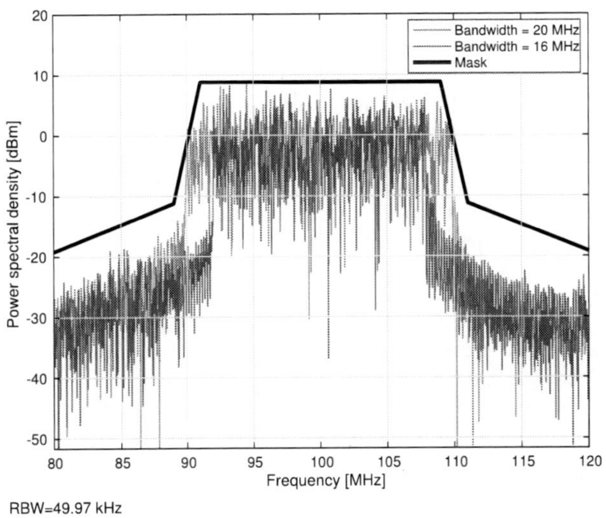

Figure 8. Spectrum for proposed system

same as that of single-carrier signals through simulations using MATLAB/Simulink. Therefore, we expected that the CAZAC scheme would approximately improve the power-added efficiency of the PA for a 16-QAM OFDM system with 52 sub-carriers from 10 to 30% because it reduced the PAPR of 5 dB while the system imposed no penalties on BER. The system satisfied the spectrum mask defined by the IEEE 802.11 a/g standards, while maintaining the same data rate, by adjusting the symbol duration of the standards and increasing the number of data sub-carriers. Moreover, the CAZAC scheme had an advantage in reducing BER under frequency selective fading environments and not degrading BER under Rayleigh fading environments.

References

[1] IEEE, "Part 11: Wireless LAN Medium Access Control (MAC) and Physical Layer (PHY) Specifications," IEEE Std 802.11-2012 (Revision of IEEE Std 802.11-2007), Mar. 2012, pp. 1–2695.

[2] A. Ghosh, R. Ratasuk, B. Mondal, N. Mangalvedhe, and T. Thomas, "LTE-advanced: Next-generation Wireless Broadband Technology," IEEE Wireless Communications, vol. 17, no. 3, June 2010, pp. 10–22.

[3] H. Seung, Hee and L. Jae, Hong, "An Overview of Peak-to-average Power Ratio Reduction Techniques for Multicarrier Transmission," IEEE Wireless Communications, vol. 12, no. 2, Apr. 2005, pp. 56–65.

[4] J. Joung, C. K. Ho, K. Adachi, and S. Sun, "A Survey on Power-Amplifier-Centric Techniques for Spectrum- and Energy-Efficient Wireless Communications," IEEE Communications Surveys & Tutorials, vol. 17, no. 1, Jan. 2015, pp. 315–333.

[5] H. Myung, J. Lim, and D. Goodman, "Single Carrier FDMA for Uplink Wireless Transmission," IEEE Vehicular Technology Magazine, vol. 1, no. 3, Sep. 2006, pp. 30–38.

[6] I. Baig and V. Jeoti, "PAPR Reduction in OFDM Systems: Zadoff-Chu Matrix Transform Based Pre/Post-Coding Techniques," in Proc. of the 2nd International Conference on Computational Intelligence, Communication Systems and Networks, July 2010, pp. 373–377.

[7] Z. Feng, M. Tang, S. Fu, L. Deng, Q. Wu, R. Lin, R. Wang, P. Shum, and D. Liu, "Performance-Enhanced Direct Detection Optical OFDM Transmission With CAZAC Equalization," IEEE Photonics Technology Letters, vol. 27, no. 14, pp. 1507–1510.

Cascade Handover Scheme in High-Speed Transport (HST) using mmWave-based Mobile Hotspot Network

Woogoo Park, Heesang Chung, and Ilgyu Kim
Mobile Wireless Backhaul Research Section
Electronics and Telecommunications Research Institute (ETRI)
Daejeon, Korea
{wgpark, hschung, igkim}@etri.re.kr

***Abstract*—Capacity and coverage improvements in mobile communication networks have evolved to accommodate increased use of broadband data. One way to enable the use of broadband data is to utilize the mmWave band. The mmWave-based mobile backhaul solution is very useful for providing broadband data traffic for mobile service providers, including carriers. However, when moving at high speed like a high-speed train, a proper handover algorithm is required in a mobile backhaul system in order to overcome the high handover shortage or delay experienced at these frequencies. Fast and efficient handover reliance on these high-speed moves has a significant impact on the control layer procedure. In this paper, we design a cascade handover method and evaluate the throughput of handover data in a Mobile Hotspot Network (MHN) using a spectrum band over 6 GHz.**

Keywords-throughput; handover; backhaul; mobile hotspot network; above 6 GHz.

I. Introduction

Mobile data traffic has grown 4,000 times over the past decade and global mobile data traffic is growing 30.6 exa-bytes per month by 2020 [1]. As more than 50 billion connected devices are expected to be launched, including 1.5 billion cars worldwide, mobile communication networks have become an important factor in meeting the needs of specific vertical industries and dramatically increasing the number of devices [2]. Cellular-type small cells below 6GHz are not the same in terms of user and system requirements to meet the need for a significant increase in data traffic when considering ultra-dense network solutions. Especially when moving at high speed, very different requirements are required. Small backhaul in urban areas is an effective solution for inter-cell interworking. However, the problem caused by mobility in high-speed is still under investigation in the mmWave-based backhaul network [3], [4]. Especially, it can provide low cost and small architecture, such as mmWave backhaul, channel feasibility, use of large scale MIMO, measurement of mmWave propagation, and combination of multi beam antenna for outdoor mmWave mobile communication [5]-[7]. MmWave-based technology has evolved over the last few decades and has contributed to reducing the number of cells required. Backhaul and fronthaul networks for 5G transport are also presented in the Xhaul architecture, which allows for flexible and reconfigurable all network elements.

For high-speed transport (HST), such as subways and trains, some results with high data rates of up to 350 km/h have been presented [9]-[10]. At 60 km/h at 60 GHz, the Doppler spread is over 3 kHz and is several hundred microseconds faster than today's cellular systems. Also, high shadowing conditions can overcome beam conditions, but channel conditions force mmWave beam blocking due to large changes in path loss in mobile environments [3]. We design and implement a cascade handover scheme, which enables faster and more efficient handover. Through this simulation, we tried to confirm the relationship between packet generation and handover at high speed. We propose this method and evaluate the performance of the method according to data throughput. The rest of this paper is mentioned as follows. Section II introduces related work and Section III outlines the MHN system. Section IV presents the proposed cascade handover scheme including window. Then, procedures and performance evaluations for synchronization and handover execution are described in Sections V and VI. The conclusion is in Section VII.

II. Related Work

To provide broadband access, such as virtual reality and augmented reality services for users in these HSTs, it is imperative to overcome the challenges of poor channel conditions and large numbers of simultaneous handovers. As the number of small cell layout increases in 5G, fast handover is required at cell edge [8], [11]. Reference [11] shows two improvements in handover performance in LTE systems. One is to prevent radio link failure in the handover, which provides the reliability of the transmission of the handover procedure while the user equipment is under poor radio channel conditions. The other is to define an early handover preparation through an Early Handover Preparation with Ping-Pong Avoidance (EHOPPPA) handover to ensure reliable transmission of the handover procedure in good radio channel conditions. In order to apply this in HST, we face some problems, such as mmWave-based beam processing and high mobility. Thus, an mmWave-based Distributed Antenna System (DAS) for mobile communication systems is introduced and can transmit data up to 1 Gbps at distances of up to 1 km using the 27 GHz spectrum band [12]. In addition, having a network of moving connected terminal devices can support faster and higher functionality.

Since the advent of new technologies for mobile communications for HST, multiple base stations have been designed for low interference and low handover times. For this purpose, MHN is a mobile backhaul based on mmWave, and several base stations are installed at intervals of 1km next to the railway for users who boarded in HST, and trains pass through MHN's mRUs along the railways in turn. The focus of this paper is on the subway of the city and in the HST placement in rural areas and is designed to have a cell radius that is wider than the current small cell size for city radius and small cell placement, i.e., a radius of 500 m. The coverage of this arrangement is such that the spacing between the two mRUs is less than 1 km due to the mmWave characteristics such as propagation loss, shadowing (e.g., humidity, rain fades and blockage) and Doppler spread [12].

The LTE physical layer is designed to support high throughput data delivery of 350 km/h and even 500 km/h in rural areas than 3G systems. However, the situation of HST can still suffer from LTE networks. First, the wireless channel status changes greatly in HST environment. Second, handover between cells is often apt to occur in terms of speed. To solve this problem, LTE-based cell array technique was introduced in [10]. While cell arrays may be effectively active on the approaching LTE cell, there are some difficulties in supporting seamless handover that does not interfere with the multimedia stream. LTE-based solutions are limited in meeting Gbps multimedia services. The handover decision procedure in LTE network between two eNBs is typically initiated by the eNBs without communicating with the MME. The decision of the home eNB that moves the UE to the target eNB is based on a measurement report for the UE, such as a Channel Quality Indicator (CQI), the target eNB is ready to prepare radio resources before confirming the handover. As soon as a handover is completed, the target eNB indicates the home eNB to release its resources.

III. Mobile Hotspot Network

Since MHN typically spans geographical areas, it is not economically feasible to build specific networks for users who are always in the HST. Therefore, a mobile wireless backhaul network that can be accessed even during high-speed movement between Wi-Fi and the network is needed so that users can connect to the network via Wi-Fi installed in the HST without changing the specifications of the terminal. In the MHN, the 27 GHz band was designed and used to provide mobile wireless backhaul to the HST. An mmWave backhaul data traffic is converted to Wi-Fi data traffic inside the HST. In Figure 1, the MHN architecture based on mmWave communication for HST is introduced. The overall architecture consists of multiple mobile radio units (mRU), multiple mobile vehicular equipment (mVE), and mobile digital devices (mDU) connected to the mobile gateway (mGW). Each mDU communicates with multiple mRUs over fiber optics and is responsible for baseband signal processing. Each mRU function is an important part of the RF transmission at the base station with unique cell identity. Beamforming can support multiple independent wireless links between mRU and mVE. One mDU and several mRUs belong to mNBs. The handover procedure is established between the home mNB and the target mNB via the M2 interface. Other Packet Data Unit (PDU) streams can be transmitted between mRU and mVE. The multi-antenna installation of mVE is designed to reduce handover latency by maintaining multiple connections to the mRU over the M-Uu interface. MVE is a relay that is connected to the mobile router using the T1 interface and the mobile router is connected to the Wi-Fi AP using the T2 interface. Passengers on board can easily access Wi-Fi via their mobile handsets. This architecture also greatly improves spectral efficiency by allowing mRUs to simultaneously use the same radio resources. The mRU in the mNB can communicate with the mVEs before and after the HST using a beam like the mmWave-based base station [12].

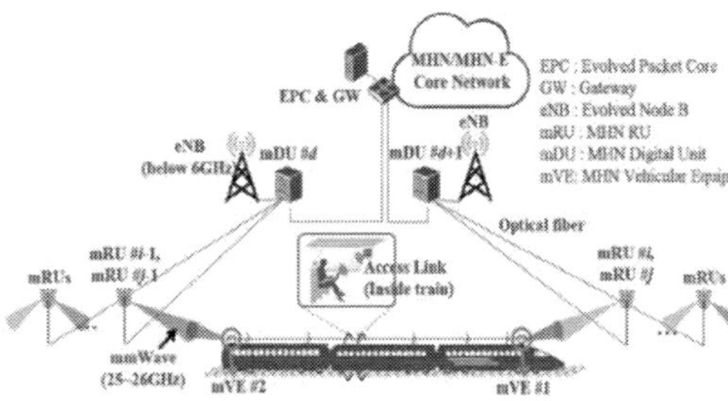

Figure 1. MHN Architecture.

IV. Handover Scheme with window

The MHN handover scheme has a synchronized channel structure and a cell search algorithm that can reliably process neighbor cell search when the interference of the home channel is 25 dB or more. The MHN proposed a cell search algorithm in which the offset and the reserved region are located at positions of synchronized channel symbols according to cell ID [12]. In this paper, we propose a handover method for fast movement between mVE and mRU. The handover procedure of cell 3 must be triggered at the maximum power of the assumed mRU_3 before entering the next cell 4 in the target mRU_4 due to the sudden drop of the received power at the cell edge of cell 3. From the viewpoint of high-speed movement, the faster the handover time, the lower the data transmission rate. Further, if the handover time is too late, the received power of the target mRU_4 received by the mVE is too low, which may cause a handover failure as shown in Figure 2. In [12], it provides an LTE-based solution that can support high throughput and continuous multimedia services for HST users, in order to ensure that wireless channel conditions change rapidly and connections are not interrupted frequently for fast handovers.

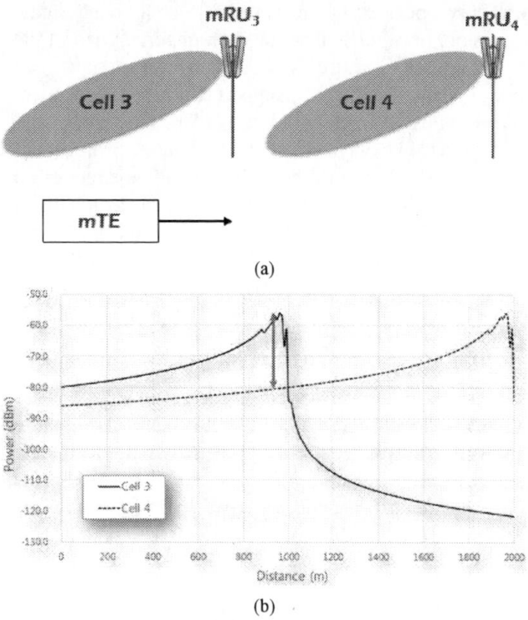

Figure 2. Cell search and time scheme for fast handover in MHN [13]. (a) Concept and (b) Scheme.

The solution uses a "cell array" that can organize continuous cells along the railway in cooperation with the femtocell service through Wi-Fi communication that collects traffic demand within a train [10]. The cascade handover method uses the window based on the moving speed of the HST, and the size of the window is determined by the HST's speed. As the moving speed increases, the size of the window increases. When the speed decreases, the size of the window decreases. Equation (1) determines the size of the W window based on the moving speed and shows how to calculate the window size through each moving speed (= *velocity*):

$$W_{size} = \left| 2^{(\log_{10} velocity)-1} + \frac{1}{2} \right| \quad (1)$$

where W_{size} represents the window size being shipped. The *velocity* indicates the moving speed in km/h. From the point of view of the handover between the two mRUs, the corresponding window size was calculated using the moving speed received from the HST.

TABLE I. WINDOW SIZE WITH RESPECT TO MOVING SPEED OF TRANSPORT

velocity (km / hour)	window size (W_{size})	moving distance (m / sec)	moving speed between mRUs (sec / 1 km)
100	2	27.8	36
500	3	138.9	7.2
750	4	208.3	4.8

Table I shows the results of a simple method of calculating the window size according to each HST mode with different moving speeds (e.g., the speed of the subway is 100 km/h, about 500 km/h for HST and about 750 km/h for future HST). This minimizes interrupt times for handover and cell search times (e.g., mVE and target mRU should find best handover timing). Therefore, depending on the speed characteristics of the HST over 500 km/h, which is a condition experienced by the system, the connection to be sustained is affected by the long downtime that can be very intermittent between mRUs.

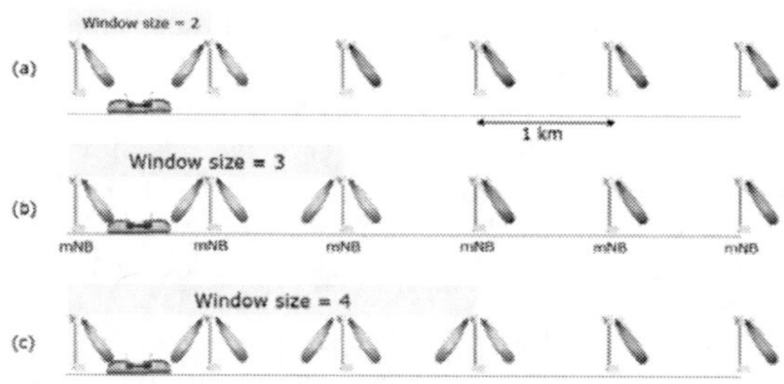

Figure 3. Assigned cases for window size. (a) Velocity is 100 km/hour as shown in subway. (b) Velocity is about 500 km/hour as shown in HST. (c) Velocity is about 750 km/hour for future HST.

V. CASCADE HANDOVER PROCEDURE

We use neighboring cell search and handover structure in the region where the power of the home cell is very large. In our procedure, a cascade handover concept and technique with window is used as shown in Figure 3. The window considers the special features of the mRU to determine the moving speed, coverage and radio resource management. The handover scheme aims at selecting and transmitting the target mRU without interruption. The shorter the duration of the unnecessary handover procedure, the more efficiently the handover mechanism will be implemented. Also, as shown in Figure 2-(b), the home mRU decides to handover the UE moving to the target mRU when the signal strength is high. To use this technique, the mRU must be synchronized within the calculated window size before performing the handover procedure. An improved handover procedure is shown in Figure 4.

A. Synchronization for handover preparation

Synchronization between home mRU and target mRU has been introduced to minimize handover interruption time due to high speed. If the home mRU in source mNB is mRU_0 and mRU_0 is followed by target mRU_1, mRU_2, ... mRU_n, then the target mRU_1 to mRU_n are the neighbor cells to be handed over. First, we calculate the window size according to the speed of movement by HST, as in (1). In addition, a synchronous channel structure / cell search algorithm is required to stably perform neighbor cell search even when the interference of the home cell is higher than 25 dB. In this paper, we introduce a synchronization procedure between mRUs on the assumption that the synchronous channel structure and the cell search algorithm are operating.

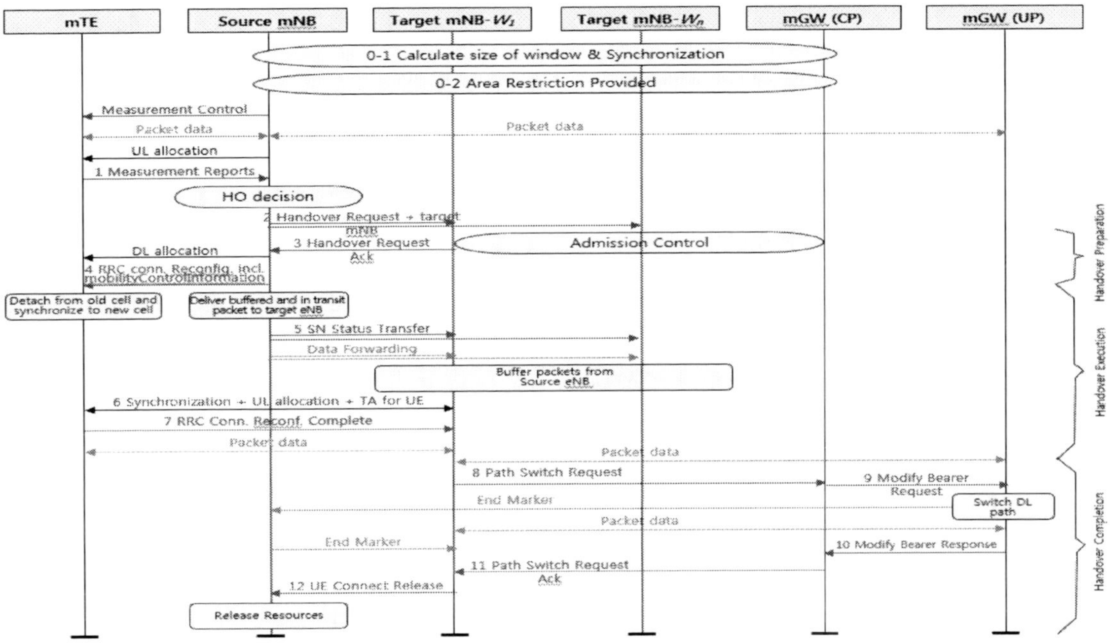

Figure 4. Handover procedure using window between mVE and mNBs.

The home mRU then sends a handover ready message to each target mRU corresponding to the window size calculated as the handover preparation information. Note that the mRU belongs to the mDU, and because the mDU and mRU belong to the mNB, the message is received by the mDU in the mNB. If window size is 3, it is assumed that the moving speed of the HST between the home mRU and the target mRU is about 500 km/h. In case of synchronization for handover between home mRU and target mRU, improvement of Radio Resource Control (RRC) message and application of window use are performed in terms of time and location.

target mRUs at Home mRU$_{(=\text{mRU}_0)}$ $\rightarrow$ {mRU$_1$, mRU$_2$, mRU$_3$} (2)

target mRUs at Home mRU$_{(=\text{mRU1})}$ $\rightarrow$ {mRU$_2$, mRU$_3$, mRU$_4$} (3)

:

target mRUs at Home mRU(= mRU$_{n\text{-}3)}$ $\rightarrow$ {mRU$_{n\text{-}2}$, mRU$_{n\text{-}1}$, mRU$_n$} (4)

Equation (2) to (4) list the sequence of target mRUs according to the change of the home mRU when the window size according to the HST speed is determined. The overall value for this can be explained by the following (5). The mRU not participating in the handover is in the sleep mode in order to block the power consumption, and the value "0" in (5) means the mRU corresponding to the sleep mode. For efficient operation of the sleep mode, inter-mRU synchronization by the RRC in the mDU is most important.

$$A_{i,j} = \begin{vmatrix} a_h & a_{t,1} & a_{t,2} & a_{t,3} & 0 & 0 & 0 & 0 & 0 & 0 \\ 0 & a_h & a_{t,1} & a_{t,2} & a_{t,3} & 0 & 0 & 0 & 0 & 0 \\ 0 & 0 & a_h & a_{t,1} & a_{t,2} & a_{t,3} & 0 & 0 & 0 & 0 \\ 0 & 0 & 0 & a_h & a_{t,1} & a_{t,2} & a_{t,3} & 0 & 0 & 0 \\ 0 & 0 & 0 & 0 & a_h & a_{t,1} & a_{t,2} & a_{t,3} & 0 & 0 \\ 0 & 0 & 0 & 0 & 0 & a_h & a_{t,1} & a_{t,2} & a_{t,3} & 0 \\ 0 & 0 & 0 & 0 & 0 & 0 & a_h & a_{t,1} & a_{t,2} & a_{t,3} \\ 0 & 0 & 0 & 0 & 0 & 0 & 0 & a_h & a_{t,1} & a_{t,2} \\ 0 & 0 & 0 & 0 & 0 & 0 & 0 & 0 & a_h & a_{t,1} \\ 0 & 0 & 0 & 0 & 0 & 0 & 0 & 0 & 0 & a_h \end{vmatrix} \quad (5)$$

where $A_{i,j}$ represents status of mRUs associated with time (i), j is location of each mRU. a_h is home mRU and $a_{t,(1,2,3)}$ is target mNBs. $A_{i,j}$ is calculated according to the conditions of the following equation.

$$A_{i,j} = \begin{cases} 1, & \text{if } A_{i,j} \in a_h \text{ and } A_{i,j} \in a_{1..W_{size}}; \\ 0, & \text{otherwise,} \end{cases} \quad (6)$$

where window size can be considered as $0 < W_{size} \leq j$. There is the number of mRU and velocity for HST. For the considered simulation practical environment, we select the velocity for train is below 750 Km/h and the number of stations is more than 3 respectfully.

B. Handover preparation in home mRU in mNB

As soon as the handover decision is complete, the home mRU of the mNB sends a "handover request" message containing target mRU IDs to target mRUs equal to the window size for admission control when dynamic resource allocation by the scheduler is activated. MRU compares its mRU ID with the target mRU ID sent from the home mRU. An mRU with a different ID does not send a “handover request confirmation” message to the home mRU. In this way, the moving speed of the HST is stably maintained even when the moving speed changes between 0 km/h and the maximum speed.

C. Handover execution in home mRU in mNB

For handover performance, in order to ensure smooth mobility between the home mRU and the target mRU in the mNB, the home mRU and all target mRUs within the window size need to share the optimal resource allocation. The home mRU sends resource allocation information to the target mRUs for fast handover execution. When the handover procedure is complete, the role of the home mRU is taken by the target mRU and the window move is moved to the next mRU. This approach is done so that the neighboring target mRUs of the home mRU are pre-assigned with the logical network entities by the control entity of the peer mRUs to the users accessing the Wi-Fi via the mVE in the HST. In particular, cooperating peer mRUs can centralize the architecture associated with the handover procedure that controls the data service of the target mRU, thereby contributing to a reduction in seamless service and handover interruption time.

D. Sleep mode for less power consumption in mRU

Due to the characteristics of subways and trains, the ratio of the total running area to the whole area is very limited depending on the moving speed and position of the train. The train passes the waiting status for a certain period of time and then the next train passes. Therefore, since the base stations located between the train and the next train continue to consume electric power, the electric power is cut off after the train has passed and the entrance of the train is received from the neighboring home RU in the vicinity of the RRC message in advance, which will contribute to power saving. The data delivery in home mRUs is typically done using a point-to-multi point approach, which is deployed in a dense arrangement. This scheme ensures a high data rate between the mVE and the mRU and at the same time minimizes intra-system interference that may occur between different cells of the MHN. Therefore, mRUs that do not participate in the handover procedure are put into sleep mode without power consumption. The home mRU enters the sleep mode as soon as it receives the "handover complete" message. In particular, if the mDU to which the home mRU belongs is different from the mDU to which the target mRU belongs, the base station handover must occur. At this time, the entire mNB (its mDU and mRUs) serving as the base station transits to the sleep mode.

VI. Performance Evaluation

A simulation based on a MHN in the mmWave range assumes that the train will run on a straight rail. The simulation model presented in this paper is evaluated on trains as an on-off model, and the possibility of access interception has a great influence on fast handover and scheduler design. Because the test cannot be performed in a real environment like a train running at a speed of 500 km/h, this simulation has replaced train speed by adjusting the interval of packets occurring between two mRUs. The design of on-off model for the application level depends on exactly how the access is described at the link level. In probabilistic modeling, each on-off source can be characterized by a two-state Markov chain with a Poisson ratio. Under this assumption, the analysis of the IP traffic model between mNB and mVE is mainly performed using the on-off model. The data streams exchanged between the mRU and the mVE can be described by an on-off model, which indicates that the processing time of each "on" model represents the generation of one data stream at a constant rate of 500 Mbps and the processing period of each "off" model is indicated the inactivity period between adjacent data streams. The configuration and flow of the on-off model for evaluating the handover procedure is shown in Figure 5.

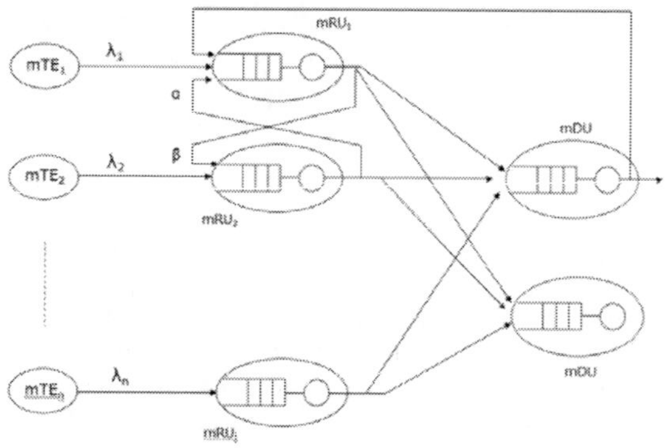

Figure 5. On-off Model to generate packets for handover

This model shows the operational status of the mVE, which provides a different set of performance than the 3GPP common User Equipment (UE). MVE converts the data received from multiple UEs into a packet stream through Wi-Fi which is an access point (AP) operating in the HST, and transmits the data stream to mRU. When the transmitted packet stream arrives at the mRU, the mRU may select it based on the exponential distribution. In probabilistic modeling, individual on and off modes can be characterized by a two-state Markov chain with a Poisson's rate, λ. The sojourn times of the two states can be exponentially distributed by the exponents α and β. This means that the model is related to the next interaction. ① mRUs receiving the users' data streams from the mVE send the data stream to the connected mDU. ② the gateway is connected not only to the home mDU, but also to the target mDU, which is the neighbor mDU of the home mDU to control the data stream. Each data stream is distributed within the mNBs in the home and target mDU. The distribution between mVE and mRU means the capacity of mRU and handover triggering, and the distribution between mRU and mDU includes handover at the cell boundary. mDU orchestrates those interactions and make sure of keeping session connection without interruption.

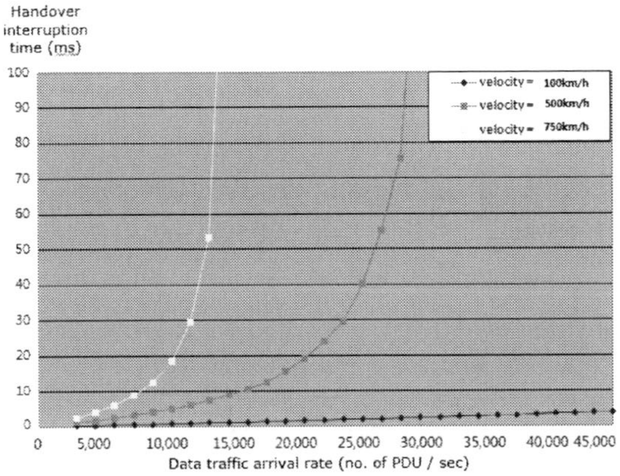

Figure 6. Handover interruption time according to traffic arrival rate.

In Figure 6, it can be shown that the handover downtime increases from 100km/h to 750km/h according to the data traffic arrival rate, when the window size requiring minimum handover interruption time is expected. The data traffic arrival rate is generated by PDUs that occur per second. When HST is operating at 500 km/h or less, the handover interruption time is maintained steadily according to the traffic, but the performance is drastically degraded as the traffic gradually increases at 750 km/h. This means that if the HST speed exceeds 500kh/h, the data traffic arrival interval is less than 1msec, or the data arrival rate is more than 12,500, the proposed handover method cannot provide proper window size. Therefore, we need another approach for handover that depends on window size. For example, as the HST operates at a speed of 750 km/h, the cell radius between the two mRUs must be at least 500 m to solve the performance degradation.

VII. CONCLUSION

The large bandwidth available at mmWave frequencies can greatly increase the capacity of the fifth generation wireless systems based on wireless backhaul. However, when moving at high speeds, utilizing the optimal handover algorithm in the MHN system to overcome the high handover shortage rate or delay experienced at these frequencies, a suitable handover algorithm is required. In particular, a fast moving mVE ahead of the target mRU will require a decision as to when to initiate a handover, and if this determination is made too fast or too late, a delay or short circuit of the session may occur. In this paper, we propose a method for providing information about target mRUs through a window to determine timing to start a fast and efficient handover. The results show that cascaded handover with windows improves cell search and extends link range to reduce handover interruption time. This procedure provides the user of the HST with an efficient handover scheme from the home mRU to the target mRU in the window according to the rate, and can be performed without collaboration with the evolved packet core (EPC). A prepared message communicates directly with the target mRU and the home mDU to which the home mRU belongs. It also analyzes both the MHN using the 27 GHz range and shows all of the measurement and simulation results to verify the use of the handover method with the MHN window. In addition to supporting high speeds of over 500 km/h, many technical issues remain. We will improve the proposed handover method by extending the simulation environment for further research.

ACKNOWLEDGMENT

This work was supported by Institute for Information & communications Technology Promotion (IITP) grant funded by the Korea government (MSIP) (No. 2014-0-00282, Development of 5G Mobile Communication Technologies for Hyper-connected smart services).

REFERENCES

[1] Cisco, ''Cisco visual network index: Global mobile traffic forecast update,'' 2016.

[2] Ericsson, "More than 50 billion connected devices," White Paper. 284 23-3149, February 2011.

[3] S. Rangan, T. S. Rappaport, and E. Erkip "Millimeter-Wave Cellular Wireless Networks: Potentials and Challenges," Proceedings of the IEEE | vol. 102, no. 3, March 2014, pp. 366-385.

[4] J. Hansryd, "Non-line-of-sight microwave backhaul for small cells," Ericsson Review, March 2013.

[5] S. Rajagopal, S. Abu-Surra, and M. Malmirchegini, "Channel Feasibility for Outdoor Non-Line-of-Sight mmWave Mobile Communication," IEEE Vehicular Technology Conference, pp1-6, September 2012.

[6] S. Sun, T. S. Rappaport, R. W. Heath, A. Nix, and S. Rangan "MIMO for Millimeter-Wave Wireless Communications: Beamforming, Spatial Multiplexing, or Both?," IEEE Com. Magazine, vol. 52, issue 12, pp.110-121, December 2014.

[7] S. Sun, G. R. MacCartney Jr., M. K. Samimi, S. Nie and T. S. Rappaport, "Millimeter Wave Multi-beam Antenna Combining for 5G Cellular Link Improvement in New York City," IEEE ICC 2014 - Wireless Communications Symposium, pp. 5468-5473, August 2014.

[8] A. De La Oliva, "Xhaul: Towards an Integrated Fronthaul / Backhaul Architecture in 5G Networks," IEEE Wireless Communications, vol. 22, Issue 5, pp.32-40, October 2015.

[9] K. Guan, "Mobile Channel Characterization in Typical Subway Tunnels at 30 GHz," IEEE P802.15 Working Group for Wireless Personal Area Networks, September 2015.

[10] O. B. Karimi, J. Liu, and C. Wang, "Seamless wireless connectivity for multimedia services in high speed trains," IEEE Journal on Selected Areas In Comm., vol. 30, No. 4, pp. 729-739, May 2012.

[11] H. S. Park, Y. S. Choi, B. C. Kim, and J. Y. Lee, "LTE Mobility Enhancements for Evolution into 5G," ETRI Journal, vol. 37, no. 6, pp. 1065-1076, December 2015.

[12] S. N. Choi, J. H. Kiml, I. G. Kim and D. J. Kim, "Development of Millimeter-Wave Communication Modem for Mobile Wireless Backhaul in Mobile Hotspot Network," IEIE Transactions on Smart Processing and Computing, vol. 3, no. 4, pp. 212-220, August 2014.

The Impact of Regulatory Frameworks and Obligations on Telecommunication Market Developments

Analysis of the European and Asian Broadband Markets and Regulatory Frameworks

Erik Massarczyk, Peter Winzer
Faculty of Design – Computer Science – Media
RheinMain University of Applied Sciences
Wiesbaden, Germany
Email: erik.massarczyk@hs-rm.de, peter.winzer@hs-rm.de

***Abstract*—Based on the rising numbers of broadband Internet users and the resulting higher importance of broadband infrastructures, previous analyses often focused on the relation between competitive market behavior and the development of customer broadband penetration rates. Additionally, some prognoses also consider the relation between the development of market concentration and customer prices. Taking into account the focus on both of these connections, the influence of competitive intensities, regulatory frameworks and the broadband development are rarely considered. Here, this paper will especially examine the interrelation between the development of market concentrations and regulatory frameworks on broadband access speeds and different customer prices and price models. Furthermore, impacts of the national regulatory frameworks are not considered in depth. Previous analyses have often examined the influence of regulatory behaviors and decisions on the development of market concentration. However, the impact of national regulatory frameworks on the other named factors is not considered in detail. Therefore, in this paper, we start addressing the named open issues. Due to the paper's status as a work in progress, it will mostly indicate some theoretical background, literature, methodology and some first results of the competitive analysis. Despite increasing competition (based on Hirschmann-Herfindahl values), approximately half of the considered fixed broadband markets still demonstrate huge discrepancies between the incumbent and competitive network operators.**

Keywords-broadband development; market concentration; Hirschmann-Herfindahl-Index; broadband access speeds, prices and penetration.

I. INTRODUCTION

As a result of the increasing use of Internet services within broadband Internet infrastructures in daily business and private life, the availability of these services is becoming increasingly important as a location factor [1][2].

In the world and particularly in the considered European and Asian broadband markets, different standards for the provision of broadband infrastructures subsist [3], which are responsible for the various broadband developments. On this account, in each regional/national market, different technical standards of broadband infrastructures, broadband penetrations, market situations and regulatory obligations in fixed-line telecommunication markets can be observed [1][4]. These differences result by the following reasons: (a) customer broadband demand, (b) prices for broadband services, (c) quality and combination of technologies providing broadband infrastructures (availability of wires and ducts), (d) implementation costs, (e) competition policy, (f) competition, and (g) demography and culture [1][4][5].

Most publications on this topic focus on the analysis of the relationship between: (a) regulatory and governmental frameworks, (b) competition, (c) broadband diffusion and adoption, (d) coverage and (e) penetration [6][7]. Furthermore, various papers deal with considerations regarding (a) the relations between implementation costs and customer prices, (b) operators and different broadband infrastructures, and (c) demand and supply of broadband Internet services [8][9][10]. Yet, the development of broadband does not only depend on the customer adoption and diffusion of broadband infrastructures. Broadband developments include all services and benefits which are targeted to strengthen and process: (a) higher broadband coverage and penetration, (b) higher broadband connection speeds, (c) higher number of offered services, (d) a higher technical standard of the infrastructures, and (e) measures to create acceptable prices for customers and to induce customer broadband demand. The following relations have been rarely considered so far: (a) the influence of competition (market concentration) on the development of broadband access speeds, (b) the influence of competition on the development of customer prices for broadband services, (c) the impact of regulatory frameworks on the market concentrations in broadband networks, (d) the impact of regulatory frameworks on the development of broadband penetration rates, and (e) the influence of regulatory behavior on the customer prices. The regulatory frameworks are considered solely as drivers for the different kinds of competition and the impact of this competition on the development of broadband penetration rates. As mentioned, the other impacts are not considered.

This study will firstly examine the impact of market concentrations on the fixed-line broadband development. Based on this relationship, we will analyze the different types of regulatory frameworks and their influence on competition. In the further steps, we will focus on the influences of the aforementioned factors with the focus being on broadband access speeds. For the evaluation, we have collected secondary data of fixed-line broadband markets in Europe and Asia to conduct a combined cross-sectional and longitudinal panel data analysis with ordinary least square regressions. The chosen time range of said data will include the years between 2004 and 2015 in order to reflect on the reasons for the different country-specific broadband developments, levels of competition/market concentration and regulatory behaviors over time. Apart from the different regression models, the intensity of competition will be – in a first step – measured through the usage of different economic concentration models. Following this approach, we will discuss how the regulatory frameworks can be examined.

The paper will proceed as follows: based on the introduction, Section 2 will present the literature review and the hypotheses. Section 3 will include the research methodology. Section 4 will indicate the first results of the examinations. After all, we will conclude the paper in Section 5.

II. LITERATURE REVIEW

Due to the various influence factors described, broadband market conditions and issues of broadband provision, the term of broadband development includes: the development of coverage and penetration of the existing broadband infrastructures, the expansion/upgrade of new and old infrastructures, the changing customer prices for broadband services and the quality of the broadband networks (broadband connection speeds).

Based on liberalizations of the fixed-line broadband markets in developed and emerging countries, various network operators and service providers compete in the provision of broadband Internet accesses and services. In order to address potentially large customer base and to quickly get back the effected expenditures, the operators often focus on broadband developments in regions with high population densities and low implementation costs [9][11], which count as economic efficient areas [10]. This approach significantly reduces the incentives for investments, implementations and upgrades of the existing broadband infrastructures in rural regions with lower population density significantly.

However, in situations when competitors get access to the broadband infrastructure of the incumbent or when the competitors have their own broadband access infrastructure (cable or fiber), the customer prices for broadband services, the broadband diffusion and provision respectively are influenced. Especially in cases of providing access for new entrants and controlled prices, regulatory decisions and behaviors by the governmental authorities could possibly strongly influence the existing market situations.

The opening of existing broadband infrastructures creates an intense price competition, which strengthens the broadband adoption by customers [6][7].

In case of competitive situations in broadband markets, the prices for broadband services decrease and the broadband diffusion and provision increase strongly [6][7]. The competition of different network operators and service providers exert a positive influence on customer adoption of broadband access networks and can be named as one of the key drivers to reach high broadband penetration rates [7].

To sum up the previous findings [6][7], the first hypothesis will examine the relationship between broadband diffusion and the development of market concentrations.

H1: A stronger competition (higher competitive intensity) leads to higher broadband penetration rates.

The relationship between (1) competitive intensities and (2a) the development of broadband connection speeds and (2b) customer prices for broadband services has thus far not been considered in greater detail. As a result of the mentioned market conditions, one can assume that competition is a main driver for the development of broadband infrastructures and broadband services. It can be expected that a competitive broadband market structure leads to higher connection speeds, since competitors invest financial resources in new infrastructures and equipment in order to differentiate from existing market players and to get in a better market position in comparison to the incumbent.

H2: Regional telecommunication markets with a higher level of broadband competition have higher broadband connection speeds.

The hypothesis expects that more competition leads to faster broadband connection speeds, lower prices and higher penetration rates. If the hypothesis turns out to be true, it can be concluded that in broadband markets with higher concentrations usually strong monopolists and oligopolists try to hold and increase their market shares instead of investing into new infrastructures and push further broadband developments. In the past incumbents are often not forced to grant possible market entrants access to their broadband network. Based on the missing fear of a possible new market entry of a new competitor, the incumbent has no incentive to develop a new or better infrastructure.

Only if the monopolist fears a competitor's market entry or the incumbent is forced to grant the access for new market entrants, it will have an incentive to upgrade the current infrastructure in order to improve the quality of its broadband networks and services.

In addition to the first two described hypotheses, existing competitive intensities in broadband markets could positively impact customer prices for broadband services [8][9][12]. Price reductions influence individual market shares and market power compared to the competitors. In addition, the market entry is made more difficult by the fact that the (potential) new providers achieve lower sales with their end customers at constant costs for the use of the infrastructure of the incumbent [5]. Due to these circumstances, the following hypotheses H3 and H4 will investigate and capture the open issue: *Do customer prices have an impact on broadband developments in regional markets?* Currently, measurements of the relationship between competition, customer broadband prices and broadband penetration are not considering the achieved and the delivered broadband connection speeds [8].

In competitive market situations, competitors decrease their prices to reach a broader customer base. Therefore, the broadband adoption can be positively influenced and will increase over time. This relationship turns out to be one of the driving indicators for broadband penetration [9]. But operators and providers in competitive market structures have to deal with the issue that enterprises lead a price competition based on the margin of cost coverage, which results in decreasing customer revenues. The influence of competition on customer revenues leads to problems if the network operators have difficulty to provide the financial resources for new investments in broadband infrastructures. Furthermore, companies try: (a) to differentiate their products and (b) to invest in the broadband infrastructure to get into a better market position than competitors [9]. In general, a weaker competition (higher market concentration) leads to higher customer broadband prices and lower investments in infrastructure [9].

Generally, it can be ascertained that prices for broadband services and the adoption of accesses are negatively related [6][13]. However, the prices also depend on the customer's willingness to pay and the demand for broadband services. Since customers are price sensitive, a declining price induces a higher willingness to adopt and use broadband access [9]. So far, researchers have only considered the influence of broadband prices on the development of penetration rates. However, there is currently no evidence regarding the relation between broadband prices and the development of broadband connection speeds.

H3: A stronger competition leads to lower monthly customer prices for broadband access.

H4: Lower customer prices for broadband access lead to a faster development of broadband connection speeds.

Following the introduction of the presented competitive considerations, the relationships of the regulatory frameworks on the development of (a) market concentrations, (b) customer prices, (c) penetration rates, and (d) broadband connection speeds need to be analyzed too.

Based on the vast range of governmental initiatives and regulatory instruments (e. g., implementation of market liberalization), it is normally intended that the competitive forces rule the market power and market shares on their own [14]-[17]. However, in some cases the market forces are not strong enough to regulate the market and regulatory authorities have to intervene [16]. On the base of different kinds of regulations (especially access regulations), Kiesewetter et al. [18], and Waverman and Koutroumpis [19] found out that regulations directly influence the market concentration in broadband markets. Regulations are able to force the incumbent to open the networks for competitors [20]. Therefore, the existing market structures and especially the market position of the incumbent can be influenced by the implementation of regulations. In this situation, the regulations shall remove burdens and constraints and may overcome the lack of competitive behavior [7][16][20]. A possible change of market structures allows new entrants to enter the market and take the risk of a foreclosure of the incumbent [20]. Hence, the acceleration of competition should induce a stronger competition with a higher rate of broadband adoptions [6].

H5: Regulatory behavior and mandatory access regulations will positively enhance competitive market behaviors.

Supporting the previous explanations, Gruber and Koutroumpis [7], and Wallsten [21] mention the fact that the implementation of regulations (especially unbundling) stimulate higher broadband penetration rates. However, Briglauer and Gugler [5] found that only few regulatory decisions influence broadband penetration rates directly. Possibly, regulations can also negatively impact the development of broadband penetration rates [3].

H6: Regulatory behavior and mandatory access regulations will positively relate to broadband penetration.

Furthermore, regulatory authorities are able and allowed to set price regulations. Therefore, they have to check if the incumbent is trying to use his market power to set higher prices than a market with competitive structures. If the incumbent cannot force higher prices, the gained revenues, financial resources and the incentives for further broadband investments will decrease. Also, the new entrants are not willing to invest high amounts, because they cannot set higher prices as the incumbent to get customers [7][20]. On one hand, regulatory authorities have to verify whether the prices are based on the long incremental or opportunity costs [20]. This behavior could discourage possible investments in broadband infrastructures, because the companies do not gain high revenues. On the other hand, governmental authorities support the roll-outs of new infrastructures with different offers of funding [5]. Based on these explanations, we originate the following two hypotheses.

H7: Regulatory behavior and mandatory access regulations will positively impact stronger broadband developments and higher broadband connection speeds.

H8: Regulatory behavior and mandatory access regulations will negatively relate to customer prices.

III. METHODOLOGY

As the previous explanations indicate, we will analyze relationships between broadband developments, the respective market concentrations and broadband market regulations in particularly Western European and Southeast Asian markets.

The focus lies on countries of the European Union 28 (EU28) and the Association of Southeast Asian Nations (ASEAN), as well as additional countries such as Switzerland, Japan and the Rep. of Korea. The reason why said regions of the world were selected are as follows: (1) EU28 and ASEAN are regions with (a) multiple countries, (b) a comparable number of inhabitants, and (c) national territories. (2) Like the EU28, the ASEAN system is also developing to get in the position of a central commission for economic, social, regulatory and juridical resolutions.

For the cross-sectional and longitudinal panel data analysis of the described relationships, we have collected secondary data from: (a) the regulatory authorities of the considered countries, (b) the International Telecommunication Union (ITU), (c) the Organization for Economic Cooperation and Development (OECD), (d) the European Union, (e) telecommunication authorities and ministries, and (f) national institutions and governments. Due to the different sources, the elicitation of the data can vary. Therefore, we test the data validity and reliability with exploratory factor analysis and Cronbach's Alpha to verify the trust in the collected secondary data [22]-[24]. Nevertheless, some discrepancies between the collected data and the anticipated time trend of the data cannot be excluded. Due to few data errors and issues, some of the considered countries are not considered in detail.

The evaluation of the competitive intensities follows different concentration models, (Hirschmann-Herfindahl-Index (HHI), Linda-Index (LI)) which measure the intensity and disparity of the national broadband markets' competition and to compare the different operators' market shares [25]-[28].

The HHI, as one of the most popular models to evaluate market concentrations, will be used to measure the intensity of competition based on absolute key figures. The collected market shares illustrate the number of customers of each of the biggest three providers in relation to the total number of customers in the specific national broadband market [25][26]. The HHI describes the weighted average of concentration and squares the collected market shares (see (1), S describes the market share of each specific network operator, i describes the considered operator) [26]-[28].

$$HHI = \sum_{i=1}^{m} S_i^2 \times 10.000 = \sum_{i=1}^{m} (100 \times S_i)^2 \quad (1)$$

The LI does not reach the same usage and awareness level but the results show how much the market varies from perfect competition (LI-value of 1). Generally, the LI is used to examine the disparity between the biggest and following companies. Therefore, the disparity measures an existence of market dominance and describes if the inequalities between the operators lead to significant changes in the competitive behavior [26]. The LI value is based on a two times calculation and presents a double average index (see (2) and (3), CR stands for the Concentration Ratio, which is the single sum of the market shares of the considered number of network operators, i describes the considered operator) [26], which separates the enterprises with significant and insignificant impact on the market enterprises, where the quotient of the market shares reaches the maximum.

$$V_{i,m} = \frac{\frac{CR_i}{i}}{\frac{CR_m - CR_i}{m-i}} \quad (2)$$

$$L_m = \frac{1}{m-1} \times \sum_{i=1}^{m-1} V_{i,m} \quad (3)$$

Nevertheless, we may also use the Exponential-Index and Horvath-Index (a) to investigate the collected data with alternative concentration models, (b) to cover the results of the previous named concentration models, and (c) to establish some other possible interpretations of the data base.

Furthermore, we will only examine the developments in the fixed-line broadband markets. Analyses of the market concentration and competitive situation are based on the three largest network operators (according to customers). This is justified by the fact that: (a) there are only three network operators in some of the individual markets [29]; and (b) in markets with a larger number of network operators the influence of these other / smaller network operators is of secondary importance for the competition situation.

The longitudinal analysis, which spans a time range from 2004 to 2015, will also cover some cross-sectional elements to conduct comparisons between the various countries in consideration. The needed data is composed of the network operators' market shares, broadband penetration rates, customer prices and some basic economic facts like Gross Domestic Product (GDP), exchange rates, price parities, households and population density. The hypotheses will be analyzed and estimated using various econometric and panel data techniques. Generally, each hypothesis will be tested by an ordinary least square regression to figure out if the results are significantly able to present the named relationships. For each hypothesis, we define the following regression equations, which can be seen in Table 1. All stated equations will be calculated twice. In the first attempt, we test the regression equation assuming single/multiple linear relationships between the dependent and independent variables. In the second step, we analyze the collected data with logarithmic equation models. Both approaches will be utilized to get a broader understanding of the collected data and the possible relationships.

TABLE 1. REGRESSION EQUATIONS

H1: a) $PE_t = \alpha + \beta_1 CI_t + \beta_2 SF_t + \beta_3 PD_t + \varepsilon$ b) $TPE_t = \alpha + \beta_1 TCI_t + \beta_2 SF_{t-1} + \beta_3 PD_t + \varepsilon$ c) $PE_{t+1} = \alpha + \beta_1 CI_t + \beta_2 SF_t + \beta_3 PD_t + \varepsilon$	PE – value of the broadband penetration TPE – trend based value of the broadband penetration CI – values of the competition index (HHI. LI etc.) TCI – trend based values of the competition index SF – monthly subscription fee PD – population density BS – broadband connection speeds IF – installation fee GDPC – Gross Domestic Product per Capita RI – regulatory index DM – years of membership in EU28 or ASEAN B – changing variable term ε – error term α – constant t – year of consideration t-1 – past year of consideration
H2: a) $BS_t = \alpha + \beta_1 CI_t + \beta_2 PE_t + \varepsilon$ b) $BS_t = \alpha + \beta_1 TCI_t + \beta_2 PE_{t-1} + \varepsilon$ c) $BS_t = \alpha + \beta_1 CI_{t-1} + \beta_2 PE_{t-1} + \varepsilon$	
H3: a) $SF_t = \alpha + \beta_1 CI_t + \beta_2 GDPC_t + \beta_3 IF_t + \varepsilon$ b) $SF_t = \alpha + \beta_1 TCI_t + \beta_2 GDPC_{t-1} + \beta_3 IF_t + \varepsilon$ c) $SF_t = \alpha + \beta_1 CI_{t-1} + \beta_2 GDPC_{t-1} + \beta_3 IF_t + \varepsilon$	
H4: a) $BS_t = \alpha + \beta_1 SF_t + \beta_2 GDPC_t + \varepsilon$ b) $BS_t = \alpha + \beta_1 SF_t + \beta_2 IF_t + \varepsilon$ c) $BS_t = \alpha + \beta_1 SF_{t-1} + \beta_2 GDPC_{t-1} + \varepsilon$	
H5: a) $CI_t = \alpha + \beta_1 RI_t + \beta_2 GDPC_t + \beta_3 DM_t + \varepsilon$ b) $CI_{t-1} = \alpha + \beta_1 RI_{t-1} + \beta_2 GDPC_{t-1} + \varepsilon$ c) $TCI_t = \alpha + \beta_1 RI_t + \beta_2 GDPC_t + \beta_3 DM_t + \varepsilon$	
H6: a) $PE_t = \alpha + \beta_1 RI_t + \beta_2 DM_t + \varepsilon$ b) $TPE_t = \alpha + \beta_1 RI_t + \beta_2 DM_t + \varepsilon$ c) $PE_{t+1} = \alpha + \beta_1 RI_t + \beta_2 DM_t + \varepsilon$	
H7: a) $BS_t = \alpha + \beta_1 RI_t + \beta_2 DM_t + \varepsilon$ b) $BS_t = \alpha + \beta_1 RI_{t-1} + \beta_2 DM_t + \varepsilon$	
H8: a) $SF_t = \alpha + \beta_1 RI_t + \beta_2 GDPC_t + \beta_3 IF_t + \varepsilon$ b) $SF_t = \alpha + \beta_1 RI_t + \beta_2 GDPC_{t-1} + \beta_3 IF_t + \varepsilon$ c) $SF_t = \alpha + \beta_1 RI_{t-1} + \beta_2 GDPC_{t-1} + \beta_3 IF_t + \varepsilon$	

IV. FIRST RESULTS

In order to analyze the relationship between competition, broadband connection speeds, customer broadband penetration rates and prices, the intensity of competition (HHI) and the disparity (LI) between the market players will be examined.

For the analysis of the broadband market concentrations, the considered values of the HHI will be separated into the three parts: (1) HHI below the value of 2,000 (low concentration), (2) HHI between the values of 2,000 and 4,000 (moderate concentration), and (3) HHI above the value of 4,000 (high concentration), based on [25]-[28].

Ideally, the fixed-line broadband markets should have stable HHI market concentration values which do not exceed 1,800 overt time.

Apart from Japan (divided consideration of NTT East and West), all European countries with low HHI-values below 2,000 are European countries situated in the continent's Northern or Eastern parts (Lithuania, Denmark, Sweden, UK) (see Figure 1, 3, and 4). These countries are also in the Global top ten of highest average broadband connection speeds [30]-[34].

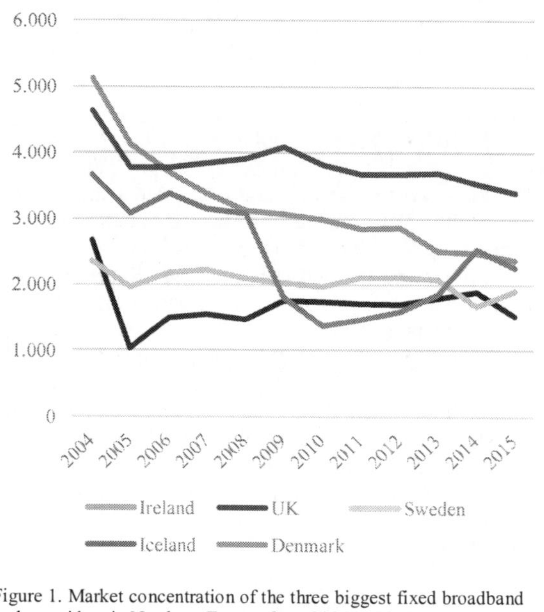

Figure 1. Market concentration of the three biggest fixed broadband network providers in Northern Europe from 2004 to 2015 (x-axis: years; y-axis: HHI values)

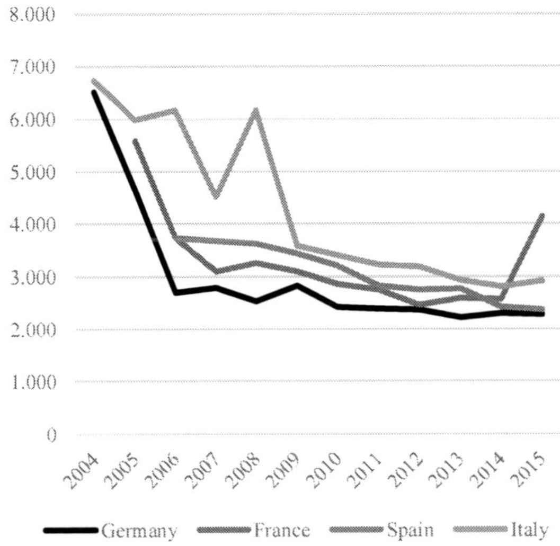

Figure 2. Market concentration of the three biggest fixed broadband network providers in the biggest four Western European countries (except UK) from 2004 to 2015 (x-axis: years; y-axis: HHI values)

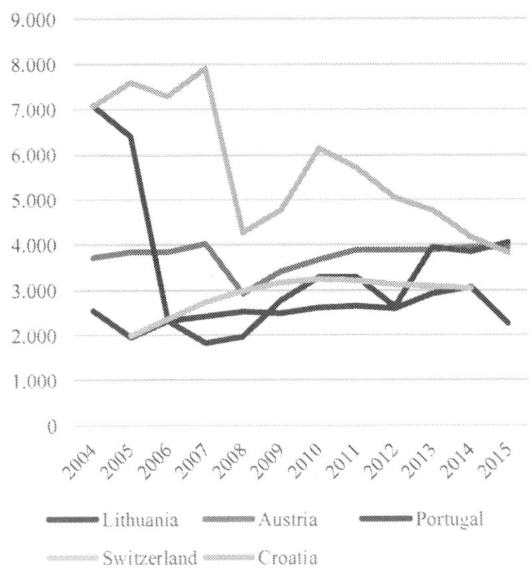

Figure 3. Market concentration of the three biggest fixed broadband network providers of further European countries from 2004 to 2015 (x-axis: years; y-axis: HHI values)

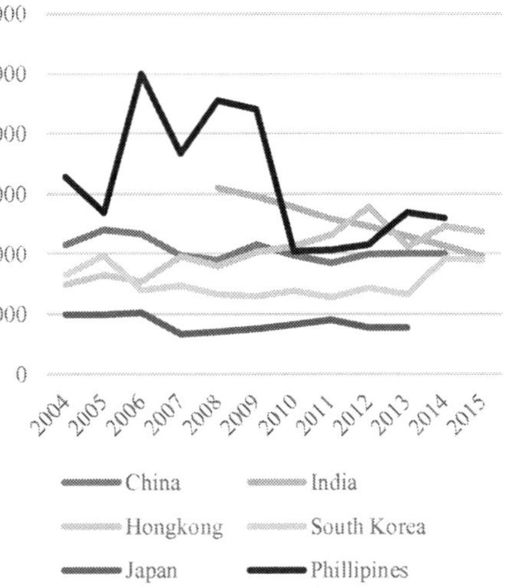

Figure 4. Market concentration of the three biggest fixed broadband network providers of Asian countries from 2004 to 2015 (x-axis: years; y-axis: HHI values)

In general, most fixed-line broadband markets of the EU28 and ASEAN now reach HHI-values between 2,000 and 4,000 and are moderately concentrated. When considering the named period, it can be concluded that market concentrations in most countries have decreased from HHI-values above 4,000 (high concentrated) to moderate concentrated market structures. This development presents diminished market forces and the change of strong monopolistic into rising competitive market structures. Generally, the considered broadband markets are moderately concentrated (e. g., Ireland, Germany, Portugal, South Korea) (see Figure 1, 2, 3, 4). Nevertheless, some countries (Croatia, Iceland, India, Philippines) still have HHI-values above 4,000, which implies that the biggest operators were able to hold their market powers and avoid strong competitive structures (see Figure 1, 3, 4).

Generally, the moderate or high market concentrations in the broadband markets suggest that national regulatory authorities should review the current market behaviors of the existing network operators. To create better competitive and network access opportunities, regulatory authorities could introduce access regulations, which secure possible market entries by competitors.

Nevertheless, two different developments can be mainly comprehended. (1) During the last ten years, the intensity of competition in the most considered broadband markets increased and the previous monopolistic structures could be diminished. (2) In the developed countries, the reduction of the power of the monopolistic incumbent is stronger than in the developing countries and the developed countries also have stronger competitive broadband market structures.

The used Linda-Index describes the disparity between the biggest three operators. In general, higher market concentrations translate into higher disparities between the operators. The disparity can be measured in two different ways. On one hand, the LI examines the discrepancy between the biggest and second biggest companies in the market and on the other hand, the LI can evaluate the discrepancy between the biggest, the second biggest and third biggest companies in the considered market. Based on the evaluation of the three biggest operators in the broadband markets, we will consider the second option with the inclusion of the second and third biggest companies.

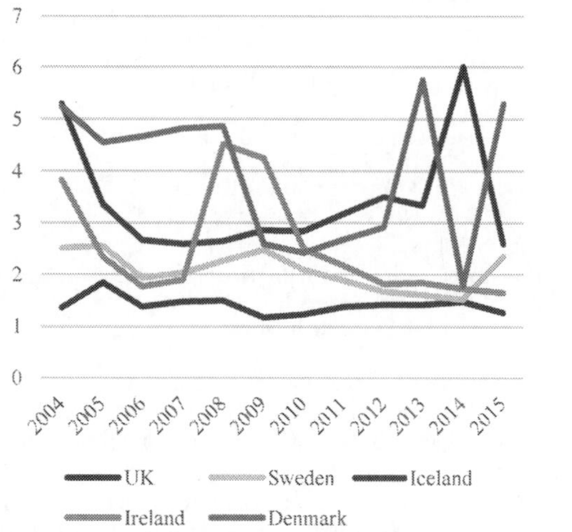

Figure 5. Market concentration of the three biggest fixed broadband network providers in Northern Europe from 2004 to 2015 (x-axis: years; y-axis: LI values)

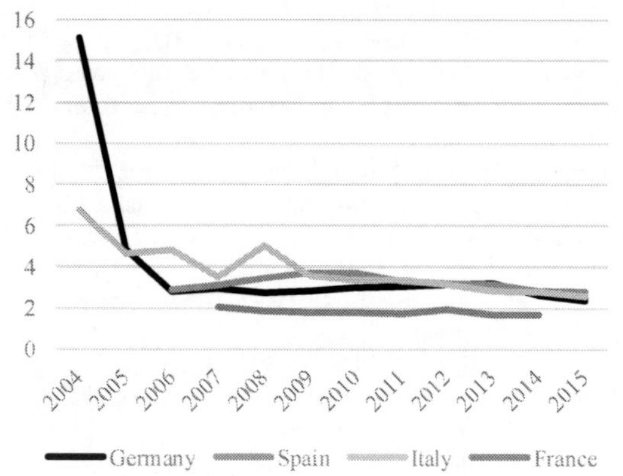

Figure 6. Market concentration of the three biggest fixed broadband network providers in the biggest four Western European countries (except UK) from 2004 to 2015 (x-axis: years; y-axis: LI values)

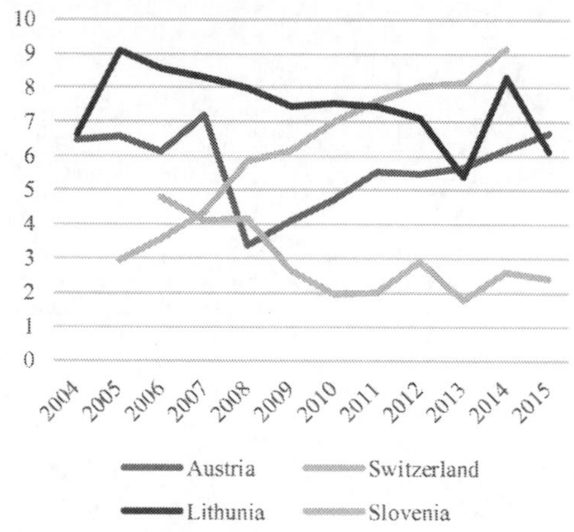

Figure 7. Market concentration of the three biggest fixed broadband network providers of further European countries from 2004 to 2015 (x-axis: years; y-axis: LI values)

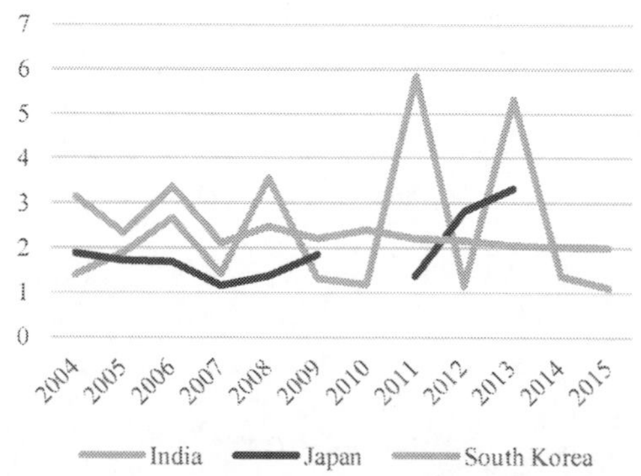

Figure 8. Market concentration of the three biggest fixed broadband network providers of Asian countries from 2004 to 2015 (x-axis: years; y-axis: LI values)

The consideration of the European and Asian fixed-line broadband markets yields LI-values between 2 and 5 for the most countries (see Figures 5, 6, and 8), which indicates that discrepancies between the operators still exist. Nevertheless, the declining trend of the LI-values shows that in most countries the differences between the incumbents and the new market entrants decrease (e. g., Germany, Italy, Slovenia, see Figures 6 and 7). In the future, these broadband markets could reach a nearly equal distributed market power. However, the results also show that the disparities between the network operators in some markets increase (e. g., Austria, Switzerland, see Figure 7). Only in the British market the LI-value is close to 1 and indicates a nearly equal distributed broadband market (between the different market operators) (see Figure 5). Combining this result with the fact that the British market has the oldest history of liberalization, it can be concluded that longer open access market could lead to more equally distributed market shares. This issue needs verification by hypothesis testing and we will include this in their evaluations. Furthermore, a couple of countries show nearly the same LI-values over the whole-time frame (e. g., France, South Korea, see Figure 6 and 8). The reasons why, on one hand, the disparities are very stable and, on the other hand, they vary, will be investigated in the future.

The variations between European and Asian markets are quite low, but nonetheless the LI-values of a couple of countries present higher values. Therefore, network operators in these countries should compensate more inequalities as far as possible. These discrepancies are not sufficiently to draw conclusions from since the results of the LI-values also vary too strongly among network operators in a couple of countries. In general, the disparity (difference in market power and influence) between the incumbent and the competitors cannot be taken as reason for the different broadband connection speeds and developments. It can be just estimated that a more equal distribution of market power could lead to higher broadband connection speeds.

In the beginning of the regression analyses, the evaluation of the correlations shows that the calculated market concentrations correlate significantly (p-values below 0.05) with the development of the broadband connection speeds. The result supports the assumption that a stronger competition could lead to higher broadband connection speeds.

In addition, the same significant correlations between broadband penetration rates and market concentrations exist (p-values below 0.05). The correlations imply that higher competitive intensities and stronger competitive behaviors lead to rising broadband penetration rates.

Due to the correlative relations, it is necessary to prove if a regressive context between the mentioned factors exists.

V. CONCLUSIONS AND FUTURE WORK

As aforementioned, the status of the paper is a work in progress and therefore, improvements in the results and in ongoing research will be necessary. Currently, we have collected the needed secondary data and have started to analyze the competitive intensities. Following this first overview, we will evaluate the above-mentioned hypotheses using the ordinary least square regressions to test the established regression equations. Additionally, we will measure the different regulatory behaviors of the considered countries and to be able to examine the named relationships in the regression equations.

Despite the named conditions and the different developments in the national broadband markets, the general trend presents increasing competitive structures in the fixed broadband markets. Combining the results of the HHI and LI analysis, the incumbents in each national broadband market have lost market shares and the disparity between the different providers is decreasing. As shown in the results, few countries (especially in Asia) still have very powerful incumbents and a general statement concerning all considered countries cannot be done at this status of work.

At this time in evaluation work, the results are on a preliminary stage, which will be a starting point for the ongoing research.

REFERENCES

[1] International Telecommunication Union, "The state of broadband 2014: broadband for all", Report from the broadband commission, pp. 16-23, 2014. (http://www.broadbandcommission.org/Documents/reports/bb-annualreport2014.pdf), [retrieved: 05.2017]

[2] P. Koutroumpis, "The economic impact of broadband on growth: A simultaneous approach", Telecommunications Policy, Volume 33 (9), pp. 471-485, 2009.

[3] W. Briglauer, "The impact of regulation and competition on the adoption of fiber-based broadband services: recent evidence from the European Union member states", Springer Verlag, pp. 450-468, 2014.

[4] Monopoly Commission, "Special Report 61 – Telcommunication 2011: Strengthen investments and secure the competition", in German: Monopolkommission "Sondergutachten 61 – Telekommunikation 2011: Investitionsanreize stärken, Wettbewerb sichern", pp. 24, 40-41, 55, 76-86, 2011. (http://www.monopolkommission.de/sg_61/s61_volltext.pdf), [retrieved: 05.2017]

[5] W. Briglauer, and K. Gugler, "The deployment and penetration of high-speed fiber networks and services: Why are EU member states lagging behind?", Telecommunications Policy, Volume 37, pp. 819-835, 2013.

[6] W. Distaso, P. Lupi, and F. M. Maneti, "Platform competition and broadband uptake: Theory and Empirical evidence from the European Union", Information Economics and Policy, Volume 18 (1), pp. 87-106, 2006.

[7] H. Gruber, and P. Koutroumpis, "Competition enhancing regulation and diffusion of innovation: the case of broadband networks", Springer Science + Business Media, New York, Volume 43 (2), pp. 168-195, 2013.

[8] R. L. Katz, "The present and future of the telecommunication in Costa Rica", in Spanish: "El presente y futuro de las telecommunicaciones de Costa Rica", 4ta Expo-Telecom Costa Rica – Telecom Advisory Services, LLC, pp. 14, 2011.

[9] R. L. Katz, and T. A. Berry, "Driving demand for broadband networks and services, signals and communication technology", Springer Verlag, pp. 5-40, 135-200, 2014.

[10] U. Stopka, R. Pessier, and S. Flößel, "Broadband study 2030 – Prospective services, broadband adoption and demand", in German: "Breitbandstudie 2030 – Zukünftige Dienste, Adoptionsprozesse und Bandbreitenbedarf", pp. 42-50, 60, 166-164, 2013.

[11] T. Tjelta, et al., "Research topics and initial results for the fifth generation (5G) mobile network", 1st International Conference on 5G Ubiquitous Connectivity (5GU), pp. 267-272, 2014.

[12] R. L. Katz, and F. Callorda, "Mobile broadband at the bottom of the pyramid in Latin America", Telecom Advisory Services, LLC, pp. 23-25, 2013.

[13] H. Gruber, "European sector regulation and investment incentives: European options for NGA deployment", In I. Spiecker and J. Krämer (Eds.), Network neutrality and open access Baden-Baden: Nomos, pp. 191-202, 2011.

[14] Bundesnetzagentur, "Annual Report 2013 – Strong networks – consumer protection", in German: "Jahresbericht 2013 – Starke Netze im Fokus – Verbraucherschutz im Blick", pp. 70-81, 2013. (http://www.bundesnetzagentur.de/SharedDocs/Downloads/DE/Allgemeines/Bundesnetzagentur/Publikationen/Berichte/2014/140506Jahresbericht2013Barrierefrei.pdf?__blob=publicationFile&v=4), [retrieved: 05/2017]

[15] Bundesnetzagentur, "Definition of market regulation", in German: "Definition von Marktregulierung", 2013. (http://www.bundesnetzagentur.de/DE/Sachgebiete/Telekom

munikation/Unternehmen_Institutionen/Marktregulierung/marktregulierung-node.html) [retrieved: 05/2017]

[16] I. Cava-Ferreruela, and A. Alabau-Munoz, "Evolution of the European broadband policy: Analysis and perspective", pp. 1-17, 2005.

[17] W. Kerber, "Competition Policy – Vahlens compendium for economic theory and economic policy", in German: "Wettbewerbspolitik. Vahlens Kompendium der Wirtschaftstheorie und Wirtschaftspolitik", Volume 2 (8), p. 302, 2003.

[18] W. Kiesewetter, L. Nett, and U. Stumpf, "Regulation and competition in European mobile telecommunication markets", in German "Regulierung und Wettbewerb auf europäischen Mobilfunkmärkten", WIK – Wissenschaftliches Institut für Kommunikationsdienste, 2002.

[19] L. Waverman, and P. Koutroumpis, "Benchmarking telecoms regulation – The Telecommunications Regulatory Governance Index (TRGI)", Elsevier – Telecommunications Policy, Volume 35, pp. 450-468, 2011.

[20] J. Bouckaert, T. van Dijk, and F. Verboven, "Access regulation, competition, and broadband penetration: An international study", Elsevier – Telecommunications Policy, Volume 34, pp. 661-671, 2010.

[21] S. Wallsten, "Broadband and unbundling regulations in OECD countries", AEI-Brookings Joint Center Working Paper No. 06-16, pp. 1-28, 2006.

[22] L. J. Cronbach, "Coefficient Alpha and the internal structure of tests. Psychometrika, Volume 16, pp. 297-334, 1951.

[23] A. Field, "Discovering statistics using SPSS", Sage Publications Ltd., Volume 4, 2013.

[24] J. F. J. Hair, and R. E. Anderson, R. L. Tatham, and W. C. Black, "Multivariate data analysis", Macmillan, New York, NY, Macmillan, Volume 3, 1995.

[25] T. Apolte, et al., "Vahlens compendium for economic theory", in German: "Vahlens Kompendium der Wirtschaftstheorie und Wirtschaftspolitik", Verlag Franz Vahlen, Volume 9 (2), pp. 404-411, 2007.

[26] I. Schmidt, "Competition Policy and law", in German: "Wettbewerbspolitik und Kartellrecht", Volume 7, Stuttgart, pp. 49-55, 2001.

[27] M. Motta, "Competition policy – theory and practice", Cambridge University Press, Cambridge, United Kingdom, 2004.

[28] W. K. Viscusi, J. E. Harrington Jr., and J. M. Vernon, "Economics of regulation and antitrust", MIT Press, Volume 4, Cambridge, Massachusetts, pp. 155-162, 2005.

[29] S. Bicheno, "South Korea to add fourth mobile operator", Telecoms, 2015. (http://telecoms.com/423611/south-korea-to-add-fourth-mobile-operator/), [retrieved: 05.2017]

[30] D. Belson, "Akamai's State of the Internet", Akamai Technologies Q1 2012 Report, Volume 8 (1), pp. 5-32, 2012. .

[31] D. Belson, "Akamai's State of the Internet", Akamai Technologies Q1 2013 Report, Volume 8 (1), pp. 5-32, 2013.

[32] D. Belson, "Akamai's State of the Internet", Akamai Technologies Q1 2014 Report, Volume 8 (1), pp. 5-32, 2014.

[33] D. Belson, "Akamai's State of the Internet", Akamai Technologies Q3 2015 Report, Volume 8 (1), pp. 5-32, 2015.

[34] International Telecommunication Union, "Yearbook of Statistics 2014 – Telecommunication/ICT Indicators 2004-2013", 2014.

Integrating Social Media Concepts as Tools in a Pedagogical Approach for a Technology-enhanced Learning Environment

Manal Assaad
Faculty of Information and Technology
Hochschule Emden/Leer
Emden, Germany
Email: manal.assaad@hs-emden-leer.de

Tiina Mäkelä
Finnish Institute for Educational Research
University of Jyväskylä
Jyväskylä, Finland
Email: tiina.m.makela@jyu.fi

Abstract— **The use of social networking sites and social media tools is on the rise, as the most common activity of today's youth. Thus, leveraging social media concepts in learning can make education more relatable to the youth in this digital era. This paper identifies key current social media concepts, such as user profiles, activity streams, and status updates, among others, and analyses how they support pedagogical learning approaches, with the progressive inquiry-based model used as an example. The preliminary study serves as an introduction to a series of future research and empirical studies on the integration of key existing social media concepts and the development of novel ones in a hybrid educational environment, called Science, Technology, Innovation, Mathematics, Engineering for the Young (STIMEY). The STIMEY environment will combine social media components, robotic artefacts, and radio, and connect students, educators, parents and organisations, based on a pedagogical framework researched and developed to increase the European youth's interest and engagement in Science, Technology, Engineering and Mathematics (STEM) education and careers.**

Keywords-E-Learning; Pedagogy; Social Media; STEM; Technologies.

I. INTRODUCTION

In a world that is becoming more technology-oriented, it is getting difficult to engage and maintain the interest of young learners in formal settings. Contemporary educational systems fail to successfully awaken the desire for active and responsible learning. Learners' levels of engagement during their years of schooling are low and many students report feeling bored or even hating school [1]. On the other hand, the popularity of social media continues to rise each year, currently with over 2.3 billion active social media user accounts globally, at a penetration rate of 31% of total global population [2]. Thus, leveraging social media concepts can be key in attracting the students' interest for Science, Technology, Engineering, and Mathematics (STEM) education and careers, and making it more relatable to them from a young age. This paper presents a preliminary concept of integrating social media concepts in the pedagogical framework for a hybrid educational environment with multi-level components, called Science, Technology, Innovation, Mathematics, Engineering for the Young (STIMEY) [3]. The STIMEY project is funded by Horizon 2020 H2020-SEAC-2015-1 program, ongoing between September 2016 and August 2019, with partners in Germany, Spain, Finland, Greece, and Belarus. It aims to make STEM education and careers more attractive for 10- to 18-year-old students in Europe, with a hybrid learning environment that combines social media components in its Web platform, robotic artefacts, and radio broadcasting. The socially motivational environment for emotional and educational engagement is being designed and developed based on a pedagogical framework to educate, engage and increase the youth's interest in STEM [4].

The STIMEY environment will also provide the necessary modern tools for teachers, parents and organizations to take part in the students' progress and development, such as social media tools, gamification, collaborative and creative tools, entrepreneurial tools, serious games, and tools for challenges, activities and competitions. Thus, universities, schools, teachers, students, parents, business and media partners come together to complete a circle in which STEM becomes a part of the daily life of youth in an educational environment that also prepares them for future careers [4].

A. Research Objectives

The overall objective of the STIMEY project is to contribute to the increase in competitiveness of the European Union economy, with results that will enable young people, ages 10 to 18, to become highly competent in STEM topics and be motivated to pursue STEM careers [4].

The specific objectives, stemming from the general goal, in relation to social media components, are to:

- create a pedagogical framework that exploits the full potentials of social media for STEM topics in formal and informal contexts;
- create a Web platform for multimodal communication, social media concepts and tools, and professional identity development. The e-profile and social media tools of the STIMEY Web platform will support students' needs to communicate, share and interact with peers, STEM event organizers, academic members, professionals, companies, etc.
- create electronic portfolio presentation tools to support students in promoting their STEM activities and achievements – participation in relative activities in formal (e.g., schools) and non-formal (e.g., science centre activities, competitions, etc.) education, STEM project completion, competition awards, etc. – with

multimedia and social media tools that also enable them to receive feedback from the STIMEY members.

The STIMEY project addresses the specific challenges in achieving the objectives by creating a shift from traditional towards innovative and effective methods [5] to increase the attractiveness of STEM education and careers, and boost the interest of young people in STEM.

Based on extensive research, testing and European-wide collaboration, the STIMEY project is then developing a set of novel pedagogical approaches grasping a holistic vision of existing challenges to offer an educational multi-channel solution that integrates social media, robotic artefacts, radio broadcasting, entrepreneurial tools and serious gaming, into a complex learning environment [4].

In Section 2, a literature review on the use of social media in learning and education serves as a starting point when researching and developing a technology-enhanced learning environment for raising European youth's interest and attraction towards STEM studies and careers. An overview of the research and development of the pedagogical framework follows in Section 3. In Section 4, key social media concepts are identified and their role as learning tools is discussed in detail. The risks of social media use and strategies to mitigate them are briefly introduced in Section 5, while Section 6 presents a conclusion of the research with an outlook on future research within the project.

II. SOCIAL MEDIA USE IN LEARNING AND EDUCATION

Social media concepts are forms of electronic communication, such as Web sites for social networking and microblogging, through which users create online communities to share information, ideas, personal messages, and other content (as videos). That is only one of the various definitions of social media across different disciplines and points of views [6]. While many may think of social media exclusively as social networks like Facebook [7], its landscape is far more inclusive of basic forms, such as microblogging (e.g., Twitter [8] and Snapchat [9]), blogs (e.g., Tumblr [10] and Wordpress [11]), wikis (e.g., Wikipedia [12]), podcasts (e.g., Apple iTunes [13]) and content communities (e.g., Instagram [14] and Youtube [15]). And those are only some of the current modern forms of social media. As it is seemingly difficult to pinpoint a single definition of social media, it is better to understand it as a group of new kinds of online media, which share most or all of the following characteristics [16]:

- Participation: social media encourages contributions and feedback from everyone who is interested. It blurs the line between media and audience.
- Openness: most social media services are open to feedback and participation. They encourage voting, comments and the sharing of information. There are rarely any barriers to accessing and making use of content – password-protected content is frowned on.
- Conversation: whereas traditional media is about "broadcast" (content transmitted or distributed to an audience), social media is better seen as a two-way conversation.
- Community: social media allows communities to form quickly and communicate effectively. Communities share common interests, such as a love of travel, an environmental issue or a favorite artist.
- Connectedness: Most kinds of social media thrive on their connectedness, making use of links to other sites, resources and people.

Teenagers are among the most prolific users of social networks and social media tools. While they primarily use them to communicate with friends, they also use them and other interactional technologies to gather information and aid in decision-making. These advances are expanding the world of today's youth in ways that have yet to be fully understood [17]. Additionally, studies show that young people learn differently with social media and online technology tools, and as a result, the need for more flexible education and online interaction has become critical [18].

Given its increasing popularity and significance, various literature has researched the use of social media in different disciplines, such as business, marketing, software engineering, collaboration, etc. Special focus has also been given to researching the use of social media in education, as it is increasingly being leveraged as a learning and teaching tool. Yet, there is not much research and literature published on the intellectual and social practices that the youth demonstrate—either in top social networks, such as Facebook—or in niche social network sites, social gaming, or mobile networking applications designed for educational purposes. Preliminary research results indicate that [19]:

- 96% of students with Internet access report using social networking technologies
- 75% of students in 7th through 12th grades have at least one social media profile
- 59% of students who use social networking talk about education topics online
- 50% of students who talk about education topics online, talk specifically about schoolwork
- 59% of schools say their students use social networking for educational purposes
- 27% of schools have an online community for teachers and administrators

Other studies have found that some school tutors have embraced smartphones and social media as mobile learning devices [20]. While critics say that social media discourages communication, supporters feel that it can enhance learner interactions, particularly for those learners who are too shy to fully participate in class [21].

Nonetheless, only few studies examine the influence of social media features and their attendant social practices on learners. Although educational research devoted to understanding young people's purposes for using social media is increasing, research on the features they find most engaging, the socio-technical practices they employ, and ways to define and assess learning and communication using social media, is still lacking. Thus, so far, educators, researchers, and designers remain unclear about whether social media can support or inhibit learning, how and under what conditions [22]. The STIMEY project thus aims to clear that out, by researching how key social media concepts can be integrated in an e-learning environment based on pedagogical framework to support learning. The following section examines in detail how a pedagogical model can be adopted then integrated with social media concepts and tools.

III. Pedagogical Framework Research and Development

In the development of a pedagogical framework for the STIMEY environment, various pedagogical models, such as project-based, problem-based, inquiry-based, exploratory, experiential, and expansive learning are analyzed in the context of technology-enhanced STEM learning environments. However, in the initial phase of the project, and for this research paper, the progressive inquiry model [23] is used as an example to demonstrate how social media concepts can be integrated to support its elements [24] in a general learning environment:

- *Creating the context*: A study project is connected to its context (e.g., real-world problem to be solved) and its meaningfulness to learners is made clear.
- *Setting up research questions*: Learners formulate questions which arise from their own attempts to understand and explain the problem.
- *Constructing working theories*: Learners formulate hypotheses and initial intuitive conceptions based on their background knowledge.
- *Critical evaluation*: Learners evaluate strengths and weaknesses of their working theories.
- *Searching deepening knowledge*: More information is searched so as to examine better the working theories in the light of new information.
- *Generating subordinate questions*: New, more specific questions are formulated so as to progressively deepen the inquiry.
- *Constructing new working theories*: More articulated working theories are formulated and displayed based on progressive inquiry.
- *Shared expertise*: All aspects of inquiry can be shared with other learners. Through social interaction, contradictions, inconsistencies and limitations can be made evident. Further, instructors play an important role in guiding and scaffolding learners' process of inquiry.

Understanding and developing pedagogic theories and approaches under the pedagogical framework allows for better reflection on learning, and its implications for the design of a social media-powered learning environment. Thus, for this paper, a mix of learning approaches is developed and adopted, as seen in Figure 1, and then further explored, as an example of how it can be supported with social media concepts. The learning approach covers the set of theories and underlying

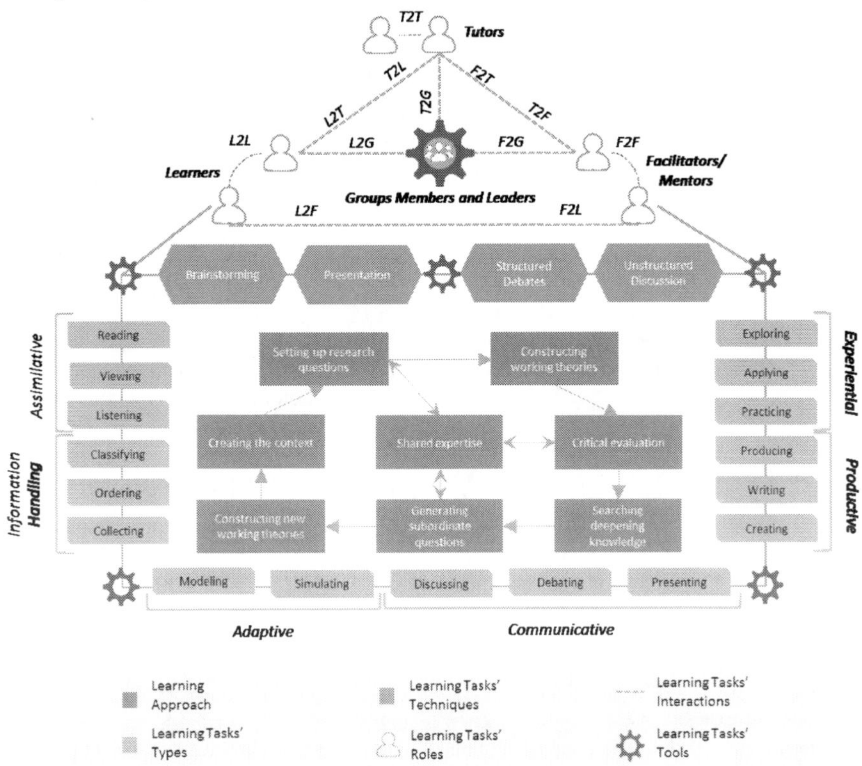

Figure 1. Learning Approach Model Development

models adopted for this research, while the learning tasks relate to the different components of learning activities [25]. Based on this model and the STIMEY project objectives, the learning tasks' components are divided as follows:

- *Types*: assimilative, information handling, adaptive, communicative, productive, and experiential.
- *Technique*: brainstorming [26], presentation, structured debate, and unstructured discussion.
- *Roles*: learner, tutor, facilitator or mentor (referring also to parents, organization members, etc., in the STIMEY environment), and group leader or member.
- *Interaction*: individual, 1 to 1 learner to learner, 1 to 1 learner to tutor (and vice versa), 1 to 1 learner to facilitator (and vice versa), 1 to 1 tutor to facilitator (and vice versa), individual to many and many to many (as in groups and discussions), etc.
- *Tools*: can be interactive, adaptive, communicative, productive or narrative. These include social media concepts suggested in the next section based on how they can support and enable this learning model.

In the following section, key social media concepts are proposed as the tools (see Figure. 1) to enhance and facilitate learning, based on their significance in supporting the progressive inquiry model as an example. As the pedagogical framework research continues, with detailed literature review, focus groups and testing, STIMEY will develop a learning approach specifically suitable for a STEM learning environment, which will form the basis of the social media concepts integration in the final stages.

IV. Identifying Key Social Media Concepts and Their Role as Learning Tools

As the STIMEY project aims to investigate the use of social media in supporting learning activities, the research is initiated by evaluating key contemporary social media concepts and how they can support a pedagogical learning model. These concepts are intuitively derived from common features in popular social networking sites, such as Facebook [7] and Google Plus [27], and e-learning platforms, such as Khan Academy [28], Digischool [29] and Edmodo [30].

A. User Profile

A user profile is the visual display of personal data associated with a specific user in a platform. The profile refers, therefore, to the explicit digital representation of a user's identity [31]. This feature allows users to add personal information, and showcase their knowledge and skills, while also controlling the visibility and privacy of the profile. This form of self-presentation satisfies several human needs, as a study by MySpace has shown [32]. The profile is also the cornerstone of a user's activity on STIMEY, containing a timeline of their activities and progress, connections, status updates, and other content as explained in detail hereafter. The user profile's role in teaching and learning, as shown in Figure 1, is, therefore, indirect but elementary in enabling the rest of the concepts and supporting activities. User profiles can also help, for example, to identify learners' interests so as to choose study projects which are personally meaningful for them (creating the context) and to group learners based on their expertise areas (shared expertise).

B. Status Updates

A status update is a feature that allows users to discuss their thoughts, opinions, or important information with their connections. Similar to a Tweet on Twitter, or a status on Facebook, a status is usually short and generally gives information without going into too much detail as a blog post, but may also contain other types of media, such as image or link. When the status is updated, it posts on the user's profile, as well as in the activity stream of their connections [33]. This feature enables the most basic form of communication, yet most crucial, in support of various phases of inquiry-based learning, see Figure 1. For example, through status updates, users can post information about the context they are working on or share their research questions or working theories, as well as generate context based on other users' posts and updates, contributing to shared expertise. It also supports various learning tasks' types, such as reading and viewing (other users' statuses), writing (text updates), creating and presenting (media status updates), and discussing (through Social Feedback, seen next). Moreover, it enables the techniques of brainstorming, presenting and unstructured discussions.

C. Social Feedback

In a social media environment, it is critical for users to have the ability to add their opinions about the quality or relevance of the content. Common examples are "like/not like," "thumbs up/thumbs down," star ratings, social commentary, tagging, flagging and reporting. Feedback has long been utilized as an effective tool to enhance learning, and social media concepts serve as a platform for effective feedback communication to improve relationships and performance in a learning environment [34]. Social feedback is most significant in supporting the co-creating of working theories and in critical evaluation, but overall plays an important role throughout sharing the expertise in inquiry-based learning, in Figure 1, especially in enabling discussing (through comments and replies), reading and viewing (of other users' comments and replies), and writing and presenting (of comments and replies, with media).

D. Social Connecting

The essence of social media, as well as the STIMEY project, is being used by people to build social networks or social relations with others who share similar personal or career interests, activities, backgrounds or real-life connections [35]. Thus, functions, such as "invite friend", "add friend", "follow account", etc., are at the cornerstone of social media concepts, to enable communication, collaboration and knowledge sharing among members. Young people particularly value social and interactive opportunities for learning [36]. This concept, therefore, drives multiple pedagogical frames that depend on the interactions of various roles (learners, tutors and facilitators/mentors), such as brainstorming, critical evaluation (by exchanging feedback), and sharing expertise.

E. Activity Stream

With the development of social media, the activity stream has become a common way to present a list of recent activities and aggregated information to users. Essentially, it is a digital interface component that lists activities or events relevant to a person, group, topic or everything in the environment in which it is built [37]. Thus, it is a central component in a social learning environment where users can keep track of their connections' and communities' updates (whether in benefit of generating context or critical evaluation), platform's news and updates, and any other elements' updates they subscribe to. In relation to inquiry-based learning (see Figure 1), the activity stream sets the stage for most steps, especially in generating context from activity updates, and receiving/providing feedback on those updates for critical evaluation.

F. Social Messaging

Instant messaging (IM) is not a new concept, or one that is specific to social media, yet it has become an essential integrated part of the experience. It refers to the exchange of text messages through a software application in real-time [38]. Popular features of social messaging applications include text chat, group chat, message notifications, status updates, media (file) sharing, and most prominently, the usage of stickers or little rich images to depict mood and convey messages in non-verbal format [39]. This concept enables deeper discussions, collaboration, brainstorming and sharing expertise in inquiry-based learning. It is also most essential in enabling the interactions between the various roles, whether through one to one (bilateral chat) or many to many (group chat) communication

G. Community

Online communities are generally regarded as online 'spaces' which individuals 'feel part of' and where they can go to interact on a common topic or interest [40]. They allow users to create, post, comment to and read from their own interest- and niche-specific forums. What makes communities so appealing is the ability to control access to them, to find and connect with only "like-minded" people or people who share a common purpose. Thus, such communities have "moderators" or admins, who create them, set their privacy settings (public or private), and grant special permissions to others (to join, to comment, to post, to invite, to approve invitations, to moderate, etc.). These communities are essential in promoting a sense of community among learners, and access to them is even more important than the physical education environment [36]. Communities enable assimilative, communicative and productive learning tasks' types, all of the learning tasks' techniques, and sharing expertise among members (through contribution to setting up research questions, critical evaluation, and generating subordinate questions), all relevant to inquiry-based learning.

H. Discussion Forum

Discussion forums exist in a variety of distance learning platforms, such as e-learning platforms (Moodle [41], Blackboard [42], e-tutor [43], etc.) or mobile platforms (WhatsApp [44], etc.). These forums provide online learners opportunities to collaborate and cooperate to construct knowledge [45]. Therefore, they are not specifically a social media concept, but they are a basic form of digital socializing that is essential in a learning environment. The main difference between discussion forums and communities is that in a forum, all users are at equal level, requiring no special permissions or access to post and discuss with others. Any user is allowed to start a topic and to respond to one. Content is usually segmented by topic, rather than by people [46]. Other discussion-related concepts, such as Q&A, can also be helpful and employed to facilitate more direct question posing, searching and answering, with users given also the ability to "vote" for and feature the correct answer (relevant to "critical evaluation") to enable better and more reliable expertise sharing around a specific topic (for e.g., courses). As in communities, discussion forums enable assimilative, communicative and productive learning tasks' types, all of the learning tasks' techniques, and sharing expertise among members.

V. Risks of Social Media Use and Mitigation Strategies

Although social media presents many benefits and opportunities, as demonstrated earlier, it can also pose some risks and challenges, especially when children and adolescents are involved. The main risk they face online today are risks from each other, risks of improper use of technology, lack of privacy, sharing too much information, or posting false information about themselves or others [47]. These risks must be recognized, addressed and mitigated whenever possible through social media principles and guidelines. Apart from developing and enforcing guidelines and policies to mitigate these risks, educating and encouraging users to engage in risk mitigation activities is considered good practice. By providing users with functions, such as privacy settings, controlling user permissions (adding or blocking users), flagging and reporting abusive or illegal content and users (as part of the social media concepts' features presented earlier), they gain better control over their own security and privacy. Thus, raising awareness among users about these risks, and empowering them to take more control over their privacy and security, are among the top mitigation strategies that will be researched and employed in STIMEY.

VI. Conclusion and Future Research

While the use of social media in learning and education is still open and in need of much research, early indications show very promising results. With most European youth using social media increasingly in many aspects of their lives, it is critical to research its uses and benefits. In the context of education, social media must be based on strong fundaments to leverage its benefits as a learning tool. Thus, it is essential that the social media concepts designed and employed in an e-learning environment are based on and emerge from a well-developed pedagogical framework. As demonstrated in this paper, social media concepts can be investigated to be used as tools that can support the various learning tasks in learning approaches, such as the progressive inquiry model. Key social media concepts, such as user profiles, activity streams, and communities, can enable and facilitate learning through discussions, collaborations, sharing expertise, and other learning fundaments.

As the project evolves, with more concrete research results on the pedagogical framework, end-user involvement, the STIMEY platform's requirements engineering, and a structured analysis of e-learning and blended learning environments, additional social media concepts will arise and be further investigated, and quantified experiment results will be conducted for verification. Moreover, research will be carried out on the technical integration of the social media concepts as learning tools within the STIMEY environment's multiple technological components.

ACKNOWLEDGMENT

This project has received funding from the European Union's Horizon 2020 research and innovation programme, Science Technology Innovation Mathematics Engineering for the Young 2016-2019, under grant agreement No 709515.

Any opinions, findings, and conclusions or recommendations expressed in this material reflect only the authors' views and the Union is not liable for any use that may be made of the information contained therein.

REFERENCES

[1] S. Buckingham Shum and R. Deakin Crick, "Learning Dispositions and Transferable Competencies: Pedagogy, Modelling and Learning Analytics," in *2nd Int. Conference on Learning Analytics and Knowledge*, Vancouver, British Columbia, Canada, 29 April - 02 May 2012, pp. 92-101.

[2] WeAreSocial. *Digital in 2016.* [Online]. Available from http://www.slideshare.net/wearesocialsg/digital-in-2016/, retrieved: February, 2017.

[3] Cordis.europa.eu, "Science Technology Innovation Mathematics Engineering for the Young," [Online] Available from: http://cordis.europa.eu/project/rcn/203161_en.html, retrieved: February, 2017.

[4] M. Assaad, et al., "Attracting The European Youth to STEM Education and Careers: A Pedagogical Approach to a Hybrid Learning Environment," in *19th Int. Conference on Advanced Learning Technologies*, Paris, France, 19 – 20 October 2017, forthcoming.

[5] N. Fachantidis, "ICT Frontiers: Educational Robotics in Greek Schools and Teacher's Training," in *13th Int. Conference of ICT in the Education of the Balkan Countries*, Varna, June 17–19, 2010, pp. 338-341.

[6] H. Cohen. *Social Media Definitions.* [Online]. Available from http://heidicohen.com/social-media-definition/, retrieved: February, 2017.

[7] Facebook, [Online]. Available from http://facebook.com/, retrieved: February, 2017.

[8] Twitter, [Online]. Available from http://twitter.com/, retrieved: February, 2017.

[9] Snapchat, [Online]. Available from http://snapchat.com/, retrieved: February, 2017.

[10] Tumblr, [Online]. Available from http://tumblr.com/, retrieved: February, 2017.

[11] Wordpress, [Online]. Available from http://wordpress.com/, retrieved: February, 2017.

[12] Wikipedia, [Online]. Available from http://wikipedia.org/, retrieved: February, 2017.

[13] Apple Inc., [Online]. Available from https://www.apple.com/lae/itunes/, retrieved: February, 2017.

[14] Instagram, [Online]. Available from http://instagram.com/, retrieved: February, 2017.

[15] Youtube, [Online]. Available from http://youtube.com/, retrieved: February, 2017.

[16] A. Mayfield. *What is social media?* [Online]. Available from http://www.icrossing.com/uk/sites/default/files_uk/insight_pdf_files/What%20is%20Social%20Media_iCrossing_ebook.pdf/, retrieved: February, 2017.

[17] G. S. Mesch, "Technology and youth. New Directions for Youth Development," 2012(135), 2012, pp. 97-105. doi:10.1002/yd.20032

[18] N. R. Ghorbani and R. N. Heidari, "Effects of information and communication technology on youth's health knowledge," Asia Pacific Journal of Public Health, 23(3), 2011, pp. 363-368. doi:10.1177/1010539509340435

[19] Elearning Infographics. *The Use of Social Media in School Infographic.* [Online]. Available from http://elearninginfographics.com/the-use-of-social-media-in-school-infographic/, retrieved: February, 2017.

[20] G. Toppo. Social Media Find Place in Classroom. [Online]. Available from http://usatoday30.usatoday.com/news/education/2011-07-24-schools-social-media_n.htm/, retrieved: March, 2017.

[21] K. Lederer. Pros and Cons of Social Media in the Classroom. [Online]. Available from http://campustechnology.com/Articles/2012/01/19/Pros-and-Cons-of-Social-Media-in-the-Classroom.aspx?Page=1/, retrieved: March, 2017.

[22] C. Greenhow, "Youth, learning and social media," Journal of Educational Computing and Research, 45(2), 2011, pp. 139-146. doi:10.2190/EC.45.2.a

[23] K. Hakkarainen and M. Sintonen, "The Interrogative Model of Inquiry and Computer-Supported Collaborative Learning," Science and Education 11(1), 2002, pp. 25-43.

[24] H. Muukkonen, K. Hakkarainen, and M. Lakkala, "Collaborative Technology for Facilitating Progressive Inquiry: the Future Learning Environment Tools," In C. Hoadley and J. Roschelle (Eds.) The proceedings of the CSCL '99 conference, December 12/15, 1999, Palo Alto, pp. 406-415. Mahwah, NJ: Lawrence Erlbaum and Associates.

[25] R. Preisinger-Kleine and G. Attwell, G8WAY: Web 2.0 Enhanced Gateway to Educational Transition. [Online]. Available from http://eacea.ec.europa.eu/LLp/projects/public_parts/documents/ict/2009/mp_505596_ict_FR_G8WAY.pdf/, retrieved: March, 2017.

[26] S. Isaksen, "A Review of Brainstorming Research: Six Critical Issues for Inquiry," Monograph #302. Creative Problem Solving Group. Buffalo, New York. June, 1998.

[27] Google Plus, [Online]. Available from https://plus.google.com/, retrieved: March, 2017.

[28] Khan Academy, [Online]. Available from https://www.khanacademy.org, retrieved: March, 2017.

[29] Digischool, [Online]. Available from http://www.digischoolgroup.com/en/, retrieved: March, 2017.

[30] Edmodo, [Online]. Available from https://www.edmodo.com/, retrieved: March, 2017.

[31] User profile. En.wikipedia.org. [Online]. Available from https://en.wikipedia.org/wiki/User_profile, retrieved: March, 2017.

[32] MySpace: Never Ending Friending. April 2007. Available from http://creative.myspace.com/groups/_ms/nef/images/40161_nef_onlinebook.pdf, retrieved: March, 2017.

[33] M. Rouse, "What is Facebook status?" WhatIs.com. [Online]. Available from http://whatis.techtarget.com/definition/Facebook-status, retrieved: March, 2017.

[34] S. L. Kio, "Feedback theory through the lens of social networking," Issues in Educational Research, 25(2), 2015, pp. 135-152.

[35] Social Networking Service. En.Wikipedia.Org. [Online]. Available from https://en.wikipedia.org/wiki/Social_networking_service, retrieved: March, 2017.

[36] P. Collin, K. Rahilly, I. Richardson, and A. Third, "The Benefits of Social Networking Services: A literature review," Cooperative Research Centre for Young People, Technology and Wellbeing. Melbourne, 2011.

[37] Activity Stream - Gartner IT Glossary. Gartner IT Glossary. 2012. [Online]. Available from http://www.gartner.com/it-glossary/activity-stream/, retrieved: March, 2017.

[38] M. Rouse, "instant messaging (IM or IM-ing or AIM)" SearchUnifiedCommunications. [Online]. Available from http://searchunifiedcommunications.techtarget.com/definition/instant-messaging, retrieved: March, 2017.

[39] Messenger Wars: How Facebook lost its lead. Ondeviceresearch.com. 2013. [Online]. Available from https://ondeviceresearch.com/blog/messenger-wars-how-facebook-lost-its-lead, retrieved: March, 2017.

[40] H. Baxter. An Introduction to Online Communities. [Online]. Available from http://www.providersedge.com/docs/km_articles/An_Introduction_to_Online_Communities.pdf, retrieved: March, 2017.

[41] Moodle Pty Ltd., [Online]. Available from https://moodle.org/, retrieved: March, 2017.

[42] Blackboard, [Online]. Available from http://www.blackboard.com/, retrieved: March, 2017.

[43] E-tutor, [Online]. Available from http://www.e-tutor.com/, retrieved: March, 2017.

[44] Whatsapp, [Online]. Available from https://whatsapp.com/, retrieved: March, 2017.

[45] L. Chan, "WebCT revolutionized e-learning," UBC Reports, 51(7). 7 July 2005.

[46] J. Owyang, "Understanding the difference between Forums, Blogs, and Social Networks," Web-strategist.com. [Online]. Available from http://www.Web-strategist.com/blog/2008/01/28/understanding-the-difference-between-forums-blogs-and-social-networks/, retrieved: March, 2017.

[47] S. Barnes, "A privacy paradox: social networking in the United States," First Monday. 2006;11(9). Available at: http://firstmonday.org/htbin/cgiwrap/bin/ojs/index.php/fm/article/view/1394/1312, retrieved: May, 2017.

On the Undecidability of Mobility Prediction and What to Look at in Mobility to Improve Communication in Mobile Networks

Marco Aurélio Spohn

Federal University of Fronteira Sul
Chapecó, SC – Brazil
Email: marco.spohn@uffs.edu.br

Marcelo Cezar Pinto

UNILA
Foz do Iguaçu, PR – Brazil
Email: marcelo.pinto@unila.edu.br

Abstract—**This work presents an analysis of mobility prediction, concluding that it is an undecidable problem. Even though one cannot always predict even its own future movement actions, it does not mean that there is no use for mobility knowledge. In mobile networks, better knowledge on how and when a node (hereafter referred as a *mover*) will decide on its next movement actions might lead to near-optimum protocol performance. In such situations, before endeavoring into sophisticated analysis by way of restricted mobility traces gathered just for that purpose, one could start checking on how much we already know (or are able to find out) about mover's actions. Based on that, the next step would be to work on how to use mobility data more appropriately. As we use such data, we can increasingly better understand mobility, making space for adaptive communication protocols. Such methodology does not go against any other analytical studies for capturing mobility properties; on the contrary, it just anticipates other uses for mobility data. Even though it is not feasible yet to consider upgrading existing routing protocols, so that full mobility knowledge is taken into account, one can envision an application routing over an overlay network. There is much hope for such an approach given that mobile networks are going to be more widely available as the Internet-of-Things evolves.**

Keywords–Mobile networks; mobility metrics; communication protocols; computability; undecidability.

I. Introduction

It would be interesting to devise an algorithm for computing all future paths to be taken by a mobile node (hereafter referred to as a *mover*). Understanding mobility at such level would provide means for solving many problems in real life, including networking by way of optimum communication protocols in mobile ad hoc networks (MANETs) [1]. Nevertheless, is it really possible to construct such algorithm?

One could start by comparing such an endeavor to other similar problems already addressed in computer science. Lloyd [2] proposed a turing test for free will, which consists of determining whether one (or any other external decider) can know one's decision before the decision is even taken. He concludes that, regardless if the world is deterministic or not, the one who passes the test is inclined to believe that he is endowed with free will, because it is an undecidable problem.

A mover can be anything capable of wandering around under a given scenario, considering all its constraints, which can be as complex as we can imagine. However, one could imply that mover's actions follow some pattern, which could possibly be identified if there would be enough data on mobility traces for analysis. Such an approach has already been taken for some specific mobility targets (*e.g.*, human mobility [3] [4]). Nevertheless, the results usually provide just some probabilistic insights into mobility patterns, which are specially useful for enhancing mobility aware protocols.

A path can be thought of as a sequence of actions taken by the mover when going from point A to point B, and it is up to the mover to choose the next action. As for the whole path, one can ask if the mover is able to predict *all* future actions it will take. Of course, if the mover has the capabilities to do so, we have already answered the very first question.

What we take into account in terms of computer capabilities could also be decisive to solve this problem. Assuming that quantum computers can efficiently simulate the laws of physics, it is also possible to conceive quantum Turing machines [5]. The inner process involved in every mover's action can be thought of as a sequence of operations. The situation is such that whether the mover itself or any other mover tries to simulate such sequence of operations, it will take more time than the original mover's sequence of operations [2].

Once assured on the undecidability of mobility prediction, one should not give up on finding ways to somehow explore mobility information whenever available. This leads to laying out the underlying requirements for taking part in the network or the services' agreement the mover has agreed upon. Based on the mobility information the mover is going to make available, the next step is to identify services/protocols, which can take advantage of such information. One desirable approach would be having the basic networking services working with and without mobility information. That is, mobility knowledge should be used to improve existing networking services, basically following an on demand and software defined network approach [6] [7].

Therefore, before starting gathering mobility traces for sophisticated analytical analysis, it is worth checking what mobility data can be assumed as granted in given scenarios. It does not mean that such analytical studies are not worth the effort, but one might ask if the desired services are not achievable through simpler approaches employing information and mechanisms known to be available beforehand. In addition, getting mobility traces might end up being impractical or not so representative depending on the sampling methodology or the number of participants.

As the network evolves, mobility traces could also be stored for later processing. That is, as there will be more mobility traces over time, it will be possible to go further into the

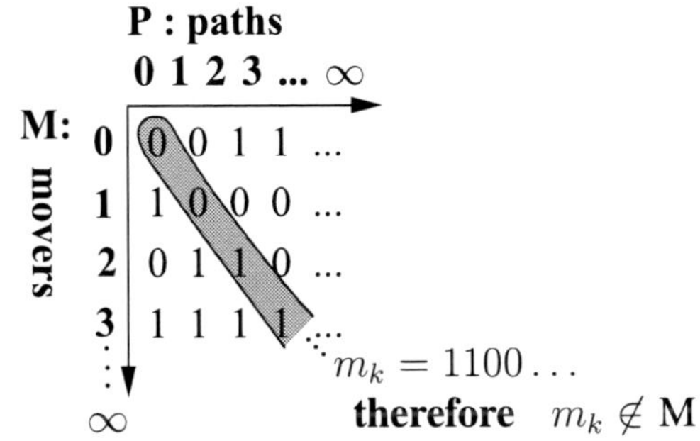

Figure 1. Cantor's diagonal argument applied to the mobility prediction problem.

analytical analysis as well (as a desirable *side effect*). In this case, mobility metrics can be employed to better capture some mobility properties [8].

Briefly, the remainder of the paper is organized as follows. In Section II, we start by showing that mobility prediction is an undecidable problem. That is, there is no way to know in advance what is the path to be taken, or not, by any mover (not even by the mover itself) in *all* situations. In Sections III and IV, we focus on how mobility awareness could improve communication in mobile networks. In Section IV, we conclude this work.

II. The Undecidability of Mobility Prediction and its Implications

Let us consider two countably infinite sets, one for all the movers,

$$M = \{m_0,\ m_1,\ \ldots\ m_i,\ \ldots\ \},$$

and the other for all the paths,

$$P = \{p_0,\ p_1,\ \ldots\ p_j,\ \ldots\ \}.$$

We are going to leverage our analysis on Cantor's diagonal argument [9], showing that it is not possible to devise an algorithm for computing whether a mover will or will not take a path *for all pairs* (m_i, p_j).

For that, we start by taking into account the Cartesian product $M \times P$ as the domain set of a function f, where every pair (m_i, p_j) is mapped to 1 or 0, showing, respectively, whether mover m_i will or will not take path p_j (see Figure 1). Therefore, each row represents the possible movement actions (*i.e.*, paths) of a mover; that is, each mover in M is represented as an infinite binary sequence.

If we can show that there is a mover, m_k, which is not present in the set of movers, we actually show that the set M is uncountably infinite. To devise such mover, for each i-th position of the sequence describing m_k we assign the complement of $f(m_i, p_i)$. By doing so, mover m_k's sequence differs by one position from every single mover in the set M and, therefore, $m_k \notin M$. This is a contradiction, because we had assumed that all movers were included in the set M.

As the number of Turing-recognizable languages (*i.e.*, decidable sets) is countable [9], there is no algorithm capable to deal with an uncountably infinite set of movers. Thus, for all possible movers and paths, it is not possible to know beforehand whether a mover will take a particular path or not. Therefore, mobility prediction is an undecidable problem.

When employing recursive reasoning, one uses a mathematical relationship between terms in a given sequence, and such recursive computation can be simulated by either classical or quantum Turing machines [5]. If any system must operate according to the known laws of physics, meaning that the world itself could be simulated by a Turing machine, one can conclude that:

1) There is no general technique to determine whether or not the mover is going to follow a given path at all (*i.e.*, the Cantor's diagonal argument).
2) In case the mover is under a time constraint, then trying to determine the movers next path sometimes takes more time than the mover takes to perform the actions.
3) A computationally universal mover can not answer all questions about its future behavior.
4) A time constrained computationally universal mover takes more time to simulate its next path than it takes it to actually perform that process directly.

Lloyd [2] employed the same reasoning for showing that one cannot prove that a decider does not possess free will; however, one cannot prove that one has free will either. Basically, one can always claim its decision as one's own choice, and behave as possessing free will.

With all that said, it does not mean that one cannot ever determine a given mover's next path. Nevertheless, it is also clear that one cannot *always* determine any mover's next path.

Next, we explore ways to take advantage of the mobility information which is already granted in many situations. That is, before taking on any complex analytical approach, start from the mobility information that can be **provided by the users/movers themselves**, and build around that the protocols/applications that can be used right away in mobile networks even when it is not possible to change the behavior of the lower layer protocols (*e.g.*, network protocols).

III. Mobility Awareness in Mobile Networks

In this section, we ask ourselves how mobility awareness might improve communication in mobile networks. It is always desirable to have the means and mechanisms to improve the network performance overall, but the focus here is just on the benefits from exploring mobility itself. Figure 2 presents an overall schematic and guidelines for the mobility information addressed in this section.

A. How much we know about mover's actions?

Taking into account mobility information when devising communication protocols may help improve the overall network performance; and this has already been done [10]–[12]! However, as it is not possible to predict *all* future movers' actions, one could well focus just on the information which is somehow related to mobility in an acceptable and predictable way for at least some situations (which might be exactly the ones we are interested in). In such cases, and before trying to gather real traces for sophisticated analytical analysis, it is worth focusing on the mover's mobility data known in advance to some acceptable degree of detail. To begin, one could pinpoint some important mobility information such as:

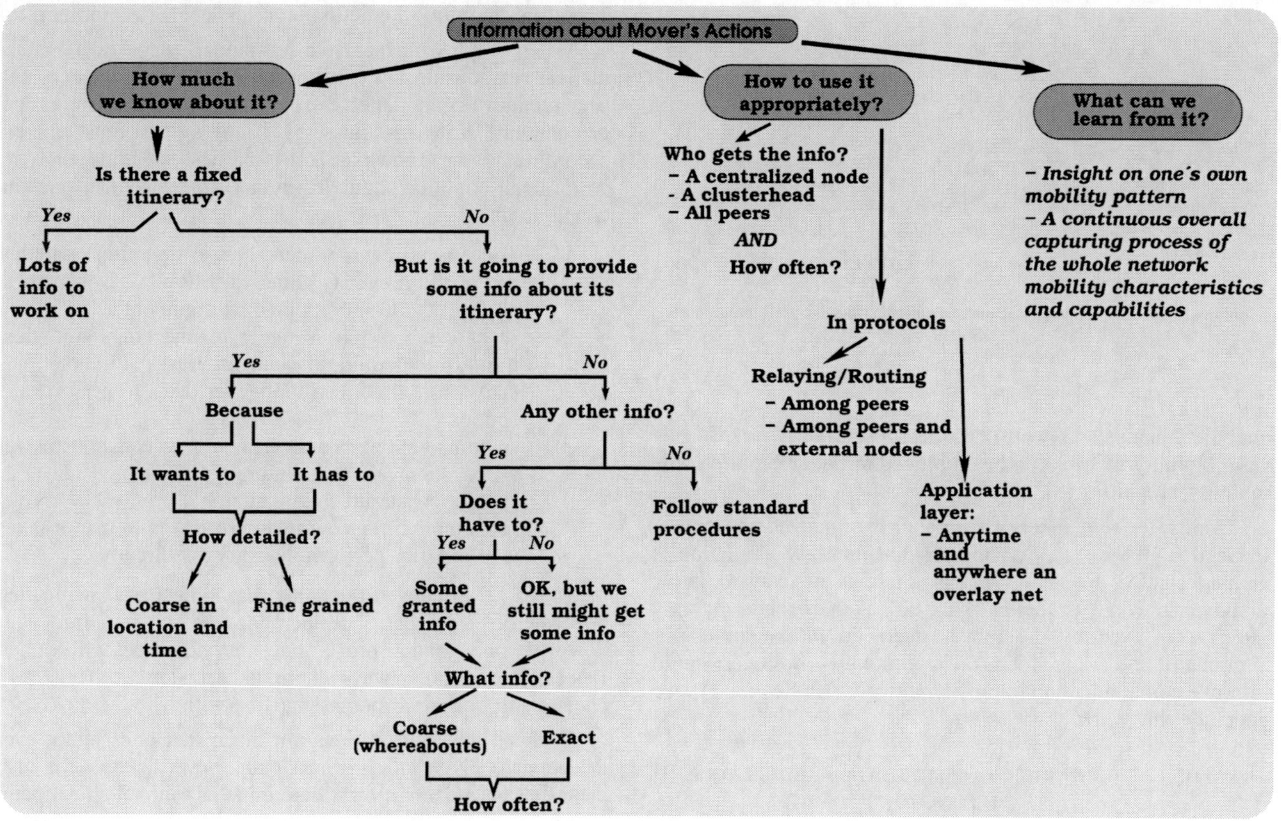

Figure 2. Overall schematic and guidelines for mobility information.

- *Is there a repeating schedule with fixed stopping points (e.g., bus terminals)?* Even though one might not know in advance all intermediary positions when a mover is going from a starting point A to a finishing point B, just having the information about where the mover should be at certain points in time is paramount if one would like to schedule a message/packet relay to well known communication agents (probably static routers) at stopping points. Note that it is not the same as not knowing when movers are expected to show up at some defined communication points (as static routers by a highway waiting for *any* mover wandering about).
- *Is the mover willing to make available its exact location or, at least, its whereabouts?* Considering there are ways to protect one's confidentiality and privacy, find ways to explore how we could enhance communication protocols given that movers are willing to help by providing some information about their location (either exact or an approximation). Even though this might sound unacceptable sometimes, the fact is that there are ways to better explore these situations specially when such information has already been made available voluntarily by users through many apps/servers (*e.g.*, Global Positioning System (GPS) location may be embedded within tweets in Twitter).
- *Must the mover provide its location periodically?* This hypothesis is stronger than the previous one, because now the mover does not get to choose if it shares its location or not. The point here is **how often** the mover does so, as well as assuming that there is a communication link at such moments (*i.e.*, it is not about recording one's position for later transmission).
- *Is the mover willing to provide some details about its itinerary?* As for the case when the mover has fixed stopping points, which are scheduled to be reached at some known points in time (with an expected variance), a mover could make available its complete itinerary. The point here is how much detail is expected to be provided by the mover (*i.e., How well characterized is the itinerary?*):
  - The mover could provide both GPS coordinates and their expected reaching times;
  - Or just GPS estimates and coarse target times.
- *Must the mover provide some details about its itinerary?* Likewise, the mover might be forced to provide its itinerary as part of the communication service itself. In this case, even though there are security concerns whenever location information is shared with a third party, there are ways to guarantee privacy, confidentiality, and integrity.

B. How to use mobility information appropriately?

With the mobility information available, one can start focusing on when and where such data should be part of any decision making process. Communication protocols must comply with safety and liveness properties, while efficiently handling the available resources. Firstly, it is necessary to address the following questions:

- *Who receives mobility data information?*
  - A centralized entity;
  - A cluster/leader (cluster-head) in the vicinity;
  - Or data gets broadcasted among *all* peers.
- *How often mobility information is obtained and sent out by movers?* This will depend on the information granularity and the imposed restrictions/requirements among the entities involved in the communication.

Secondly, it is required to sort out how mobility information might be useful for communication protocols:

- For the link layer and routing, the mover itself could act as a router/relayer:
  - Among movers, whether mobility information is shared directly among movers or it comes from a centralized node or cluster-head;
  - Among movers and external nodes (*e.g.*, any node in the Internet): for example, in situations where a centralized node acts as an access point to the Internet.
- For the upper layers (*e.g.*, application):
  - Application content can be shaped according to on demand needs as we know the mover's whereabouts or its intended destination.

C. *What can we learn from mobility?*

As mentioned before, as a sort of *good side effect*, mobility information can be gathered for further analysis in a similar fashion as mobility traces are captured just for analytical studies. However, it is not likely to produce as many details as when it is solely planned for capturing mobility traces. Considering the situations pinpointed earlier, by default, the obtained traces are going to include some but not necessarily all positions taken by the mover.

Nevertheless, even though the mover desires to or has agreed upon providing only the required mobility information, locally it can always track its own movement with more detail for later use or to make it available to analytical analysis, if desirable. At the end, it is even possible to have more and better traces compared to those obtained just for some specific purposes.

It is even worth checking how the mover might help itself when analyzing its own movement actions. For example, if the mover has a predictable behavior for the next hours or days, it could plan where and when to get and send information in advance. In addition, if the mover shares this information with other peers or a centralized node, there will be plenty of other possibilities.

According to Tanenbaum [13], "Never underestimate the bandwidth of a station wagon full of tapes hurtling down the highway". Whatever storage capabilities one can conceive, either in terms of storage capacity, size, and data transfer rates, it is always possible to imagine that data can be stored in the movers memory and be delivered later when reaching the destination or getting closer to it (in terms of communication connectivity or geographical location).

As one learns from its own behavior and from other peers, it is possible to combine traditional communication approaches with customized ones, and they could well be implemented at the application layer as an overlay network infrastructure [14]–[16]. There are many possibilities in this case: for example, considering the movers capabilities that are acceptable for a given delivery task (*i.e.*, transporting a large backup file from its own application or from another peer to the cloud), once it is known in advance that the mover will stay connected to a fast network for enough time (*i.e.*, for relaying the content or delivering it directly to the destination), such task could well be planned accordingly.

IV. Well said, but what to do then?

So far, we have been looking at how much mobility information is available, how we could possibly use it, and how we might improve our overall knowledge on mobility for enhancing communication in mobile networks. One can take for granted that there will be an ever growing number of mobile entities with computer and communication capabilities (*e.g.*, the Internet-of-Things [17] promises to contribute to that); therefore, it is reasonable to consider a richer communication environment. In such context, it is worth to take into account a software defined network approach whenever conceiving ways to take advantage of mobility information. In this sense, it might be possible to improve communication performance in mobile networks even when focusing just on the application layer itself.

When it comes to using such mobility information, one should consider it as coming from a continuous feedback process, evolving as the network advances. Once again, it does not go against any particular mobility aware protocol approach based solely on specific captured mobility patterns; however, following our proposed methodology, one could start right away from existing communication protocols by extending them or working just on the application layer. As pointed out before, movers' current locations and the next intended ones are straightforward for applying into routing processes in mobile networks.

In a wider network environment (*e.g.*, the Internet), of course it would not be an easy task to adapt the existing routing protocols to take into account mobility data in a broader sense. However, given that we expect movers to be at the last mile of the network, an application layer routing over an overlay network [18] is possibly the most attractive alternative when it comes to employing the proposed methodology. While in direct reach of each other, movers could act as routers among themselves, and whenever relaying any message/packet, decisions should be leveraged on the better expected result in terms of who can possibly make it faster to the desired destination (or fixed infrastructure leading to the destination) based on the known mobility information. This might sound like any traditional routing approach, but the difference here is that it could be based on the mobility information provided by those who know better about it: the movers.

Let us look at an example (see Figure 3 as a reference). Consider mover **A** wants to send a backup file to a restricted private cloud infrastructure accessible only to peers taking part in the group. Having the mobility information of some of **A**'s peers (*i.e.*, movers **B**, **C**, **D**, and **E**), mover **A** decides to transfer the file to mover **B** because it is going to be closer to another

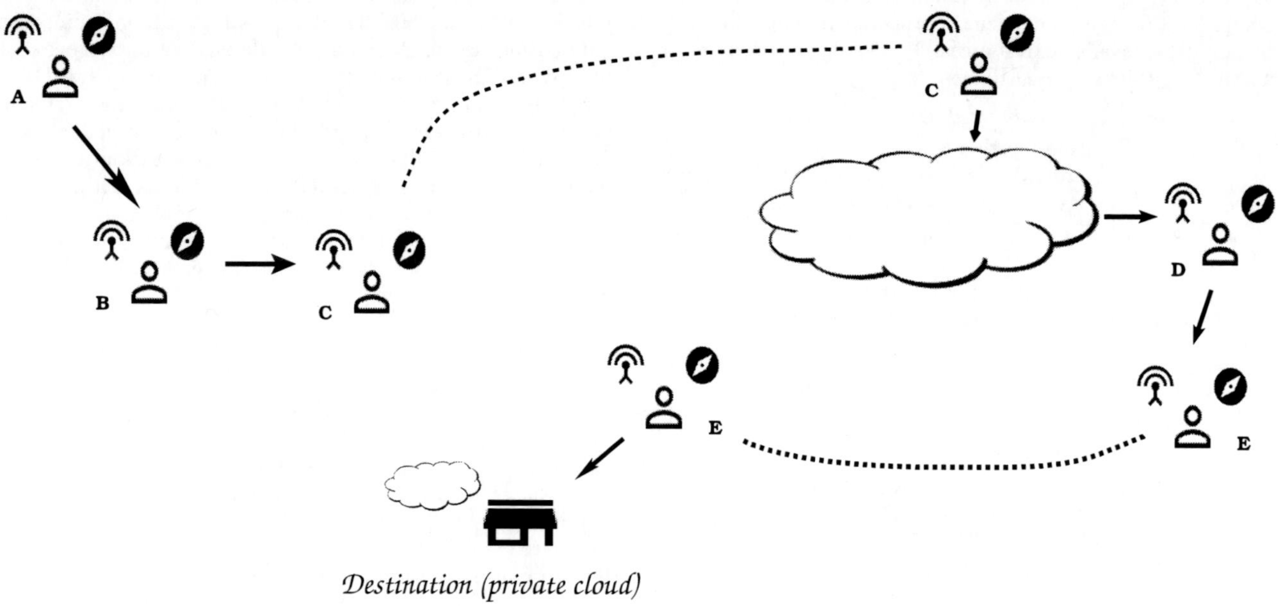

Figure 3. *What can we do then?* An example of an application routing approach based on an overlay network.

mover, **C**, for an acceptable period of time (*i.e.*, enough time for transferring the backup file). In turn, later on, mover **C** is known to shift to a place where it is going to stay connected to the Internet for some extended period of time. Besides that, it is also known that there is another peer, mover **D**, which is going to stay connected for enough time to get the backup file relayed through the Internet from mover **C**. In addition to that, mover **D** is also a good candidate because it can relay the file to another peer, mover **E**, which is known to get in touch with the destination (a private cloud infrastructure) later on.

Even though this short example might sound a little far from reality now, it is likely that such application overlay networks will become common given the infrastructure to be built on and around the Internet-of-Things.

One could as well argue that mobility awareness has been receiving plenty of attention when designing communication protocols so far [10]–[12] [19]–[21]; however, what is actually proposed here is that we could change the *starting point* when designing such protocols: first of all, analyze what useful mobility information *coming from the user/mover* is already available or otherwise could be made available, and starting to work with just that. Depending on the application requirements, and the required security protocols, we could possibly achieve better, or at least reasonable, performance results.

V. CONCLUSIONS

Even though it is impossible to predict *all* movement actions of any mover, one could possibly enhance communication considering just what one already knows about its own mobility actions, from other peers, and eventually from a centralized point of coordination.

Basically, before going through specific analytical analysis (usually based solely on a restricted set of mobility traces), we should focus on mobility information we could get spontaneously or as part of the protocol/application requirements/agreements. Again, this does not mean one cannot continuously strive to improve one's insight into mobility patterns through the analytical approach. This can also go hand in hand with the proposed methodology because mobility traces are a possible *good side effect* of collaborative mobility aware protocols/applications.

Using mobility data appropriately can improve overall mobile network performance and introduce new features and services not available yet (*e.g.*, better cloud service experience in a mobile environment) due to its intrinsic limitations. First, one must take into account who actually gets such data (*i.e.*, all peers, a centralized node, or cluster heads). Periodicity is also crucial here, because of its impact on accuracy. When thinking about protocols, depending on the granularity and accuracy of mobility data, routing can be enabled among peers or among peers and a fixed infrastructure. At the application layer, with the implementation of overlay networks, one can really expand the mobile network possibilities, and there are plenty of security mechanisms available for making it attractive even to more concerned users.

What is missing then? Essentially, when designing new mobility aware protocols, we suggest that a methodology similar to the one proposed here be followed: start from the mobility knowledge that is somehow granted given the requirements/agreements for some service. That is, one should start working on the mobility information provided by the movers themselves. It is even possible that a more sophisticated approach may end up not providing better performance results or just only marginal improvements not worth the cost. Taking into account the promises around the Internet of Things, simple solutions for mobility awareness should be strongly considered.

ACKNOWLEDGMENT

This work was partially supported by the Brazilian National Council for Scientific and Technological Development (CNPq) under grant 444610/2014-6.

REFERENCES

[1] R. Rajaraman, "Topology control and routing in ad hoc networks: A survey," *SIGACT News*, vol. 33, no. 2, pp. 60–73, Jun. 2002.

[2] S. Lloyd, "A turing test for free will," *Philosophical Transactions of the Royal Society of London A: Mathematical, Physical and Engineering Sciences*, vol. 370, no. 1971, pp. 3597–3610, 2012, retrieved: April, 2017. [Online]. Available: http://rsta.royalsocietypublishing.org/content/370/1971/3597

[3] F. Giannotti *et al.*, "Unveiling the complexity of human mobility by querying and mining massive trajectory data," *The VLDB Journal*, vol. 20, no. 5, pp. 695–719, 2011.

[4] W.-J. Hsu, T. Spyropoulos, K. Psounis, and A. Helmy, "Modeling spatial and temporal dependencies of user mobility in wireless mobile networks," *IEEE/ACM Transactions on Networking*, vol. 17, no. 5, pp. 1564–1577, 2009.

[5] S. Lloyd, "Universal quantum simulators," *Science*, vol. 273, no. 5278, pp. 1073–1078, 1996, retrieved: April, 2017. [Online]. Available: http://science.sciencemag.org/content/273/5278/1073

[6] N. Feamster, "Tomorrow's network operators will be programmers (keynote)," in *Companion Proceedings of the 2015 ACM SIGPLAN International Conference on Systems, Programming, Languages and Applications: Software for Humanity*, ser. SPLASH Companion 2015. New York, NY, USA: ACM, 2015, pp. 1–2.

[7] D. Levin, M. Canini, S. Schmid, and A. Feldmann, "Incremental sdn deployment in enterprise networks," in *Proceedings of the ACM SIGCOMM 2013 Conference on SIGCOMM*, ser. SIGCOMM '13. New York, NY, USA: ACM, 2013, pp. 473–474.

[8] S. Xu, K. Blackmore, and H. Jones, "An analysis framework for mobility metrics in mobile ad hoc networks," *Eurasip Journal on Wireless Communications and Networking*, vol. 2007, no. 1, pp. 1–16, 2007.

[9] M. Sipser, *Introduction to the Theory of Computation*, 2nd ed. Course Technology, 2006.

[10] S. J. Philip and V. Anand, "Mobility aware path maintenance in ad hoc networks," in *Proceedings of the 2009 ACM Symposium on Applied Computing*, ser. SAC '09. New York, NY, USA: ACM, 2009, pp. 201–206.

[11] L. Zhang, Z. Cai, J. Lu, and X. Wang, "Mobility-aware routing in delay tolerant networks," *Personal Ubiquitous Comput.*, vol. 19, no. 7, pp. 1111–1123, Oct. 2015.

[12] J. C. Mukherjee and A. Gupta, "Mobility aware event dissemination in vanet," in *Proceedings of the 2015 International Conference on Distributed Computing and Networking*, ser. ICDCN '15. New York, NY, USA: ACM, 2015, pp. 22:1–22:9.

[13] A. Tanenbaum, *Computer Networks*, 4th ed. Prentice Hall Professional Technical Reference, 2002.

[14] A. Nakao, L. Peterson, and A. Bavier, "Scalable routing overlay networks," *SIGOPS Oper. Syst. Rev.*, vol. 40, no. 1, pp. 49–61, Jan. 2006.

[15] ——, "A routing underlay for overlay networks," in *Proceedings of the 2003 Conference on Applications, Technologies, Architectures, and Protocols for Computer Communications*, ser. SIGCOMM '03. New York, NY, USA: ACM, 2003, pp. 11–18.

[16] R. Cohen and D. Raz, "Cost-effective resource allocation of overlay routing relay nodes," *IEEE/ACM Trans. Netw.*, vol. 22, no. 2, pp. 636–646, Apr. 2014.

[17] T. L. Koreshoff, T. Robertson, and T. W. Leong, "Internet of things: A review of literature and products," in *Proceedings of the 25th Australian Computer-Human Interaction Conference: Augmentation, Application, Innovation, Collaboration*, ser. OzCHI '13. New York, NY, USA: ACM, 2013, pp. 335–344.

[18] J. Kurian and K. Sarac, "A survey on the design, applications, and enhancements of application-layer overlay networks," *ACM Comput. Surv.*, vol. 43, no. 1, pp. 5:1–5:34, Dec. 2010.

[19] Q. Dong and W. Dargie, "A survey on mobility and mobility-aware mac protocols in wireless sensor networks," *IEEE Communications Surveys Tutorials*, vol. 15, no. 1, pp. 88–100, First 2013.

[20] P. Bellavista, M. Cinque, D. Cotroneo, and L. Foschini, "Integrated support for handoff management and context awareness in heterogeneous wireless networks," in *Proceedings of the 3rd International Workshop on Middleware for Pervasive and Ad-hoc Computing*, ser. MPAC '05. New York, NY, USA: ACM, 2005, pp. 1–8.

[21] H. Abou-zeid, H. S. Hassanein, and R. Atawia, "Towards mobility-aware predictive radio access: Modeling; simulation; and evaluation in lte networks," in *Proceedings of the 17th ACM International Conference on Modeling, Analysis and Simulation of Wireless and Mobile Systems*, ser. MSWiM '14. New York, NY, USA: ACM, 2014, pp. 109–116.

A Routing Protocol Proposal for NDN Based Ad Hoc Networks Combining Proactive and Reactive Routing Mechanisms

Ngo Quang Minh, Ryo Yamamoto, Satoshi Ohzahata, and Toshihiko Kato
University of Electro-Communications
Tokyo, Japan
e-mail: mingus@net.is.uec.ac.jp, ryo_yamamoto@is.uec.ac.jp, ohzahata@is.uec.ac.jp, kato@is.uec.ac.jp

Abstract— **In this paper, we propose a new routing protocol for named data networking (NDN) based ad hoc networks. One feature of our protocol is that it adopts a hybrid approach where a proactive routing is used in the producer side network and a reactive routing is used in the consumer side network. Another feature is that we focus only on the name prefix advertisement in the proactive routing. The result of performance evaluation focusing on the communication overhead shows that our proposal has a moderate overhead both for routing control messages and Interest packets compared with some of conventional NDN based ad hoc routing mechanisms proposed so far.**

Keywords- Ad Hoc Network; Named Data Networking; Proactive Routing; Reactive Routing.

I. INTRODUCTION

Recently, Information Centric Networks (ICNs) have been widely studied as a future Internet architecture well suited for large scale content distribution. Named Data Networking (NDN) [1] has been widely adopted as a platform for ICN research activities. The fundamental adopted in NDN is the name of required content, not the address of hosts containing content. NDN uses two types of packets in all communications: Interest and Data. A consumer requesting a piece of content sends an Interest packet containing the content name. A producer providing the corresponding content data returns a Data packet to the consumer. NDN routers transferring the Data packet cache the packet for future redistribution.

Originally, NDN was designed for wired network topology, but it can be effectively applied to wireless multi-hop ad hoc network topology. Since nodes move around in wireless ad hoc networks, the routing mechanism is a more important research topic compared with wired networks. In NDN, the purpose of routing is how to construct Forwarding Information Base (FIB) for name prefixes, which specifies the correspondence between a name prefix and a face (or a neighbor identifier) to the content with this name prefix.

There are several proposals on the routing in NDN. For the wired NDN topology, those proposed in [2] and [3] are examples introduced in an early stage. Both of them are based on the link state routing protocol, which maintains and advertises link statuses between neighbors, shares the topology information, and creates routing tables from it. The protocol in [4] is a new proposal based on the link state routing considering multipath routing.

In the case of NDN based wireless ad hoc networks, both proactive and reactive approaches are proposed [5]-[9]. This trend is the same as IP based ad hoc networks. MobileCCN [6] and TOP-CCN [7] are examples of the proactive routing mechanism. MobileCCN is an application of RIP [10] to the NDN based ad hoc routing. TOP-CCN is an application of OLSR [11]. On the other hand, E-CHANET [8] and REMIF [9] are examples of the reactive routing mechanism, which are considered extensions of Ad Hoc On-Demand Distance Vector routing (AODV) [12].

These NDN based ad hoc routing mechanisms have pros and cons. The proactive routing can create FIB in response to an up-to-date network topology, but has some overheads of routing control message exchange. On the contrary, the reactive routing has no overheads of routing, but has some overheads of Interest packet transfer.

In this paper, we propose a new NDN based ad hoc routing which has the following two features. First, in a typical ad hoc network used in a public space, such as shopping malls and museums, a content producer side has a stable network where producers and intermediate routers are located in fixed positions. On the other hand, consumers are mobile nodes which change their locations quite often. Therefore, a hybrid approach which uses the proactive and reactive routing is considered to be useful. In the IP based ad hock network, a hybrid routing is also proposed [13]. Based on these considerations, we take a hybrid approach that the proactive routing is adopted in a producer side network, because of its in-advance route setting, and the reactive routing is adopted in a consumer side network, because of its flexibility for mobility.

The second feature is about the procedure of proactive routing. The NDN proactive routing procedures proposed so far are advertising both the network topology and the name prefixes. However, the point of NDN routing is how the name prefixes are disseminated. In order to realize this requirement, it is sufficient that the shortest path information is maintained for individual producer. So, we proposes a new proactive NDN routing focusing on just the name prefix advertisement.

The rest of this paper consists of the following sections. Section II describes the related work on NDN and NDN based ad hoc routing. Section III proposes our new protocol, and Section IV shows the performance evaluation focusing on the routing control and Interest transfer overheads. Section V concludes this paper.

II. Related Work

A. Overview of named data networking

NDN nodes (consumers, NDN routers and producers) maintain the following three major data structures [1].

- Forwarding Interest Base (FIB): used to forward Interest packets toward producers of matching Data.
- Pending Interest Table (PIT): keeping track of Interest packets forwarded to producers so that returned Data packets can be sent to consumers.
- Content Store (CS): caching received Data packets temporarily.

When an Interest packet arrives on some face, the content name in the Interest is looked up. If there is a copy of the corresponding Data packet in CS, it is sent out to the face the Interest packet arrived on and the Interest packet is discarded. Otherwise, if there is a PIT entry exactly matching to the received content name, the Interest's arrival face is added to the PIT entry and the Interest packet is discarded. Otherwise, if there is a matching FIB entry, then the Interest packet is sent to the face specified in the FIB entry.

As described above, the routing mechanism in NDN is a procedure to create FIB entries for published name prefixes. As for the routing in wired NDN topology, the major protocols proposed so far [2]-[4] are based on Open Shortest Path First (OSPF) [14], which is a link state based intra-domain routing protocol used widely in IP networks. Among them, Named-data Link State Routing protocol (NLSR) [3], for example, introduces two types of link state advertisements (LSAs): Adjacency LSA and Prefix LSA. An Adjacency LSA is similar to an LSA defined in OSPF and contains a list of neighbor name and cost of the link to neighbor. A Prefix LSA is designed for NDN and contains name prefixes. An NDN node sends Periodic "info" Interest packets for neighbor detection. If it receives an "info" Content reply, it considers that a neighbor is alive. An NDN node also sends periodic "Root Active" Interest packets. If any link state information has changed, its reply is returned. After that, an Interest packet requesting a new LSA and its corresponding Data packet are exchanged.

B. NDN based ad hoc routing mechnisms

For NDN based ad hoc networks, there are a lot of research activities [5]. Among them, MobileCCN [6] and TOP-CCN [7] are typical examples of the proactive routing mechanism. In MobileCCN, NDN nodes regularly broadcast their own FIB, obtain neighbors' FIB, and re-create own FIB. The idea is similar to that of Routing Information Protocol (RIP), in which routers send their own routing table to their neighbors periodically [10]. As is in RIP, the scalability is a problem in MobileCCN.

TOP-CCN is an extension of the Optimized Link State Routing (OSLR) [11] to the NDN based ad hoc routing. TOP-CCN introduces a new packet called Content Announcement (CA). It also introduces the idea of multipoint relay (MPR) and publisher MPT (PMPR). A CA packet contains name prefixes, node id and type of sender, list of neighbors' id and type, and so on. It is used for the neighbor discovery and MPR selection, through single hop broadcast, and for the link state information announcement, through multi-hop flooding. A multi-hop CA packet is generated by PMPR and flooded by MPRs and PMPRs, and it is used to create the topology information and FIB. Since the base of TOP-CCN is OLSR used in IP networks, however, multi-hop CA packets provide over-specified information. For example, a route between consumers, which is never used in NDN, can be obtained from this information.

On the other hand, the reactive routing mechanism is original in ad hoc networks. There are many examples [5], including REMIF [9], which we use in the performance evaluation. REMIF does not use any routing control messages and therefore NDN nodes do not maintain FIBs. Instead, a route to producer is detected during Interest packet flooding. In order to avoid a broadcast storm problem, REMIF adopts differed re-broadcasting with remaining energy checking. Although REMIF has better performance than E-CHANET [8] as for the Interest forwarding overhead [9], the overhead may increase depending on the node density and the average hops between consumers and producers.

III. Proposal

A. Design principles

We have adopted the following design principles for our hybrid NDN based routing mechanism.

- As described above, we divide a whole NDN network into the producer side and the consumer side. In the producer side, NDN nodes including producers and intermediate routers have their location fixed. So, a proactive routing mechanism is introduced in this part. On the other hand, the consumer side includes mobile nodes working as consumers or intermediate routers. Those nodes move around and the network configuration often changes. In this part, a reactive routing mechanism is introduced.
- For the producer side, our proactive routing focuses only on the name prefix advertisement. It constructs a directed acyclic graph (DAG) starting from each producer. An FIB entry for a specific name prefix is given by pointing upstream nodes so as to traverse the corresponding DAG in a reverse direction. If there are more than one upstream nodes, all of them are registered in the entry and used for multipath forwarding [15].
- In order to create a DAG for a specific name prefix, the corresponding producer issues a *Name Prefix Announcement Request* (*NPAreq*) packet. It is broadcasted, and if any receiving NDN nodes are on the corresponding DAG, they return a *Name Prefix Announcement Reply* (*NPArep*) packet by unicast.
- As for the consumer side, NDN nodes do not use any control packets for routing. Instead, the FIB entry is created by the first Interest packet for a name prefix. The first Interest packet is flooded throughout the consumer side, and after it reaches some node in the producer side, this Interest packet is transferred to the

TABLE 1. PARAMETERS IN NPAreq AND NPArep PACKETS.

packet	parameters
NPAreq	producer node ID, nonce, name prefix list, hop count, number of downstream nodes.
NPArep	producer node ID, nonce.

producer. When the corresponding Data packet returns, a temporary FIB entry is created at the nodes in the consumer side. For the following Interest packets for the same name prefix, this FIB entry is used.

B. Detailed design for producer side

Table 1 shows the parameters contained in NPAreq and NPArep packets. *Producer node ID* is the MAC address of the producer node, and NPAreq and NPArep packets can be uniquely identified using this ID and *nonce*. A producer periodically generates NPAreq packets containing the *name prefix list* which it is publishing. *Hop count* is the number of hops from the producer. When a producer side node receives an NPAreq packet, it rebroadcasts the received packet with incrementing hop count and setting the *number of downstream nodes*, and returns an NPArep packet to the sender of the NPAreq packet, according to the procedure described below.

Figure 1 shows the structure of FIB used by producer side nodes. An FIB entry is created for an individual name prefix, and it may contain multiple forwarding candidates. Each candidate has the forwarding parameters and the routing parameters. The forwarding parameters are the ID (MAC address) of upstream node and other performance related values as defined in [14]. The routing parameters are used both to select and rank the upstream node providing shortest path to the name prefix and to compose a NPAreq packet to be rebroadcasted.

A node receiving an NPAreq packet follows the below.

1. The node checks whether there is an FIB entry for the name prefix specified in the received NPAreq packet.
2. If there are no such entries, it adds a new entry with the MAC address of the sender of the NPAreq packet set in the upstream node ID. It sends an NPArep packet to the NPAreq sender, and rebroadcasts the NPAreq packet.
3. Otherwise, it checks whether there is a forwarding candidate which has the same producer node ID. If there is such a candidate, then look for candidates in which the nonce is the same as that in the NPAreq packet.
   (3-1) If there are no such candidates, handle this NPAreq as a new advertisement. That is, it deletes the producer node ID and nonce pair from the list in all of found candidates. If the list becomes empty, it deletes the candidate and adds the producer node ID and nonce with creating a new candidate when necessary. It sends an NPArep packet to the NPAreq sender, and rebroadcasts the NPAreq packet.
   (3-2) Otherwise, that is, when there are some candidates having the same pair of producer node ID and nonce with the NPAreq packet, it compares the hop count in the entry with that in the NPAreq.
      (3-2-1) If the hop count in the entry is smaller, then ignore the received NPAreq packet.
      (3-2-2) If two hop counts are the same, then it checks whether there are any candidates which have the upstream node ID identical to the NPAreq sender address.
         A) If there is such a candidate, it ignores the received NPAreq packet.
         B) Otherwise, that is, when the NPAreq is sent by a new upstream node, it adds a new forwarding candidate, and returns an NPArep and rebroadcasts the NPAreq.
      (3-2-3) Otherwise, that is, when the hop count in the entry is larger than that in NPAreq packet, it handles this NPAreq as a new advertisement, and acts as specified in step (3-1).
4. Following the first part of step 3, the last step is for when there are no candidates with the producer node ID specified in the NPAreq packet, that is, when an NPAreq with the same name prefix from a new provider. In this case, it compares the hop count in the FIB entry with that in the received packet, and acts in the same way as (3-2-1) through (3-2-3) according to the result.

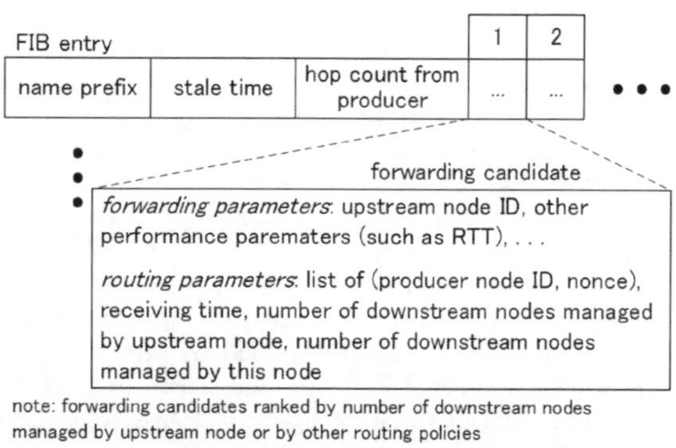

Figure 1. Structure of FIB at producer side.

When a forwarding candidate is created or modified, the number of downstream nodes managed by upstream node needs to be modified according to the received NPAreq packet.

When a node receives an NPArep packet, it looks for a forwarding candidate with the producer node ID and nonce in the packet, and increments the number of downstream nodes managed by this node by one.

Figure 2 shows an example of this protocol. As shown in Figure 2(a), there are six producer side nodes connected with wireless links shown in dashed lines. Among them, node 2 is a producer and the others are NDN routers. As shown in Figure 2(b), in the beginning, node 2 broadcasts an NPAreq packet with producer node ID = 2, nonce1, "name", hop count = 1, and number of downstream nodes = 0. Nodes 1, 2, and 5 receive this packet, create an FIB entry as shown in the figure, and return an NPArep packet individually. Then

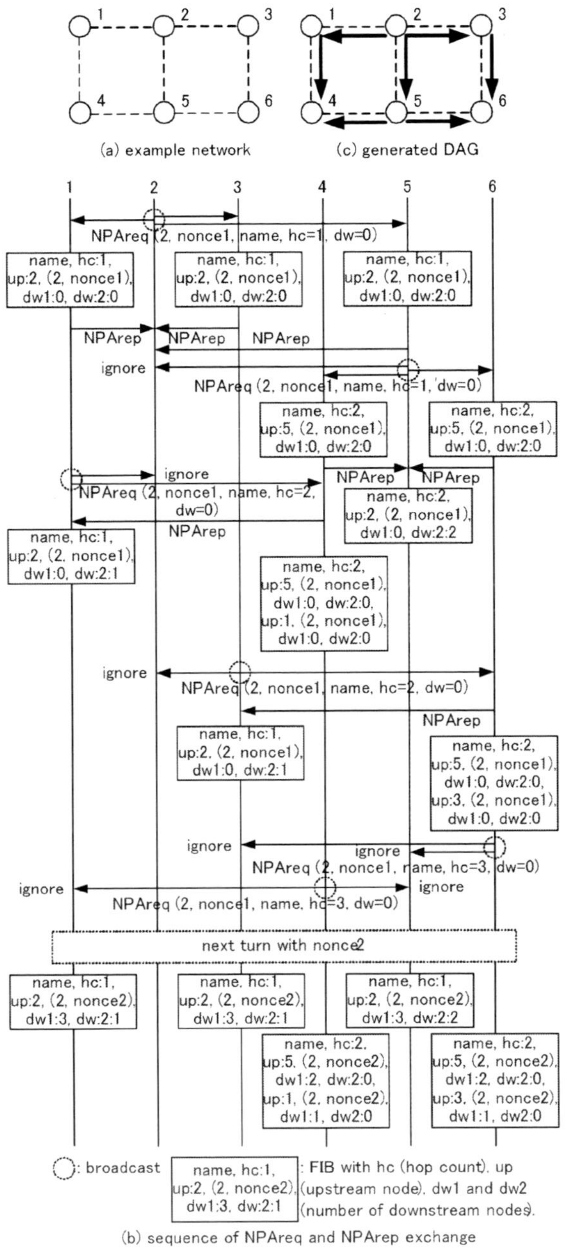

Figure 2. Communication sequence at producer side.

node 5 rebroadcasts the NPAreq packet with changing hop count to 2, and nodes 4 and 6 respond it. Node 2 receives the packet but ignores it. When node 5 receives the NPArep packets from nodes 4 and 6, the number of downstream nodes in this node is set to 2.

Next, node 1 rebroadcasts the NPAreq packet, to which node 4 responds. As a result, the FIB entry in node 4 has two forwarding candidates to node 1 and 5. Similarly, the NPAreq packet rebroadcasted by node 3 is handled by node 6. In the end of this advertisement, the NPAreq packets are rebroadcasted by nodes 4 and 6, but nobody responds to them. The generated DAG is shown in Figure 2(c).

After some periods, node 2 broadcasts a new NPAreq packet with nonce2. After this new NPAreq packet is disseminated, the FIBs of individual nodes are set as shown in the figure. It should be noted that the FIBs in nodes 4 and 6 have two forwarding candidates with node 5 and nodes 1/3 as the upstream nodes, respectively. These candidates are ranked by the number of downstream nodes managed by upstream node ("dw2"). Since node 5 has two downstream nodes, the forwarding candidate to node 5 is ranked first.

So far in this subsection, we do not mention PIT in producer side nodes. The PIT structure in producer side nodes is identical to that used in original NDN nodes [15], except that the face ID is replaced by the neighbor node ID (MAC address).

C. Detaild design for consumer side

We introduce a reactive routing mechanism to the consumer side network in the following way. FIB is not set in the consumer side in the beginning. When a node starts to retrieve a specific content, the first Interest packet for the content is flooded among consumer side nodes. When an Interest packet reaches some producer side node, it will be transferred to the corresponding producer. The producer sends back the Data packet containing the requested content. It is transferred through the reverse path of the Interest packet. When it goes through the consumer side nodes, FIB entry is set in individual nodes. The following Interest packets accessing to this name prefix use the FIB arranged. For the consumer side, we use the original formats of Interest and Data packets and the original structures of FIB and PIT, except that the first Interest packet is broadcasted and that a neighbor node MAC address is used as a face ID.

Figure 3 shows an example of the communication sequence between a mobile consumer and a producer. As shown in Figure 3(a), the producer side nodes are the same as in Figure 2(a), and there are three consumer side nodes (nodes *p*, *q*, *r*). The dashed line shows a wireless link.

We assume that the FIBs are arranged in the producer side nodes. As shown in Figure 3(b), node *p* starts contest retrieval for name prefix "name" and the first Interest is for "name/001". The Interest packet is broadcasted and nodes *q* and *r* receive it. Then node *q* rebroadcasts the Interest packet, and nodes 6 and *p* receive it. Node *p* ignores this Interest, because it is a duplicate one. Node 6 relays the received Interest packet to node 5 according to its FIB. On the other hand, node *r* also rebroadcasts the Interest packet, which nodes 6 and *p* receive. But both nodes ignore this Interest because of the duplication.

The Interest packet is sent to node 2, the producer, via node 5, and in response to it, the Data packet containing the content of "name/001" is returned along the reverse path of the Interest packet. That is, the Data packet goes via nodes 5, 6, and *q*, and reaches node *p*. When node *q* relays the Data packet, it creates an FIB entry for "name" which indicates that the upstream node is node 6. Similarly, when node *p*, the consumer, receives this Data packet, it creates an FIB entry for "name" indicating that the upstream node is node *q*.

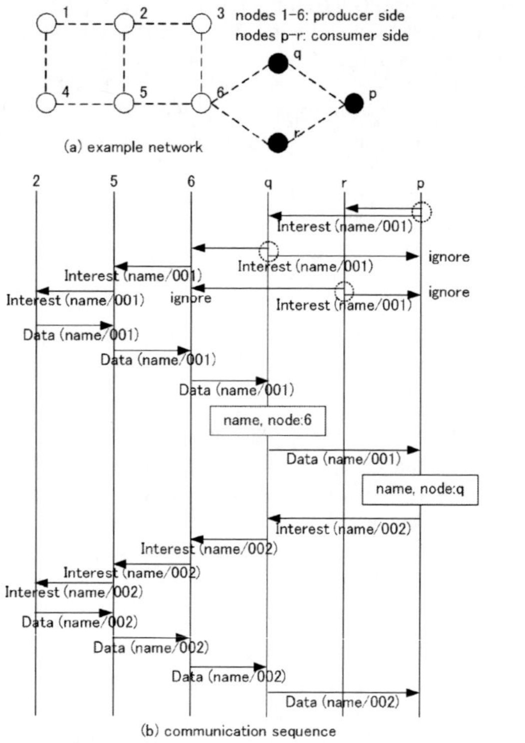

Figure 3. Communication sequence between consumer and producer.

For the following Interest packets, nodes p and q use the created FIB. That is, the next Interest packet requesting content for "name/002" is sent to node q in the unicast communication. Similarly, node q relays this Interest to node 6 directly.

When some nodes move and the communication link is broken, the Data packet is not returned and the timer for Interest packet will expire. At that time, node p will broadcast the lost Interest packet, and the similar procedure with the first Interest is performed.

IV. Performance Evaluation

This section describes the results of performance evaluation for the overhead of routing control and Interest packet transfer. We compare our proposal, TOP-CCN as an example of proactive mechanism, and REMIF as an example of reactive mechanism. Figure 4 shows the network configuration used in the evaluation. Nodes are arranged in a grid network, n nodes in the horizontal direction and 4 nodes in the vertical direction. Similarly with the examples above, the dashed line is a wireless link.

Figure 4(a) shows the detailed configuration for our proposal. The first and second rows are the producer side, and the third and fourth rows are the consumer side. Figure 4(b) shows the detailed configuration for TOP-CCN. According to [7], the light gray nodes are PMPRs and the dark gray nodes are MPRs. In REMIF, all nodes are handled equally.

We assume that some nodes in the first row work as producers. That is, the number of producers changes from 1

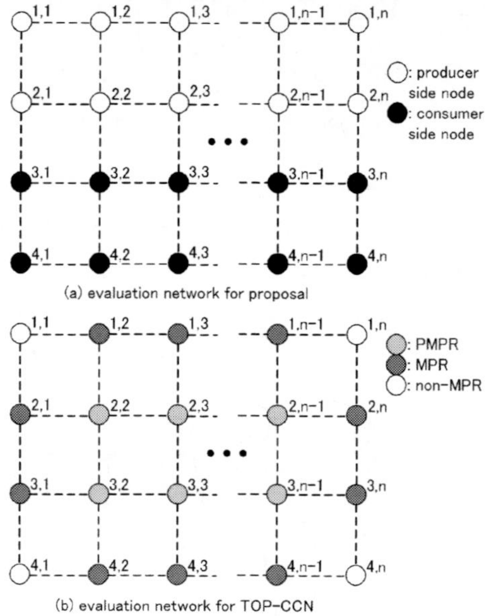

Figure 4. Evaluation network for proposal and TOP-CCN.

to n. We also assume that consumers locate in the third and fourth rows. In the evaluation, one consumer communicates with one producer for independent content. So, the cache is not effective in this evaluation.

A. *Results of routing control overhead*

Since our proposal and TOP-CCN use a proactive routing mechanism, they have some overheads in routing control. Routing control is performed periodically, but in this evaluation, we calculate the total number of control packets exchanged in one turn. We suppose there are m producers.

The details for our proposal are as follows. First, we consider the case that there is one producer (a node among 1,1 through 1,n). The producer issues an NPAreq packet, and it is rebroadcasted by any other nodes in the first and second rows, once per node. So, the total number of broadcasted NPAreq packets is $2n$. As a result of routing control, a rudder style network is generated as a DAG (see Figure 2(c)). In order to generate this configuration, one NPArep packet is transferred once over one wireless link. Therefore, the total number of transmitted NPArep packets is equal to the number of wireless links, that is, $3n-2$. So, the routing overhead for one producer is $5n-2$ in our proposal. For the case of m producers, the total number becomes m times as the case of one producer. Therefore, the result is $m(5n-2)$.

In the case of TOP-CCN, the number of control packets does not depend on the number of producers. The details for TOP-CCN are as follows. For non-MPR nodes (white nodes in Figure 4(b)), one CA packet is sent for advertising itself, and another CA packet is sent for MPR selection. So, the number of CA packets is 2 per node. For MPR nodes, a CA packet is sent after one neighbor detection, and the number of neighbors is 3. One CA packet is sent for MPR selection. For route announcement, it sends CA packets as many as the number of PMPR. Therefore, the number of CA packets is 4 + number of PMPR per node. For PMPR nodes, one CA packet is sent after one neighbor detection (there are four neighbors), and one for MPR selection. For relaying multi-hop CA packets, the number of CA packet transfer is equal to the number of PMPR nodes. Therefore, the total number is 5 + number of PMPR per node. The number of MPR and PMPR is $2n$ and $2(n-2)$, respectively. As a result, the total number is

$$2 \times 4 + 2n(4 + 2(n-2)) + 2(n-2)(5 + 2(n-2)) = 8n^2 - 6n + 4.$$

Figure 5 shows the number of routing control packets when n is 10, by changing the number of producers (m) from 1 to 10. In our proposal, the number of NPAreq and NPArep packets changes from 48 to 480 when m changes from 1 to 10. On the other hand, in TOP-CCN, the number of CA packets is always 744 independently of m. In REMIF, there are no routing control packets.

B. Results of Interest transfer overhead

In spite of the weakness in routing control overheads, the proactive mechanism provides more efficient Interest packet transfer then the reactive mechanism. Here, we suppose that there are one hundred Interest packets for one specific name prefix, and count the total number of Interest packets transmitted over wireless links (*total Interest hop count*). The calculation is done by changing the number of consumer and producer pairs from 1 to n.

In the case of TOP-CCN, the optimum route is used for all Interest packets. When there is one consumer / producer pair, the average hop count of one Interest packet is obtained

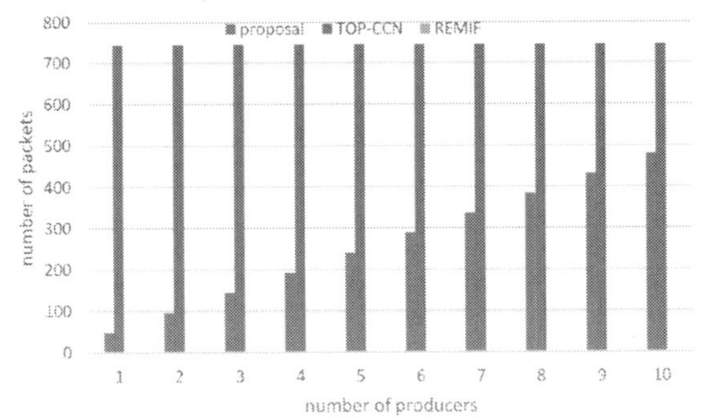

Figure 5. Number of routing control packets (n=10).

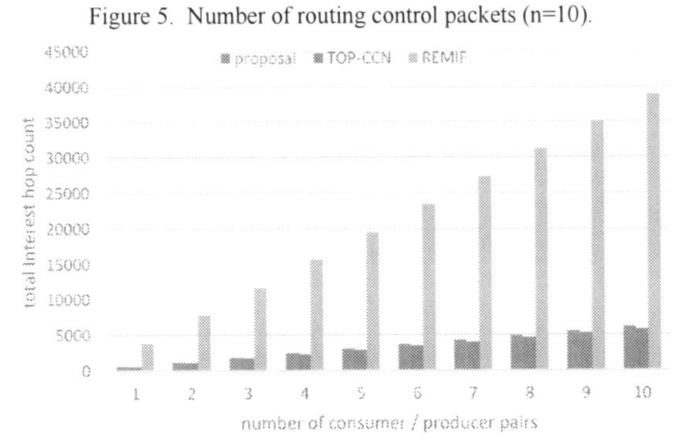

Figure 6. Total Interest hop count (average; n=10).

in the following formula. Please remember that a producer is located in the first row, and a consumer is located in the third or fourth row. The first item is an average vertical hop and the second is for horizontal transfer.

$$\frac{5}{2} + \frac{\sum_{j=1}^{n}\sum_{i=1}^{n}|i-j|}{n^2} = \frac{5}{2} + \frac{n^2-1}{3n}$$

For 100 Interests with m consumer / producer pairs, the total Interest hop count (average) for TOP-CCN is

$$100m\left(\frac{5}{2} + \frac{n^2-1}{3n}\right).$$

In the case of our proposal, only the first Interest packet is flooded among consumer side nodes and producer side nodes except the producer itself. So, the total Interest hop count (average) for our proposal is

$$(4n-1)m + 99m\left(\frac{5}{2} + \frac{n^2-1}{3n}\right).$$

In the case of REMIF, since there is no FIB, every Interest packet is flooded. In the grid configuration used here, every node except the producer will rebroadcast each Interest once. So, the result is $100(4n-1)m$.

Figure 6 shows the total Interest hop count (average) when n is 10, by changing the number of consumer /producer pairs (m) from 1 to 10. This figure indicates that the total number of REMIF is much larger than the others. The result of our proposal is slightly higher than TOP-CCN.

V. CONCLUSIONS

In this paper, we proposed a new NDN based ad hoc routing protocol, which combines the proactive and reactive approaches. We assume that, in a common ad hoc network, nodes in the information provider side are located in a fixed position and user nodes are mobile terminals. The proposed method introduces a proactive routing in the producer side and a reactive routing in the consumer side. Our proactive routing focuses only on the name prefix advertisement. Through a theoretical analysis, we showed that our proposal provides a lighter routing overhead than TOP-CCN, a proactive approach, and the similar Interest transfer overhead with TOP-CCN, which is much better than REMIF, a reactive approach.

REFERENCES

[1] V. Jacobson, et al., "Networking Named Content," Proc. of CoNEXT '09, pp.1-12, Dec. 2009.

[2] L. Wang, A. Hoque, C. Yi, A. Alyyan, and B. Zhang, "OSPFN: An OSPF Based Routing Protocol for Named Data Networking," NDN, Technical Report NDN-0003, pp.1-15, Jul. 2012.

[3] A. Hoque, et al., "NLSR: Named-data Link State Routing Protocol," Proc. of ICN '13, pp.1-6, Aug. 2013.

[4] E. Hemmati and J. Garcia-Luna-Aceves, "A New Approach to Name-Based Link-State Routing for Information-Centric Networks," Proc. of ICN '15, pp.29-38, Sep. 2015.

[5] X. Liu, Z. Li, P. Yang, and Y. Dong, "Information-centric mobile ad hoc networks and content routing: A survey," Ad Hoc Network, Available online, pp.1-14, Apr. 2016.

[6] S. Yao, X. Zhang, F. Lao, and Z. Guo, "MobileCCN: Wireless Ad-hoc Content-centric Networks over SmartPhone," Proc.of ACM International Conference on Future Internet Tech. (CFI '13), pp.1-2, Jun. 2013.

[7] J. Kim, D. Shin, and Y. Ko, "TOP-CCN: Topology aware Content Centric Networking for Mobile Ad Hoc Networks," Proc. of ICON '13, pp.1-6, Dec. 2013.

[8] M. Amadeo, A. Molinaro, and G. Ruggeri, "E-CHANET: Rouiting, fowarding and transport in Information-Centric multihop wireless networks," Conputer Communications, Vol.36, pp. 792-803, 2013.

[9] R. Rehman, T. Hieu, and H. Bae, "Robust and Efficient Multipath Interest Forwarding for NDN-based MANETs," Proc. of WMNC '16, pp.1-6, Jul. 2016.

[10] G. Malkin, "RIP Version 2," IETF RFC 2453, Nov. 1998.

[11] T. Clausen and P. Jacquet, "Optimized Link State Routing Protocol (OLSR)", IETF RFC 3626, Oct. 2003.

[12] C. Perkins, E. Belding-Royer, and S. Das, "Ad hoc On-Demand Distance Vector (AODV) Routing," IETF RFC 3561, Jul. 2003.

[13] F. Ducatelle, G. Caro, and L. Gambardella, "A New Approach for Integrating Proactive and Reactive Routing in MANETs," Proc. of MASS 2008, pp.377-383, Sep. 2008.

[14] J. Moy, "OSPF Version 2," IETF RFC 2328, Apr. 1998.

[15] C. Yi, et al., "A Case for Stateful Forwarding Plane," NDN, Technical Report NDN-0002, 2012.

Efficient Rerouting Algorithm for Optimizing Performances of WDM Transparent Networks Under Scheduled and Random Traffic

Naama Amdouni[1,2] and Taoufik Aguili[1]

[1]Université de Tunis El Manar, École Nationale d'Ingénieurs de Tunis, Laboratoire de Systèmes de Communications, 1002, Tunis, Tunisie;
[2]Université de Jendouba, Institut Supérieur de l'Informatique du Kef, 7100, Le Kef, Tunisie;
Email: naama.amdouni@gmail.com, taoufik.aguili@enit.rnu.tn

Abstract—**In this paper, we investigate further improvement in performances of Wavelength Division Multiplexing (WDM) transparent networks under scheduled and random traffic by applying traffic rerouting. Scheduled traffic corresponds to high priority traffic, whereas random traffic corresponds to best effort traffic. Indeed, in WDM transparent networks, the wavelength clash constraint along with the wavelength continuity constraint result in inefficient utilization of network resources and lead to higher rejection ratio. The traffic rerouting concept is a cost-effective and viable solution used to alleviate the inefficiency brought by the wavelength continuity, but it induces a service disruption period. Therefore, minimization of the incurred service disruption period is imperative. Our proposed rerouting algorithm proceeds in two separate phases. It first computes off-line the routing and wavelength assignment (RWA) for scheduled lightpath demands (SLDs) before considering random lightpath demands (RLDs) on the fly on the remaining network resources. Thus, if an incoming RLD cannot be established in the absence of a free wavelength-continuous path between its source and destination nodes, the proposed algorithm may reroute a minimum number of not yet routed SLDs and already routed RLDs. Rerouting of already routed SLDs is not allowed since they correspond to high priority guaranteed service. Allowing rerouting of not yet routed SLDs should lead to a shorter service disruption period. The performance of the proposed algorithm is evaluated and discussed through extensive numerical experiments. Significant improvements are demonstrated, either in terms of rejection ratio or in terms of service disruption period, in comparison with rerouting algorithms previously presented in the literature.**

Keywords–Routing and Wavelength Assignment (RWA); Service disruption period; Traffic rerouting; Wavelength continuity constraint; WDM transparent networks.

I. INTRODUCTION

An optical network provides a common infrastructure over which a variety of services, such as video on demand, video conference, distance education can be delivered [1]. The requirement for networks with high capacity is increasing. There are many ways to increase the capacity of the optical fiber and one of the ways is Wavelength Division Multiplexing (WDM). In WDM networks, an optical communication path, referred to as lightpath, is set up to support a connection between two optical wavelength-routing nodes. The problem of establishing lightpaths with the objective of optimizing the utilization of network resources is known as the Routing and Wavelength Assignment (RWA) problem [2]. The RWA problem has been extensively investigated in the literature and several approaches have been proposed either for static traffic or dynamic traffic (see [3], among others).

In the absence of wavelength converters, optical networks are referred to as transparent networks or all-optical networks [4]. In such networks, a lightpath is established before data can be transferred by allocating the same wavelength on all the fiber links in the route through which data traffic is transmitted. This constraint is called the wavelength continuity constraint [5]. Also, two lightpaths sharing at least one common fiber-link must be identified by different wavelengths to prevent the interference of the optical signals. This second constraint is called the wavelength integrity constraint. These limitations lead to inefficient utilization of wavelength channels which results in higher blocking ratios. Wavelength conversion and traffic rerouting are the two possible mechanisms that can increase the efficiency. Using wavelength converters potentially allows the network to support a larger set of Lightpath Demands (LDs). But, such converters remain too expensive. When wavelength conversion is not available, rerouting is used to improve network usage. It consists in rearranging certain existing lightpaths to free a wavelength-continuous path for the incoming LD. There are two ways to rearrange an existing lightpath. One is partially rearranging, which only changes the used wavelength and keeps the same physical route. This is also referred to as wavelength rerouting (WRR). Another is fully rearranging, which consists of finding a new physical path with possibly a new wavelength to replace the old path. This is referred to as lightpath rerouting (LRR). A taxonomy of rerouting schemes can be found in [6]. Transmission of the existing lightpaths to be rerouted must be temporarily shutdown to protect data from being lost or misrouted resulting in service disruption incurred by the longer propagation delay for transmitting signaling messages in transparent wide-area networks [7]. This period is referred to as the service disruption period. Therefore, in such networks, minimization of the incurred service disruption is imperative.

In this paper, we present a new rerouting algorithm in order to get further improvement either in terms of rejection ratio or in terms of service disruption period when two classes of traffic demands are considered:

- The first class is referred to as Scheduled Lightpath Demand (SLD). A SLD is a connection request with known setup and teardown times. The SLD model is deterministic since the demands are known in advance and is dynamic because it takes into account the evolution of the traffic load in the network over time.
- The second class is referred to as Random Lightpath Demand (RLD). A RLD, also called dynamic lightpath

demand, is a connection request that arrives randomly.

Through numerical results, we outline that thanks to rerouting, the lightpath demands' rejection ratio is improved and that our LRR algorithm selects a minimum number of established RLDs to be rerouted which should hopefully lead to a short service disruption period.

The rest of this paper is organized as follows. Section II presents related work. In Section III, we summarize our main contributions. In Section IV, some notations are given. In Section V, we present in detail the proposed rerouting algorithm. Numerical results and concluding remarks are given in Sections VI and VII, respectively.

II. Related Work

The traffic rerouting concept has been applied to WDM transparent networks to alleviate the impact of the wavelength continuity constraint. In [7], Lee et al. introduced the WRR concept by studying the rerouting problem with the objective of minimizing the disruption incurred due to WRR. In [8], Mohan and Murthy proposed a time optimal wavelength rerouting algorithm based on the Parallel Move-To-Vacant Wavelength-Retuning (MTV-WR) rerouting scheme. In [9] and [10], the authors proposed two low complexity wavelength rerouting algorithms to improve throughput and to reduce blocking probability in wavelength division multiplexed networks. The former is called the Shortest Path Wavelength ReRouting (SPWRR) algorithm while the latter is called the Lightpath ReRouting Algorithm (LRRA). The authors also demonstrated that LRRA gives better results and can be implemented in huge networks for good blocking performance. Recently, a new lightpath rerouting scheme called Sequential Routing with Lightpath Rerouting (SeqRwLR) has been proposed in [11] to improve the rejection ratio while keeping a short service disruption period. In [12] and [13], the authors investigated hybrid rerouting to increase the network throughput and minimize the incurred service disruption period. In [14], the authors compared passive, active and hybrid rerouting. They demonstrated that when there is wavelength conversion, passive rerouting outperforms active rerouting, and hybrid rerouting can only improve the performance over passive rerouting slightly. Also, they demonstrated that, in the absence of wavelength converters, hybrid rerouting can improve the blocking performance significantly. Later, two RWA algorithms applying active lightpath rerouting are presented in [15]. The authors show that, in the absence of wavelength converters and in contrast to the results announced in [14], active rerouting works much better than passive rerouting but induces a longer service disruption period. Improving the performances of transparent optical networks in terms of rejection ratio by exploiting the set-up delay tolerance specification contained in the Service Level Agreement (SLA) has already been investigated in [1][16][17][18]. The basic idea is to delay LDs instead of rejecting them due to the current network state and try to establish them after some time, since other routed LDs may leave the network and its network resources are released. While in all of the above described algorithms dynamic traffic is considered, in [19], the authors proposed a new lightpath rerouting scheme to optimize network resources allocation considering scheduled and random lightpath demands. Their scheme prohibits SLD rerouting while the establishment of a new RLD may require the rerouting of one or several RLDs. To the best of our knowledge, this is the first attempt to apply rerouting of not already established SLDs to maximize the number of established RLDs and moreover, minimize the incurred service disruption period. The performances of the proposed algorithm either in terms of rejection ratio or in terms of service disruption period are demonstrated to be promising through illustrative simulation results.

III. Contribution of the Paper

In this paper, we present an efficient RWA algorithm for WDM transparent networks working under the wavelength continuity constraint without wavelength converters. We anticipate to alleviate the inefficiency brought by the wavelength continuity constraint by the use of an efficient lightpath rerouting strategy minimizing the number of rejected LDs. A combination of two traffic classes, namely, SLDs and RLDs are considered. Permanent lightpath demands (PLD) (i.e. static lightpath demands which are preknown connection requests and if accepted, remain in the network indefinitely) are not considered in this study because, once established, these demands remain in the network indefinitely. This can be considered as a reduction in the number of available wavelengths channels on some network fiber-links.

Our proposed scheme computes the RWA for the SLDs and the RLDs separately. First, it computes the RWA for the SLDs off-line, as SLDs correspond to preknown traffic, aiming at minimizing the number of blocked SLDs. Taking the assignment of the SLDs into account, the RWA for the RLDs is computed sequentially. When an incoming RLD cannot be established in the absence of a wavelength-continuous path between the source and the destination of the RLD, we try to reroute one or several SLDs in the set of SLDs that are not yet routed and/or a minimum number of already routed RLDs aiming hopefully at freeing a wavelength-continuous path to accommodate the incoming RLD. We assume that an already established SLD cannot be rerouted since SLDs correspond to high priority guaranteed service, and only SLDs that have not been routed yet can be rerouted. Unlike SLDs, already established RLDs may be rerouted to accommodate the new incoming RLD. In order to shorten the duration of the service disruption period, our rerouting algorithm promotes rerouting of not yet routed SLDs. This is because the service disruption period incurred by rerouting a not yet routed SLD is shorter than that incurred by rerouting an already established RLD. Theoretically, the service disruption period incurred due to rerouting a not yet routed SLD is very short since the SLD is not yet routed and the data transmission is not yet started. Our proposed algorithm differs from the previously published ones in the following aspects:

- First, it considers two classes of traffic demands. Only RLDs have been considered in all the others algorithms presented in the literature. In [19], two types of traffic demands are considered.
- Second, when a new RLD is to be rejected by the routing phase, the rerouting phase selects one or several RLDs and/or not yet routed SLDs to be rerouted in order to accommodate the new RLD. Whereas, in [19], the rerouting of SLDs is forbidden once the optimal RWA for the SLDs is computed off-line and only rerouting of already established RLDs is allowed. As mentioned above, rerouting not yet routed SLDs has a

direct impact on the duration of the service disruption period.

- Third, our proposed algorithm does not construct any auxiliary graph with crossover edges to determine the set of active lightpaths that should be rerouted as in [7][8][11]. Thus, our algorithm should be less Central Processing Unit (CPU) intensive than rerouting algorithms previously presented in [7][8][11].

IV. NOTATIONS

We use the following notations and typographical conventions:

- $G = (\nu, E, \vartheta)$ is an arc-weighted symmetrical directed graph representing the network topology with vertex set ν (representing the network nodes), arc set E (representing the network fiber-links) and weight function $\vartheta : E \rightarrow R+$ mapping the cost of the links set by the network operator.
- $N = |\nu|$, $L = |E|$ are respectively, the number of nodes and links in the network.
- D is the total number of LDs (SLDs and RLDs) which arrives at the network over the considered time period.
- W denotes the number of wavelengths per fiber-link.
- $\Lambda = \{\lambda_1, \lambda_2, ..., \lambda_W\}$ is the set of available wavelengths on each fiber-link of the network.
- The ith LD, $1 \leq i \leq D$ (to be established), is defined by a 5−tuple $(s_i, d_i, \pi_i, \alpha_i, \beta_i)$. $s_i \in \nu$ and $d_i \in \nu$ are the source and the destination nodes of the LD, respectively; π_i is the number of requested lightpaths; and α_i and β_i are the setup and teardown time of the LD, respectively. Here, for the sake of simplicity, we assume that each LD requires only one lightpath between the source and the destination nodes $(\pi_i = 1)$.
- $P_{i,k}$, $1 \leq i \leq D$, $1 \leq k \leq K$, represents the kth alternate shortest path in G connecting node s_i to node d_i (source and destination of the ith LD). The hop count is used as the link metric and K-alternate (loop-free) shortest paths for each source−destination pair (LD) are computed beforehand according to the algorithm described in [20] (if as many paths exist, otherwise we only consider the available ones).
- P_i, $1 \leq i \leq D$, is the set of alternate shortest paths computed between the source and destination nodes of LD number i. Hence $|P_i| \leq K$. This computation is done in a preliminary step prior to any routing.
- P is the set of alternate shortest paths computed between the source and destination nodes of each possible node pair in the network. Clearly $|P| \leq N(N-1)K$.
- $c(i, k, w, t)$, $1 \leq i \leq D$, $1 \leq k \leq K$, $1 \leq w \leq W$ is the cost of using wavelength λ_w on the kth-alternate shortest path in G from node s_i to node d_i of LD numbered i at time t. The cost function of each considered path is determined as follows:

$$c(i,k,w,t) = \begin{cases} \varepsilon & \text{if } \lambda_w \text{ is path-free on } P_{i,k} \\ \infty & \text{if } \lambda_w \text{ is already used by another} \\ & \text{LD on at least on link of } P_{i,k} \end{cases}$$

ε is a tiny positive value corresponding to the hop count on path $P_{i,k}$.

- $\theta(i, k, w, t)$, $1 \leq i \leq D$, $1 \leq k \leq K$, $1 \leq w \leq W$, denotes the set of LDs to be rerouted when serving the incoming RLD number i at time t using wavelength λ_w on $P_{i,k}$.
- $cr(j)$, $1 \leq j \leq |\theta(i, k, w, t)|$ is the cost of rerouting the jth LD $\in \theta(i, k, w, t)$ in order to satisfy the incoming RLD on $P_{i,k}$, using wavelength λ_w.

$$cr(j) = \begin{cases} \tau, & \text{if the LD to be rerouted is a not} \\ & \text{yet established SLD} \\ \sigma, & \text{if the LD to be rerouted is an already} \\ & \text{routed RLD} \end{cases}$$

τ is a tiny positive constant and σ is a positive weighting factor indicating the penalty of rerouting an already routed RLD to accommodate the new demand. σ is chosen such that $(\sigma \gg \tau)$ to promote rerouting of not yet routed SLDs. τ and σ are chosen such that the number of RLDs to be rerouted is minimized which should lead to the minimization of the service disruption incurred by rerouting.

- $cr(i, k, w, t) = \sum_{j \in |\theta(i,k,w,t)|} cr(j)$, $1 \leq i \leq D$, $1 \leq k \leq K$, $1 \leq w \leq W$ is the cost of rerouting to set up the incoming RLD number i at time t using wavelength λ_w on $P_{i,k}$.
- $cr^{min} = min_{1 \leq k \leq K, 1 \leq w \leq W} cr(i, k, w, t)$ is the minimum cost to satisfy the new RLD number i at time t on $P_{i,k^{min}}$ using wavelength $\lambda_{w^{min}}$.

V. THE PROPOSED SCHEME

Our proposed LRR algorithm called SepRwLR, for Separate Routing with Lightpath Rerouting, handles the SLDs and the RLDs separately, as shown in Figure 1. First, it considers the RWA for SLDs before considering the RLDs. The objective is to minimize the number of blocked SLDs. No rerouting is performed when computing the RWA for SLDs. Taking the RWA of the SLDs into account, the SepRwLR then tries to route sequentially the incoming RLDs in the following two phases:

- The first phase, also called routing phase, computes the RWA for a new RLD without considering rerouting.
- If Phase I fails, rerouting phase determines which LDs (already routed RLDs and not yet routed SLDs) are to be rerouted and how they will be rerouted to accommodate the incoming RLD.

Subsection V-A details the routing and wavelength assignment algorithm for LDs (be it scheduled or random) whereas Subsection V-B details the rerouting algorithm for RLDs.

A. Routing and Wavelength Assignment for LDs

At the incoming time of a new LD, we first try to establish it without rerouting any active lightpaths according to the traditional sequential Dijkstra based algorithm. The associated K-alternate shortest paths (computed off-line and denoted P_i) are considered in turn according to their number of hops. We look for the first path-free wavelength. The LD is hence set

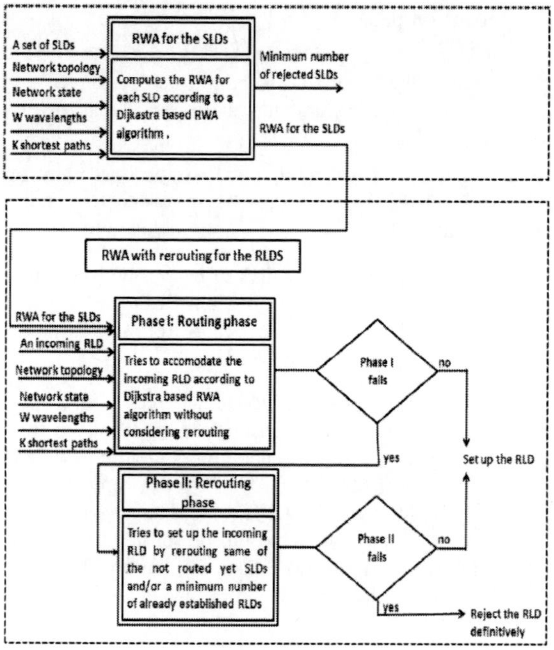

Figure 1. Block diagram of the SepRwLR algorithm.

up on the first met path-free wavelength among its K-shortest-paths if such path exists. The wavelength assigned to this path is selected according to a first-fit scheme [21] whenever multiple wavelengths are available on the considered path. If a path-free wavelength to satisfy the demand does not exist, two cases may happen: the demand is a SLD, in which case it is rejected since no rerouting is performed when computing the RWA for SLDs. The second case that may happen is that the demand is a RLD in which case the rerouting phase will be considered.

B. Rerouting algorithm for RLDs

We assume that a new RLD arrives at time t and that the routing phase fails to set it up. Thus, the rerouting phase is launched aiming hopefully to free a path along one of its K shortest paths as follows:

For each shortest path $P_{i,k}$, $1 \leq k \leq K$, associated to RLD numbered i, rejected by the routing phase, and for each wavelength λ_w, $1 \leq w \leq W$, we determine the set of RLDs, $\theta(i,k,w,t)$, that should be rerouted to establish the incoming RLD on the selected path and wavelength. The minimum cost of rerouting, cr^{min}, is then computed. If cr^{min} is finite, its associated k^{th}-alternate shortest path and the wth wavelength are hence selected. Let θ^{min} denote the corresponding set of LDs to be rerouted. Two cases may happen: all the LDs in θ^{min} can be rerouted by only changing the used wavelength whilst keeping the same path or by changing the physical path and then possibly the used wavelength. In this case, the incoming RLD is established using $P_{i,k^{min}}$ on wavelength $\lambda_{w^{min}}$. $c(i,k^{min},w^{min},t)$, the cost of using $P_{i,k^{min}}$ on wavelength $\lambda_{w^{min}}$, at time t is updated to $+\infty$, as well as the cost of all the paths in P that share at least one common link with $P_{i,k^{min}}$. We also update the costs of the new paths used by the rerouted LDs to $+\infty$ and to ε the cost of the released paths. The second case that may happen is that $P_{i,k^{min}}$ using $\lambda_{w^{min}}$ cannot be freed because one or several LDs cannot be rerouted. In that case, $cr(i,k^{min},w^{min},t)$ is updated to $+\infty$ and the minimum cost is computed again. If cr^{min} is infinite, the incoming RLD numbered i is definitively rejected.

For an illustration, we consider a graph representing a network with five nodes and bidirectional fiber-links, as shown in Figure 2, and the set of LDs described in Table I. Two shortest paths ($K = 2$) are computed for each source destination pair as shown in Table I. We assume that each fiber has only one wavelength λ_0.

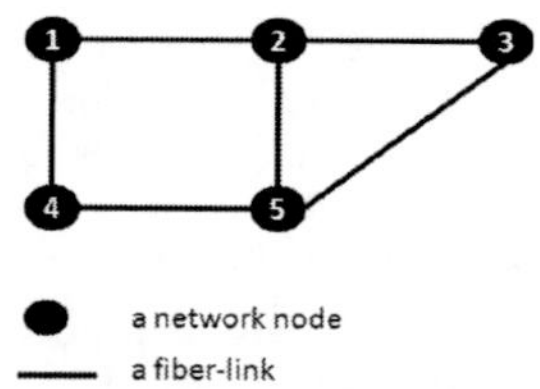

Figure 2. 5-node test network.

TABLE I. SET OF LDs TO BE SET UP.

Number	*s*	*d*	π	α	β	*K shortest paths*	*Nature*
1	5	3	1	100	808	5-3 / 5-4-1-2-3	RLD
2	2	5	1	303	1100	2-5 / 2-1-4-5	SLD
3	2	5	1	405	715	2-5 / 2-1-4-5	RLD
4	1	2	1	607	1118	1-2 / 1-4-5-2	SLD

The RWA for the SLDs is shown in Table II.

TABLE II. RWA FOR THE SLDs.

Number	*s*	*d*	π	α	β	*Path*	*Wavelength*
2	2	5	1	100	1100	2-5	λ_0
4	1	2	1	607	1118	1-2	λ_0

Now, we have to consider the RLDs taking into account the RWA for the SLDs. When RLD 1 arrives, λ_0 is selected to set it up on $P_{1,1} = 5-3$. SLD 2 arrives at time $t = 303$ and has to be set up on $P_{2,1} = 2-5$ using wavelength λ_0 according to Table II. At time $t = 607$, RLD 3 has to be set up. The routing phase fails to find a path-free wavelength and hence the rerouting phase is considered. On $P_{3,1} = 1-2-3$, the set of LDs to be rerouted is $\theta_{3,1,\lambda_0,607} = \{SLD4\}$. $SLD4$ is an SLD not routed yet, thus $cr_{3,1,\lambda_0,607} = \tau$. The set of LDs to be rerouted, on $P_{3,2} = 1-4-5-3$, is $\theta_{3,2,\lambda_0,607} = \{RLD2\}$. $RLD2$ is an already routed RLD hence $cr_{3,2,\lambda_0,607} = \sigma$. Since $\tau \ll \sigma$ the minimum cost $cr^{min} = cr_{3,1,\lambda_0,607}$ is selected and the algorithm selects the not yet routed SLD $1 \rightarrow 2$ to be rerouted on the following new physical path $1-4-5-2$. Then, it routes $RLD3$ on $P_{3,1} = 1-2-3$.

VI. NUMERICAL RESULTS

In this section, we attempt to experimentally evaluate and compare the performance of the SepRwLR scheme presented in the preceding section. We use the 14$-$node network topology shown in Figure 3. The source and destination nodes for SLDs and RLDs are chosen according to a random uniform distribution in the interval $[1, 14]$. The RLDs requests arrive as independent Poisson processes with common arrival rate $\nu = 1$ and, once accepted, hold the network resources with independent exponential times with common mean holding time $\mu = 300$. The set-up and tear-down times for the SLDs are set according to a random uniform distribution in the same interval of RLDs arrivals. We compute $K = 5$ shortest paths between each node pair in the network if so many paths exist, otherwise we consider only the available ones. We assume also that there are $W = 32$ wavelengths on each fiber-link.

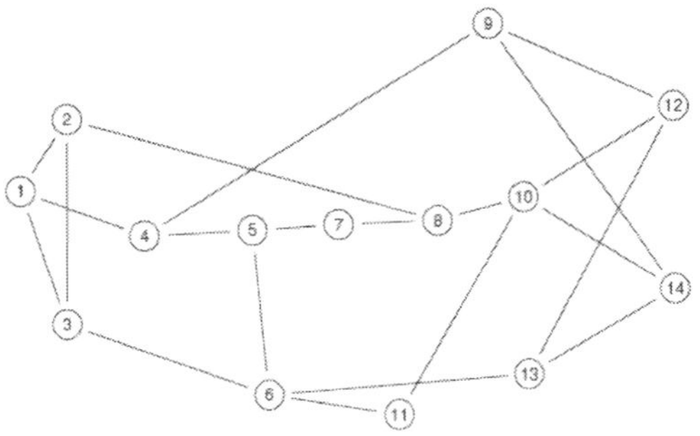

Figure 3. The 14-node network topology (NSFNET).

In order to evaluate the performance of our proposed scheme, we propose to compare the results obtained with the SepRwLR algorithm to those obtained with the following two algorithms:

- The separate routing algorithm (SepR) which computes separately the RWA for the SLDs and the RLDs according to the algorithm described in [22] without considering rerouting. The average rejection ratio obtained by this algorithm is considered in order to highlight the gain obtained thanks to rerouting.
- The separate routing with rerouting algorithm (SRWR) which routes in two separate phases the SLDs and the RLDs. To accommodate an incoming RLD rejected at the end of the first phase, the SRWR algorithm uses the rerouting algorithm described in [19]. SLD (be it routed or not yet routed) rerouting is forbidden. The SRWR algorithm is the only algorithm presented in the literature considering two types of traffic. All the others consider only random traffic.

Figure 4 shows the average rejection ratio computed when D, the total number of LDs arriving at the network during the observation period, varies. We notice that the rejection ratio increases with the traffic loading. This is because when the traffic loading increases, network resources decrease and therefore it becomes more difficult to serve a new incoming demand. The curves show that both of rerouting algorithms improve the rejection ratio significantly compared to the no-rerouting case. We also observe that the SepRwLR algorithm performs better than the SRWR algorithm. In fact, as the SepRwLR allows the rerouting of not yet routed SLDs (which is forbidden in SRWR) in addition to existing RLDs to set up an incoming RLD to be rejected by the routing phase, the number of rejected RLDs is hence minimized.

Figure 5 shows the average rejection ratio gain computed by the SepRwLR algorithm versus D. The rejection ratio gain

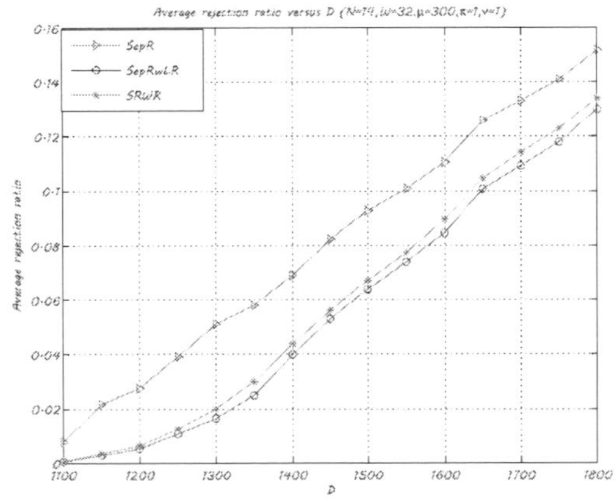

Figure 4. Average rejection ratio versus D.

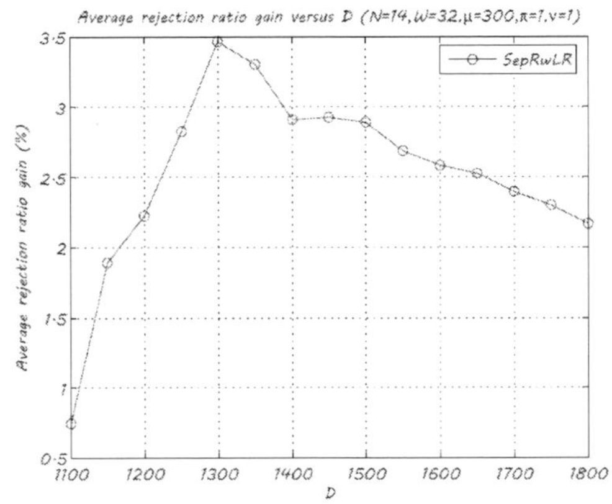

Figure 5. Average rejection ratio gain versus D.

has been computed as the difference between the average number of rejected LDs computed without rerouting i.e computed by the SepR algorithm and the average number of rejected LDs computed by the SepRwLR algorithm divided by D and multiplied by 100. A maximum rejection ratio gain of 3.5% is observed for $D = 1300$ under the aforementioned simulation parameters. The average rejection ratio gain decreases when D increases. This is mainly due to the fact that, when the number of LDs exceeds 1300 and since the number of wavelengths on each link is fixed, the network becomes saturated and it becomes impossible to accommodate more incoming LDs even by rerouting since no network resources are left.

Figure 6 shows the average number of rerouted LDs when D increases. Each group of two bars shows the average number of rerouted LDs by the SepRwLR (first bar from the left-hand side) and the SRWR algorithm (second bar), respectively. The height of the white segment indicates the average number of rerouted not yet routed SLDs whereas the height of the black one shows the average number of rerouted already routed RLDs. We observe that the SepRwLR algorithm requires fewer already routed RLDs to be rerouted than the SRWR algorithm. This is because the SepRwLR promotes rerouting of not yet routed SLDs at the expense of rerouting of already routed RLDs in order to reduce the service disruption period and that

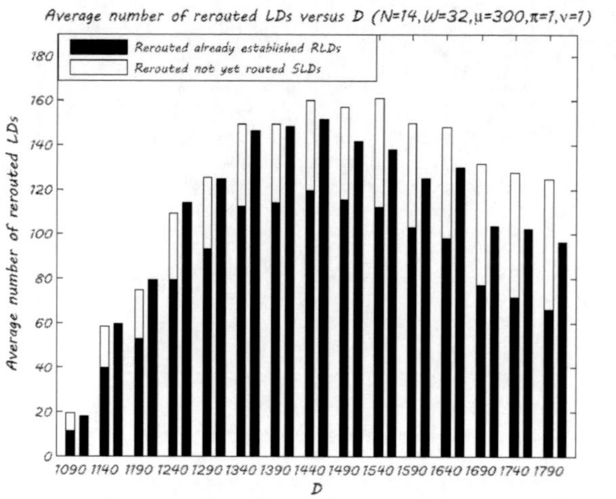

Figure 6. Average rerouted LDs versus D.

is why we can say that the service disruption period incurred by our rerouting algorithm is shorter than that of the SRWR algorithm. From Figure 6 we also notice that the number of LDs to be rerouted by the SepRwLR and the SRWR algorithms respectively decreases under heavy traffic load because the probability that an already routed RLD or a not yet routed SLD be retunable on the same path or on new path becomes infeasible. This is because the saturation regime of the network is achieved.

VII. Conclusion

In this paper, we propose a lightpath rerouting scheme to further improve the performances of transparent networks. Our algorithm considers both SLDs and RLDs. Our algorithm's objective is to further minimize the rejection ratio and the service disruption period. Simulation results show that our algorithm achieves better performance in terms of rejection ratio and reduces considerably the service disruption period since it promotes rerouting of not yet routed SLDs. Our forthcoming studies will investigate further improvement of WDM transparent networks performance by applying traffic rerouting and set up delay tolerance.

References

[1] A. Muhammad and R. Forchheimer, "Reducing blocking probability in dynamic wdm networks by rerouting and set-up delay tolerance," Proc. 17th IEEE International Conference on Networks, pp. 195-200, 2011.

[2] H. Zang, J.P. Jue, and B. Mukherjee, "A review of routing and wavelength assignment approaches for wavelength-routed wdm networks," Optical Networks Magazine, vol. 1, no. 1, pp. 47-60, 2000.

[3] X. Chu and B. Li, "Dynamic routing and wavelength assignment in the presence of wavelength conversion for all-optical networks," IEEE/ACM Transactions on Networking, vol. 13, no. 3, pp. 704-715, 2005.

[4] A.A.M. Saleh, "Transparent optical networking in backbone networks," Proc.Optical Fiber Communication Conference, pp. 62-64, 2000.

[5] I. Chlamtac, A. Ganz, and G. Karmi, "Lightpath communications: an approach to high bandwidth optical WAN's," IEEE Transactions on Communications, vol. 40, no. 7, pp. 1171-1182, 1992.

[6] E. W. M. Wong, A. K. M. Chan, and T. S. P. Yum, "A taxonomy of rerouting in circuit switched networks," IEEE Communications Magazine, vol. 37, no. 11, pp. 116-122, 1999.

[7] K.C. Lee and V.O.K. Li, "A wavelength rerouting algorithm in wide-area all-optical networks," IEEE/OSA Journal of Lightwave Technology, vol. 14, no. 6, pp. 1218-1229, 1996.

[8] G. Mohan and C. S. R. Murthy, "A time optimal wavelength rerouting algorithm for dynamic traffic in wdm networks," IEEE/OSA Journal of Lightwave Technology, vol. 17, no. 3, pp. 406-417, 1999.

[9] A. Wason and R.S. Kaler, "Rerouting technique with dynamic traffic in wdm optical networks, Journal of Optical Fiber Technology, vol. 16, no. 1, pp. 950-954, 2010.

[10] A. Wason and R.S. Kaler, "Lightpath rerouting algorithm to enhance blocking performance in all-optical wdm network without wavelength conversion," Journal of Optical Fiber Technology, vol. 16, no. 3. pp. 146-150, 2010.

[11] N. Amdouni, M. Koubàa, and T. Aguili, "Lightpath rerouting scheme for dynamic traffic in wdm all-optical networks," Proc. IEEE International Conference on Computer Systems and Industrial Informatics (ICCSII12), pp. 1-6, 2012.

[12] X. Chu, T. Bu, and X Li, "A study of lightpath rerouting schemes in wavelength-routed wdm networks," Proc. IEEE International Conference on Communications, pp. 2400-2405, 2007.

[13] N. Amdouni, M. Koubàa, and T. Aguili, "A new hybrid rerouting scheme in wdm all-optical networks under dynamic traffic," Proc. 2014 Global Summit on Computer & Information Technology (GSCIT), pp. 1-7, 2014.

[14] X. Chu, H. Yin, and X. Li, "Lightpath rerouting in wavelength-routed wdm networks," IEEE/OSA Journal of Optical Communications and Networking, vol. 7, no. 8, pp. 721-735, 2008.

[15] M. Koubàa, N. Amdouni, and T. Aguili, "Efficient traffic engineering strategies for optimizing network throughput in wdm all-optical networks," International Journal of Computer Network and Information Security, vol. 6, pp. 39-49, 2015.

[16] C. Cavdar, M. Tornatore, F. Buzluca, and B. Mukherjee, "Shared-path protection with delay tolerance (sdt) in optical wdm mesh networks", IEEE/OSA Journal of Lightwave Technology, vol. 28, no. 14, pp. 2068-2076, 2010.

[17] C. Cavdar, M. Tornatore, and F. Buzluca, "Availability-guaranteed connection provisioning with delay tolerance in optical wdm mesh networks," Journal of Optical Fiber Communication, pp. 1-3, 2009.

[18] A. Muhammad, C. Cavdar, L. Wosinska, and R. Forchheimer," Effect of delay Tolerance in wdm network with differentiated services," Journal of Optical Fiber Communication, pp.1-3, 2011.

[19] M. Koubàa and M. Gagnaire, "Lightpath rerouting strategies in wdm all-Optical networks under scheduled and random traffic," IEEE/OSA Journal of Optical Communications and Networking, vol. 2, no. 10, pp. 859-871, Oct. 2010.

[20] D. Eppstein, "Finding the k shortest paths," SIAM Journal of Computing, vol. 28, no. 2, pp. 652-673, 1998.

[21] X. Sun, Y. Li, I. Lambadaris, and Y. Q. Zhao, "Performance analysis of first-fit wavelength assignment algorithm in optical networks," Proc. 7th International Conference on Telecommunications, vol. 2, pp. 403-409, 2003.

[22] M.Gagnaire, M. Koubàa, and Nicolas Puech, "Network dimensioning under scheduled and random lightpath demands in all-optical wdm networks," IEEE Journal On Selected Areas in Communications, vol. 25, no. 9, pp. 58-67, 2007.

Code-Based Public-Key Cryptosystem Based on Bursts-Correcting Codes

E. Krouk, A. Ovchinnikov
Saint-Petersburg State University of Aerospace Instrumentation
Saint-Petersburg, Russia
email: ekrouk@vu.spb.ru, mldoc@ieee.org

Abstract—**In this paper, the public-key cryptosystems based on error-correcting codes are considered. The most known code-based public-key cryptosystem belongs to McEliece and its security is based on decoding vectors of given weight t in linear code, equivalent to some private code with minimal distance $d = 2t + 1$. Another class of code-based cryptosystems is known, whose security is based on complete decoding task (or searching through all possible error vectors). It is supposed that the security of these systems may significantly overcome those of McEliece. In the paper, the cryptosystem from this class is proposed based on bursts-correcting codes.**

Keywords–Code-based public-key cryptosystems; Cryptosystems based on complete decoding task; Bursts-correcting codes.

I. INTRODUCTION

The public-key cryptosystem, proposed in 1978 by R. J. McEliece, is based on error-correcting codes [1]. The idea of the system is to select the error-correcting code for which the effective decoding algorithm is known, and then to hide this code in linear code of arbitrary structure. The description of initial code, usually given by its generator matrix, serves as private key, while the description of obtained code with arbitrary structure is public key. Being very computationally effective, McEliece cryptosystem did not obtain much practical usage, which is mainly argued by its large key sizes.

Though the decoding task of arbitrary linear code is NP-complete [2], it should be noted that in classical variant of McEliece cryptosystem its public and private keys are equivalent codes, and in fact the adversary should solve the task of decoding in sphere of some radius, which seems simpler than arbitrary linear code decoding by minimal distance. Besides, the attacks revealing the code's structure are also possible [3]-[4].

In [5], the class of public-key cryptosystems is proposed which is based on the task of complete decoding, that is, decoding of coset leaders in the standard array [6]. However, the selection of particular system from this class requires definition of masking transformation and the set of error vectors applied during encryption. Some attacks on the variants of such definitions were considered in [7]. Practical examples of the systems based on complete decoding task are also given in [7][8].

The paper is organized as follows. Section II gives the description of McEliece cryptosystem. Section III describes the class of cryptosystems based on complete decoding task. In Section IV, the variant of the system from this class is proposed based on bursts-correcting codes. Section V concludes the paper.

II. MCELIECE CODE-BASED CRYPTOSYSTEM

The construction of McEliece public-key cryptosystem is based on linear (n, k) code for which the polynomial decoding procedure is known, providing correction of any combination of t or less errors. The family of Goppa codes are usually considered for this purpose [1][6].

In McEliece cryptosystem, each user constructs private and correspondent public keys as follows:

1) Select integers k, n, t as general system parameters.
2) Select generator $(k \times n)$ matrix $\mathbf{G}$ of linear (n, k) code, for which the effective procedure ψ of correcting any combination of t errors is known.
3) Select random binary non-singular $(k \times k)$ matrix $\mathbf{M}$.
4) Select random $(n \times n)$ permutation matrix $\mathbf{P}$.
5) Calculate $(k \times n)$ matrix $\mathbf{G}' = \mathbf{MGP}$.
6) Public key is $(\mathbf{G}', t)$, private key is $(\mathbf{M}, \mathbf{G}, \mathbf{P})$.

To encrypt the message, one should do the following:

1) Represent the message as binary k-bit sequence $\mathbf{m}$.
2) Select random n-bit binary vector $\mathbf{e}$ of weight t.
3) Calculate ciphertext $\mathbf{c} = \mathbf{mG}' + \mathbf{e}$.

To decrypt the ciphertext, one should do the following:

1) Calculate $\mathbf{c}' = \mathbf{cP}^{-1}$.
2) Obtain $\mathbf{m}'$ by decoding $\mathbf{c}'$ in code $\mathbf{G}$ using ψ.
3) Calculate $\mathbf{m} = \mathbf{m}'\mathbf{M}^{-1}$.

Decryption is correct, since $\mathbf{c}' = \mathbf{cP}^{-1} = (\mathbf{mG}' + \mathbf{e})\mathbf{P}^{-1} = (\mathbf{mMGP} + \mathbf{e})\mathbf{P}^{-1} = (\mathbf{mM})\mathbf{G} + \mathbf{eP}^{-1}$ and $\mathbf{eP}^{-1}$ is the vector of weight t.

In the next section, we will describe the class of public-key cryptosystems based on complete decoding task.

III. THE CLASS OF CRYPTOSYSTEMS BASED ON COMPLETE DECODING TASK

The straightforward attack on McEliece cryptosystem is decoding of error vector of weight t in the code $\mathbf{G}'$. The system would be significantly harder break into if decryption would require to correct not only error vectors of weight t, but all coset leaders, that is, performing complete decoding [6].

Consider the following variant of public and private keys construction [5][7]:

1) Select generator $(k \times n)$ matrix $\mathbf{G}$ of linear (n, k) code, for which the effective procedure ψ of correcting any errors from the error set E is known (for example, E may be the set of vectors of weight t).
2) Select random binary non-singular $(n \times n)$ matrix $\mathbf{M}$.
3) Calculate $(k \times n)$ matrix $\mathbf{G}' = \mathbf{GM}$.
4) Define the error set $E' = \{\mathbf{e}' : \mathbf{e}' = \mathbf{eM}, \mathbf{e} \in E\}$.
5) Public key is $(\mathbf{G}', E')$, private key is $(\mathbf{G}, \mathbf{M})$.

To encrypt the message, one should do the following:

1) Represent the message as binary k-bit sequence $\mathbf{m}$.
2) Select random n-bit binary vector $\mathbf{e}' \in E'$.
3) Calculate ciphertext $\mathbf{c} = \mathbf{mG}' + \mathbf{e}'$.

To decrypt the ciphertext, one should do the following:

1) Calculate $\mathbf{c}' = \mathbf{cM}^{-1}$.

2) Obtain $\mathbf{m}$ by decoding $\mathbf{c}'$ in code $\mathbf{G}$ using ψ.

Decryption is correct, since $\mathbf{c}' = \mathbf{cM}^{-1} = (\mathbf{mGM} + \mathbf{eM})\mathbf{M}^{-1} = \mathbf{mG} + \mathbf{e}$, where $\mathbf{e} \in E$, and the procedure ψ may be effectively used.

The security of the described class of systems is based on the fact that the adversary needs decoding in the code $\mathbf{G}'$, while $\mathbf{G}'$ is not only non-equivalent to the code $\mathbf{G}$ as in McEliece cryptosystem, but after multiplying $\mathbf{G}$ by $\mathbf{M}$ from the right the error-correction capability of public code $\mathbf{G}'$ is unknown (and may be rather low). In addition, the structure (for example, weight) of vector $\mathbf{e}'$ is unknown (and, in fact, it may not be the coset leader for $\mathbf{G}'$), thus the best attack may turn out not to perform the complete decoding, but instead to use brute force by vectors from E', which may be a more complicated task. Finally, we note that the set E itself may not be published and this may be used to further strengthen the system.

On the other hand, the described class proposes only a general approach, and not the particular cryptosystem. First, not only Goppa code may be used as private code $\mathbf{G}$, and not only vectors of fixed weight may form the set E. This is of special interest since, in the last years, code-based cryptosystems using codes other than Goppa codes have been considered [9][10]. Surely, by selecting particular classes of codes new possibilities may arise for the adversary, which should be thoroughly taken in consideration.

Next, the method of defining the set E' should be specified, which for security reasons should have exponential cardinality. In [7][8], some examples of such definition are given. In the next section, the public-key code-based cryptosystem from the described class is proposed, based on bursts-correcting codes.

IV. CODE-BASED CRYPTOSYSTEM USING BURSTS-CORRECTING CODES

Let us consider the following variant of the system from the class described in the previous section:

1) Select generator $(k \times n)$ matrix $\mathbf{G}$ of linear (n, k) code, for which the effective procedure ψ of correcting any errors from the error set E is known.
2) Select random binary non-singular $(n \times n)$ matrix $\mathbf{M}_2$.
3) Define the error set $\tilde{E}$ and $(n \times n)$ matrix $\mathbf{M}_1$ such that for any $\tilde{\mathbf{e}} \in \tilde{E}$ vector $\tilde{\mathbf{e}}\mathbf{M}_1$ belongs to E.
4) Calculate matrix $\mathbf{M} = \mathbf{M}_1\mathbf{M}_2$.
5) Calculate $(k \times n)$ matrix $\mathbf{G}' = \mathbf{GM}_2$.
6) Public key is $(\mathbf{G}', \mathbf{M}, \tilde{E})$, private key is $(\mathbf{G}, \mathbf{M}_1, \mathbf{M}_2)$.

To encrypt the message, one should do the following:

1) Represent the message as binary k-bit sequence $\mathbf{m}$.
2) Select random n-bit binary vector $\tilde{\mathbf{e}} \in \tilde{E}$ and calculate $\mathbf{e}' = \tilde{\mathbf{e}}\mathbf{M}$.
3) Calculate ciphertext $\mathbf{c} = \mathbf{mG}' + \mathbf{e}'$.

To decrypt the ciphertext, one should do the following:

1) Calculate $\mathbf{c}' = \mathbf{cM}_2^{-1}$.
2) Obtain $\mathbf{m}$ by decoding $\mathbf{c}'$ in code $\mathbf{G}$ using ψ.

Decryption is correct, since $\mathbf{c}' = \mathbf{cM}_2^{-1} = (\mathbf{mGM}_2 + \tilde{\mathbf{e}}\mathbf{M}_1\mathbf{M}_2)\mathbf{M}_2^{-1} = \mathbf{mG} + \mathbf{e}$, where $\mathbf{e} \in E$, and the procedure ψ may be effectively used.

In this variant, the set E' is defined by the vectors $\tilde{\mathbf{e}}\mathbf{M}$, which in turn requires effective definition of $\tilde{E}$. Besides, the matrix $\mathbf{M}_1$ should be defined mapping the vectors from $\tilde{E}$ to E.

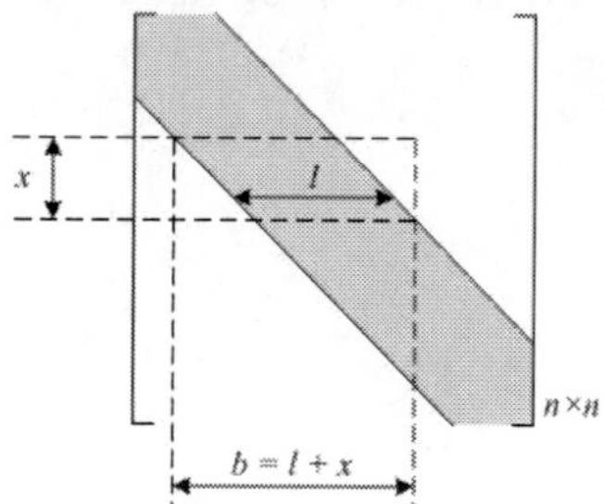

Figure 1. Definition of matrix $\mathbf{M}_1$

For example, $\tilde{E}$ and E may coincide and be formed by the vectors of some fixed weight. In this paper, we propose the system, where the set E is formed by vectors in which the number of positions between first and last non-zero elements are no greater than some value b and such error vectors are called error bursts of length b. In coding theory, the bursts-correcting codes are known to be capable of correcting single error bursts of a given length [11][12]. As the set $\tilde{E}$ we will also consider the set of error bursts of some length.

Consider as $\mathbf{M}_1$ the matrix shown in Figure 1. The gray color corresponds to positions filled by random binary elements, other positions are zeros. Clearly, such matrix defines mapping of error bursts of length x to error bursts of length b.

Then, the specification of the proposed system may be finalized by the following conditions:

- Set E: the set of bursts of length $\leq b$.
- Matrix $\mathbf{G}$ should define the code for which effective procedure of correcting single bursts of length b is known.
- Set $\tilde{E}$: the set of bursts of length $\leq x$. Clearly, x should be included in system's public key as definition of $\tilde{E}$.

Note that code $\mathbf{G}'$ has no known structure: neither its bursts-correction capability nor its minimal distance are known. Moreover, the set $E' = \{\mathbf{e}' : \mathbf{e}' = \tilde{\mathbf{e}}\mathbf{M}\}$ contains vectors of arbitrary structure, with arbitrary weights and which are not error bursts. Thus, it seems that the structure of bursts used by private code cannot be exploited by the adversary, and the best attacking strategy is to search through the elements of E'.

Quantitative estimation of system parameters: bursts lengths x and b, cardinalities of E' and $\tilde{E}$, and finally selection of k and n which define the key size depends on class of bursts-correction codes being used. This class should contain exponential number of codes for given b, k, n, and the codes should not possess the structure which may be used by the adversary to perform the structural attack. One variant for such codes is the class of low-density parity-check codes (LDPC). The bursts-correction capabilities of some LDPC codes were investigated in [13][14]. However, these codes cannot be directly applied in proposed cryptosystem since they are strongly structured, and the task of bursts-correction code selection for usage in the proposed cryptosystem may be considered as further research.

V. Conclusion

In this paper, a code-based cryptosystem using bursts-correction codes is proposed. This system belongs to the class of cryptosystems based on complete decoding task. It is supposed that cryptosystems from this class allow to achieve better security than the McEliece cryptosystem. The selection of particular codes for usage in the proposed system, which allows qualitative estimation of parameters and perhaps requires additional cryptanalysis research is the direction of further investigations.

Acknowledgment

The reported study was funded by RFBR according to the research project No. 16-01-00716 a.

References

[1] R. J. McEliece, "A Public-Key Cryptosystem Based on Algebraic Coding Theory," 1978, DSN progress report #42-44, Jet Propulsion Laboratory, Pasadena, California.

[2] E. Berlekamp, R. McEliece, and H. van Tilborg, "On the inherent intractability of certain coding problems (corresp.)," IEEE Transactions on Information Theory, vol. 24, no. 3, May 1978, pp. 384–386.

[3] V. M. Sidelnikov and S. O. Shestakov, "On insecurity of cryptosystems based on generalized Reed-Solomon codes," Discrete Mathematics and Applications, vol. 2, no. 4, 1992, pp. 439–444.

[4] E. Krouk, A. Ovchinnikov, and E. Vostokova, "About one modification of McEliece cryptosystem based on Plotkin construction," in 2016 XV International Symposium Problems of Redundancy in Information and Control Systems (REDUNDANCY), Sept 2016, pp. 75–78.

[5] E. Krouk, "A New Public-Key Cryptosystem," in Sixth Joint Swedish-Russian International Workshop on Information Theory, Moelle, Sweden, 1993, pp. 285–286.

[6] F. MacWilliams and N. Sloane, The Theory of Error-Correcting Codes. North-Holland publishing company, 1983, 782 p.

[7] E. Krouk and U. Sorger, "A Public Key Cryptosystem Based on Total Decoding of Linear Codes," in VI International Workshop "Algebraic and combinatorial coding theory", Pskov, 1998, pp. 116–118.

[8] G. Kabatiansky, S. Semenov, and E. Krouk, Error Correcting Coding And Security For Data Networks: Analysis Of The Superchannel Concept. John Wiley & Sons, 2005, 278 p.

[9] R. Misoczki, J. P. Tillich, N. Sendrier, and P. S. L. M. Barreto, "MDPC-McEliece: New McEliece variants from Moderate Density Parity-Check codes," in 2013 IEEE International Symposium on Information Theory, July 2013, pp. 2069–2073.

[10] E. M. Gabidulin, A. V. Ourivski, B. Honary, and B. Ammar, "Reducible rank codes and their applications to cryptography," IEEE Transactions on Information Theory, vol. 49, no. 12, Dec 2003, pp. 3289–3293.

[11] R. Blahut, Theory and practice of error control codes. Addison-Wesley, 1983, 500 p.

[12] W. Zhang and J. K. Wolf, "A class of binary burst error-correcting quasi-cyclic codes," IEEE Transactions on Information Theory, vol. 34, no. 3, May 1988, pp. 463–479.

[13] E. A. Krouk and S. V. Semenov, "Low-Density Parity-Check Burst Error-Correcting Codes," in 2 International Workshop "Algebraic and combinatorial coding theory", Leningrad, 1990, pp. 121–124.

[14] E. A. Krouk and A. A. Ovchinnikov, "2-Stripes Block-Circulant LDPC Codes for Single Bursts Correction," Smart Innovation, Systems and Technologies, vol. 55, June 2016, pp. 11–23.

[15] N. Sendrier, "Finding the permutation between equivalent linear codes: the support splitting algorithm," IEEE Transactions on Information Theory, vol. 46, no. 4, Jul 2000, pp. 1193–1203.

[16] E. Krouk and A. Ovchinnikov, "About one structural attack on McEliece cryptosystem," in 2016 XV International Symposium Problems of Redundancy in Information and Control Systems (REDUNDANCY), Sept 2016, pp. 71–74.

RSMA Receiver

Sergei Semenov
HiSilicon/Huawei
Lund, Sweden
e-mail: sergei.semenov@huawei.com

***Abstract*—In this paper, we propose a new algorithm for the detection of Resource Spread Multiple-Access (RSMA) signal. The proposed algorithm provides a significant performance gain in comparison with other algorithms for the high spectral efficiency case with affordable complexity.**

Keywords-RSMA; NOMA; OLMA; message passing algorithm; projection based IC.

I. INTRODUCTION

Resource spread multiple access (RSMA) is an overloaded multiple-access (OLMA) strategy, which is closely related to code-division multiple access (CDMA) [7] and interleave-division multiple-access (IDMA) [8]. RSMA was proposed in [1][2] as a candidate for new radio (NR) uplink (UL) multiple access. Current assumption for RSMA receiver implementation is that very low rate channel coding is used in the system. In this case, quite simple approaches can be used for the RSMA receiver implementation. In [3], the use of two types of receivers was proposed:

1. Match filter (MF): Each layer descrambles and de-spreads the signal before passing it to the decoder. Detection is done by the Hermitian transpose of spreading/scrambling sequence matrix, which can be viewed as a match filter.
2. MF+successive interference cancellation (SIC): Once a packet is decoded, then its waveform can be cancelled from the received waveform. The receiver re-attempts to decode unsuccessful packets. The iteration stops when no new packet needs to be decoded.

This type of receiver can be used in Ultra Reliable Low Latency Communications (URLLC) scenario and to some extent in Massive Machine Type Communications (mMTC) scenario but it hardly can be used for Enhanced Mobile Broadband (eMBB) transmission since in this case, low spectral efficiency (SE) caused by usage of very low code rate is a drawback. Joint maximum likelihood (ML) detection provides the optimum performance but the complexity of this type of the receiver grows exponentially with the number of users.

The message passing algorithm (MPA) can be used in the receiver for non-orthogonal MA employing low-density signatures like LDSMA [4] or SCMA and it provides good performance with affordable complexity. However, it cannot be applied directly to RSMA detection since RSMA does not use low-density signatures, i.e., the number of users colliding over one resource element (RE) is equal to the number of all users.

In this paper, we propose to use a combination of MPA and projection based interference cancellation (IC) for RSMA signal detection.

The rest of this paper is organized as follows. Section II describes the application of MPA for OLMA detection and the projection based IC. Section III describes the hybrid receiver combining MPA and projection based IC for RSMA detection. Simulation results are represented in Section IV. The conclusions close the article.

II. MPA FOR OLMA DETECTION AND PROJECTION BASED IC

A. MPA for LDSMA signal

The application of MPA for the detection of the LDSMA signal is described in [4]. This application is based on the structure of the LDSMA signal. Users in LDSMA share the available REs in such a way that only limited number of users can transmit over a particular RE.

The structure of this system can be described with the help of indicator matrix $\mathbf{F}_{N\times K}$ defining the signals of K users spreading their signals over N REs. An example of indicator matrix for $N = 12$ and $K = 16$ is presented in Figure 1.

$$
\mathbf{F}_{12\times 16} = \begin{bmatrix}
0 & 0 & 1 & 0 & 0 & 0 & 0 & 1 & 0 & 1 & 0 & 0 & 1 & 0 & 0 & 0 \\
0 & 0 & 0 & 1 & 0 & 0 & 1 & 0 & 0 & 0 & 0 & 0 & 1 & 0 & 1 & 0 \\
0 & 1 & 0 & 0 & 1 & 0 & 1 & 0 & 0 & 1 & 0 & 0 & 0 & 0 & 0 & 0 \\
0 & 0 & 0 & 1 & 0 & 1 & 0 & 0 & 0 & 0 & 1 & 0 & 0 & 1 & 0 & 0 \\
0 & 0 & 1 & 0 & 0 & 0 & 0 & 0 & 1 & 0 & 0 & 0 & 0 & 0 & 1 & 1 \\
1 & 0 & 0 & 0 & 0 & 1 & 0 & 0 & 0 & 1 & 0 & 0 & 0 & 0 & 1 & 0 \\
0 & 0 & 0 & 1 & 0 & 0 & 0 & 1 & 1 & 0 & 0 & 1 & 0 & 0 & 0 & 0 \\
0 & 1 & 0 & 0 & 0 & 1 & 0 & 0 & 0 & 0 & 0 & 1 & 0 & 0 & 0 & 1 \\
1 & 0 & 0 & 0 & 0 & 0 & 1 & 0 & 0 & 0 & 0 & 0 & 0 & 1 & 0 & 1 \\
0 & 0 & 1 & 0 & 1 & 0 & 0 & 0 & 0 & 0 & 0 & 1 & 0 & 1 & 0 & 0 \\
0 & 1 & 0 & 0 & 0 & 0 & 0 & 0 & 1 & 0 & 1 & 0 & 1 & 0 & 0 & 0 \\
1 & 0 & 0 & 0 & 1 & 0 & 0 & 1 & 0 & 0 & 1 & 0 & 0 & 0 & 0 & 0
\end{bmatrix}
$$

Figure 1. Indicator matrix, $\boldsymbol{K = 16, N = 12, d_u = 3}$ and $\boldsymbol{d_c = 4}$. [4].

The position of ones in the nth row of the indicator matrix $\mathbf{F}_{N\times K}$ denotes the set of users who contribute their data at the nth symbol, while its kth column represents the set of symbols over which the user spreads his/her data. The maximum number of ones in each column d_u indicates the maximum number of nonzero spread symbols, which can be located for each user among the N possible time-frequency resources. It is also clearly seen that each spread symbol will collide in the channel with d_c (maximum number of ones in row) symbols from other users.

If the indicator matrix has the same number of ones in each column, i.e., d_u and also the same number of ones in each row, i.e., d_c, but is not necessarily equal to d_u, then the structure is called regular indicator matrix, otherwise, it is called irregular indicator matrix.

As can be seen from the description of the indicator matrix it corresponds to the description of the parity-check matrix of the LDPC code. Due to this fact, the idea of MPA used for decoding LDPC codes is applicable for LDSMA signal detection.

An indicator matrix can be represented by a bidirectional bipartite factor graph. In Figure 2, the graph for the LDPC matrix shown in Figure 1 is illustrated.

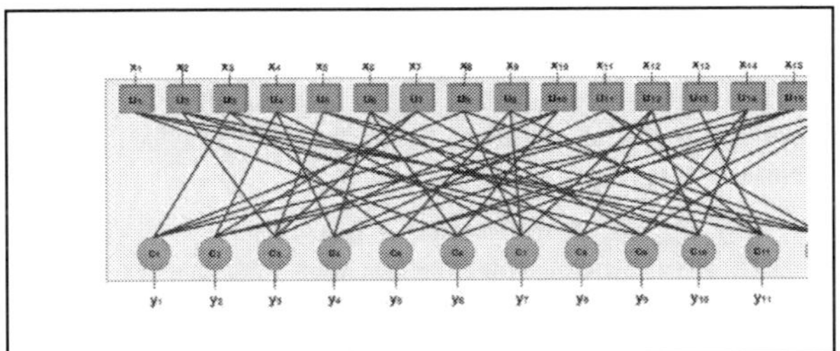

Figure 2. Factor graph representation of the indicator matrix shown in Figure 1 [4].

In this graph, the upper (variable) nodes $\{u_k\}, k = 1, \dots, K$ are connected to the K user transmitted symbols; the lower (function) nodes $\{c_n\}, n = 1, \dots, N$ represent N REs carrying the encoded information and being connected to the observations at these REs $\{y_n\}, n = 1, \dots, N$; the edges between indicate which REs are occupied by a user. From this graph, we find that there is an edge between pair (c_i, u_j) if and only if the matrix element F_{ij} is nonzero. We see also that each node c_n is connected to d_c nodes and each node u_k is connected to d_u nodes.

Let edge $e_{n,k}$ be the edge that connects a function node c_n to a variable node u_k. At the function node c_n, the local channel observation at the corresponding RE y_n is made and is given by

$$p(y_n|\mathbf{x}^{[n]}) = \frac{1}{\sqrt{2\pi}\sigma}\exp\left(-\frac{1}{2\sigma^2}\left\|y_n - \mathbf{g}^{[n]^T}\mathbf{x}^{[n]}\right\|^2\right), \tag{1}$$

where $\mathbf{g}^{[n]}$ and $\mathbf{x}^{[n]}$ is the set of channel coefficients and the set of transmitted symbols corresponding to non-zero elements in the nth row of the indicator matrix, i.e., corresponding to the users contributing to the nth RE.

Each message being exchanged must be in the form of a vector of size $|\mathcal{A}|$ comprising the reliability values for each of the possible values taken from the symbol constellation alphabet $\mathcal{A}$. Note that, the message must be normalized such that the sum of all probability values for all alphabet symbols is one. LLRs can be used instead of probabilities. Then, the size of message is $|\mathcal{A}| - 1$.

Let symbol y_n be the symbol of observation. The message being sent from function node c_n onto edge $e_{n,k}$ is the product of the messages received from edges $e_{l,n}$ ($l \in \varepsilon_n\backslash k$, where ε_n is the set of d_c variable nodes connected to the function node c_n defined by the nth row of index matrix $\mathbf{F}_{N\times K}$ (variable node u_k must be excluded from this set)) with the local function at c_n and being summarized for the variable associated with the edge, i.e., x_k. Similarly, the variable node u_k will send onto edge $e_{n,k}$ a message, which is the product of the messages received from edges $e_{m,k}$ ($m \in \xi_k\backslash n$, where ξ_k is the set of d_u function nodes connected to the variable node u_k defined by the kth column of index matrix $\mathbf{F}_{N\times K}$ (function node c_n must be excluded from this set)).

Let $\mu_{c_n\leftarrow u_k}$ and $\mu_{c_n\rightarrow u_k}$ be the message sent along edge $e_{n,k}$ from variable node u_k and function node c_n, respectively. The message $\mu_{c_n\leftarrow u_k}$ gives an updated inference of x_k based on the observation taken at symbols y_m, $m \in \xi_k\backslash n$:

$$\mu_{c_n\leftarrow u_k}(j) = \log\frac{P_{ext,n}(x_k = a_j)}{P_{ext,n}(x_k = a_0)} = \sum_{m\in\xi_k\backslash n} \mu_{c_m\rightarrow u_k}(j), \quad j = 1, \dots, |\mathcal{A}| - 1, \tag{2}$$

where $a_j \in \mathcal{A}$ is the corresponding element of the constellation alphabet $\mathcal{A}$.

Appending the set of equations (2) with the additional restriction

$$\sum_{j=0}^{|\mathcal{A}|-1} \lambda_{n,k} P_{ext,n}(x_k = a_j) = 1, \tag{3}$$

where $\lambda_{n,k}$ is a normalizing coefficient, and solving this set of equations, we obtain

$$P_{ext,n}(x_k = a_j) = \frac{\exp\left(\mu_{c_n\leftarrow u_k}(j)\right)}{\lambda_{n,k}\left(\sum_{i=0}^{|\mathcal{A}|-1}\exp\left(\mu_{c_n\leftarrow u_k}(i)\right)\right)}, \quad \mu_{c_n\leftarrow u_k}(0) = 0. \tag{4}$$

The denominator in (4) is constant for all $P_{ext,n}(x_k = a_j)$, $j = 0, \dots, |\mathcal{A}| - 1$. Then (4) can be simplified to

$$P_{ext,n}(x_k = a_j) = \exp\left(\lambda'_{n,k}\mu_{c_n\leftarrow u_k}(j)\right), \quad \mu_{c_n\leftarrow u_k}(0) = 0. \tag{5}$$

where $\lambda'_{n,k}$ is the normalization coefficient and is chosen to satisfy (3), $\lambda'_{n,k} = -\log\lambda_{n,k}$.

At the function node c_n, the inference of x_k is updated and is given by

$$\mu_{c_n\rightarrow u_k}(j) = \log\frac{p_{ext,n}(x_k = a_j|y_n, \mathbf{x}^{[n]}\backslash x_k)}{p_{ext,n}(x_k = a_0|y_n, \mathbf{x}^{[n]}\backslash x_k)}, \quad j = 1, \dots, |\mathcal{A}| - 1. \tag{6}$$

Applying Bayes' rule to the nominator and the denominator of (6) and taking into account that the a priori pmf of x_k should not be included in the computation of a posteriori pmf of x_k, we obtain

$$\begin{aligned}&\mu_{c_n\to u_k}(j)\\&=\log\frac{p_{ext,n}(x_k=a_j|y_n,\mathbf{x}^{[n]}\backslash x_k)}{p_{ext,n}(x_k=a_0|y_n,\mathbf{x}^{[n]}\backslash x_k)}\\&=\log\frac{p_{ext,n}(y_n|\mathbf{x}^{[n]},x_k=a_j)P(\mathbf{x}^{[n]}\backslash x_k)}{p_{ext,n}(y_n|\mathbf{x}^{[n]},x_k=a_0)P(\mathbf{x}^{[n]}\backslash x_k)},\\&j=1,\dots,|\mathcal{A}|-1.\end{aligned}\tag{7}$$

Combining (1), (2), and (5) into (7), we can write a complete message being sent from the function node c_n to the variable node u_k onto the edge $e_{n,k}$ as follows:

$$\begin{aligned}&\mu_{c_n\to u_k}(j)\\&=\log\frac{\sum_{\mathbf{x}^{[n]}\in\mathcal{A}^{d_c},\,x_k=a_j}\exp\left(\sum_{l\in\varepsilon_n\backslash k}\lambda'_{n,l}\mu^{[\mathbf{x}^{[n]}]}_{c_n\leftarrow u_l}(j)-\frac{1}{2\sigma^2}\left\|y_n-\mathbf{g}^{[n]^T}\mathbf{x}^{[n]}\right\|^2\right)}{\sum_{\mathbf{x}^{[n]}\in\mathcal{A}^{d_c},\,x_k=a_0}\exp\left(\sum_{l\in\varepsilon_n\backslash k}\lambda'_{n,l}\mu^{[\mathbf{x}^{[n]}]}_{c_n\leftarrow u_l}(j)-\frac{1}{2\sigma^2}\left\|y_n-\mathbf{g}^{[n]^T}\mathbf{x}^{[n]}\right\|^2\right)}\\&=\max_{\mathbf{x}^{[n]}\in\mathcal{A}^{d_c},\,x_k=a_j}{}^{*}\left(\sum_{l\in\varepsilon_n\backslash k}\lambda'_{n,l}\mu^{[\mathbf{x}^{[n]}]}_{c_n\leftarrow u_l}(j)-\frac{1}{2\sigma^2}\left\|y_n-\mathbf{g}^{[n]^T}\mathbf{x}^{[n]}\right\|^2\right)\\&-\max_{\mathbf{x}^{[n]}\in\mathcal{A}^{d_c},\,x_k=a_0}{}^{*}\left(\sum_{l\in\varepsilon_n\backslash k}\lambda'_{n,l}\mu^{[\mathbf{x}^{[n]}]}_{c_n\leftarrow u_l}(j)-\frac{1}{2\sigma^2}\left\|y_n-\mathbf{g}^{[n]^T}\mathbf{x}^{[n]}\right\|^2\right),\\&j=1,\dots,|\mathcal{A}|-1,\end{aligned}\tag{8}$$

where $\mu^{[\mathbf{x}^{[n]}]}_{c_n\leftarrow u_l}$ denotes the message from variable node u_l to function node c_n corresponding to vector $\mathbf{x}^{[n]}$ and function max* is defined as

$$\max{}^*(a,b)=\log(e^a+e^b)=\max(a,b)+\log\left(1+e^{-|a-b|}\right).\tag{9}$$

After the message arriving to variable nodes u_k, $k=1,\dots,K$ have converged or the maximum iteration number has been reached, the variable nodes will use all messages received from all connected edges to calculate the final estimated inference for symbol x_k, because now we are calculating the symbol estimate rather than an extrinsic information, and, except this detail, this is done in the same way as in (2)

$$\begin{aligned}&P(x_k=a_j)=\exp\left(\sum_{n\in\xi_k}\lambda'_{n,k}\mu_{c_n\to u_k}(j)\right),\\&\mu_{c_n\to u_k}(0)=0.\end{aligned}\tag{10}$$

B. Projection based IC

Another method used in hybrid RSMA receiver is the interference cancellation based on projection techniques.

Consider the system model

$$\mathbf{y}=\mathbf{Gx}+\mathbf{n},\tag{11}$$

where $\mathbf{y}$ is the received signal, $\mathbf{x}$ is the vector, composed of the transmitted symbols of all users and $\mathbf{n}$ is the noise vector. Matrix $\mathbf{G}$ is the generalized channel matrix including both channel coefficients and user signatures.

We denote the part of vector x corresponding to signal of interest by $\mathbf{x_T}$ and the other part of vector $\mathbf{x}$ corresponding to the interference by $\mathbf{x_Q}$. Then, the matrix $\mathbf{G}$ can also be split into two parts corresponding to signal of interest and interference. Without loss of generality, we can assume that the first Δ elements of vector $\mathbf{x}$ and correspondingly first Δ columns of matrix $\mathbf{G}$ correspond to the signal of interest. Then, the matrix $\mathbf{G}$ can be represented as follows:

$$\mathbf{G}=[\mathbf{T},\mathbf{Q}].\tag{12}$$

And (11) can be represented as

$$\mathbf{y}=\mathbf{Gx}+\mathbf{n}=\mathbf{Tx}_T+\mathbf{Qx}_Q+\mathbf{n}.\tag{13}$$

The simplest solution to (13) wrt $\mathbf{x}_T$ is to apply a ZF type receiver. It can be done with the help of the following correlation operation

$$\begin{aligned}(\mathbf{T}^H\mathbf{T})^{-1}\mathbf{T}^H\mathbf{y}&=(\mathbf{T}^H\mathbf{T})^{-1}\mathbf{T}^H(\mathbf{Tx}_T+\mathbf{Qx}_Q+\mathbf{n})\\&=(\mathbf{T}^H\mathbf{T})^{-1}\mathbf{T}^H\mathbf{Tx}_T\\&+(\mathbf{T}^H\mathbf{T})^{-1}\mathbf{T}^H\mathbf{Qx}_Q+(\mathbf{T}^H\mathbf{T})^{-1}\mathbf{T}^H\mathbf{n}\\&=\mathbf{x}_T+(\mathbf{T}^H\mathbf{T})^{-1}\mathbf{T}^H\mathbf{Qx}_Q\\&+(\mathbf{T}^H\mathbf{T})^{-1}\mathbf{T}^H\mathbf{n}.\end{aligned}\tag{14}$$

The main problem with the ZF type receiver solution (14) is the term corresponding to interference $(\mathbf{T}^H\mathbf{T})^{-1}\mathbf{T}^H\mathbf{Qx}_Q$.

The main idea of interference mitigation is to project the received signal y onto a vector subspace that is orthogonal to the interference vector subspace (the subspace spanned by the columns of matrix $\mathbf{Q}$).

The projection is a linear transformation $\mathbf{P}$ from a vector space to itself such that it is idempotent, i.e., $\mathbf{P}^2=\mathbf{P}$.

Let W be an underlying vector space. Suppose the subspaces U and V are the range and null space of $\mathbf{P}$ respectively. Then, the projection has these basic properties:

1. $\mathbf{P}$ is the identity operator $\mathbf{I}$ on U: $\forall\mathbf{x}\in U:\ \mathbf{Px}=\mathbf{x}$.
2. W is a direct sum $W=U\oplus V$. This means that every vector $\mathbf{x}\in W$ may be decomposed uniquely in the manner $\mathbf{x}=\mathbf{u}+\mathbf{v}$, where $\mathbf{u}\in U$ and $\mathbf{v}\in V$. The decomposition is given by
   $\mathbf{u}=\mathbf{Px},\ \mathbf{v}=\mathbf{x}-\mathbf{Px}=(\mathbf{I}-\mathbf{P})\mathbf{x}.$

If the range U and the null space V are orthogonal subspaces, the projection $\mathbf{P}$ is an orthogonal projection. For orthogonal projection matrix $\mathbf{P}$ is Hermitian matrix, i.e., $\mathbf{P}=\mathbf{P}^H$. If $\mathbf{u}_1,\dots,\mathbf{u}_k$ is a basis of U, and $\mathbf{A}$ is the matrix with these vectors as columns, then the projection is

$$\mathbf{P_A}=\mathbf{A}(\mathbf{A}^H\mathbf{A})^{-1}\mathbf{A}^H.\tag{15}$$

Then the projection onto interference vector space, i.e., vector space spanned by columns of $\mathbf{Q}$ is defined by the matrix

$$\mathbf{P_Q}=\mathbf{Q}(\mathbf{Q}^H\mathbf{Q})^{-1}\mathbf{Q}^H,\tag{16}$$

and, correspondingly, the projection onto null vector space is defined by matrix

$$\mathbf{P}_{\mathbf{Q}}^{\perp} = \mathbf{I} - \mathbf{P}_{\mathbf{Q}} = \mathbf{I} - \mathbf{Q}(\mathbf{Q}^{H}\mathbf{Q})^{-1}\mathbf{Q}^{H}. \quad (17)$$

After projecting the received signal $\mathbf{y}$ onto the null space of $\mathbf{Q}$, we obtain:

$$\begin{aligned}\mathbf{P}_{\mathbf{Q}}^{\perp}\mathbf{y} &= \left(\mathbf{I} - \mathbf{Q}(\mathbf{Q}^{H}\mathbf{Q})^{-1}\mathbf{Q}^{H}\right)\mathbf{y} \\ &= \mathbf{T}\mathbf{x}_{T} + \mathbf{Q}\mathbf{x}_{Q} + \mathbf{n} - \mathbf{Q}(\mathbf{Q}^{H}\mathbf{Q})^{-1}\mathbf{Q}^{H}\mathbf{T}\mathbf{x}_{T} - \mathbf{Q}\underline{\underline{(\mathbf{Q}^{H}\mathbf{Q})^{-1}\mathbf{Q}^{H}\mathbf{Q}}}\mathbf{x}_{Q} \\ &- \mathbf{Q}(\mathbf{Q}^{H}\mathbf{Q})^{-1}\mathbf{Q}^{H}\mathbf{n} = \mathbf{P}_{\mathbf{Q}}^{\perp}\mathbf{T}\mathbf{x}_{T} + \mathbf{P}_{\mathbf{Q}}^{\perp}\mathbf{n}.\end{aligned} \quad (18)$$

Denote vector $\mathbf{P}_{\mathbf{Q}}^{\perp}\mathbf{y}$ as $\bar{\mathbf{y}}$, vector $\mathbf{P}_{\mathbf{Q}}^{\perp}\mathbf{n}$ as $\bar{\mathbf{n}}$ and matrix $\mathbf{P}_{\mathbf{Q}}^{\perp}\mathbf{T}$ as $\bar{\mathbf{G}}$. Then (18) can be written as

$$\bar{\mathbf{y}} = \bar{\mathbf{G}}\mathbf{x}_{T} + \bar{\mathbf{n}}. \quad (19)$$

Then, any appropriate method can be used to solve (19). For example, in [5] [6], RAKE receiver is used to solve (19).

III. HYBRID RSMA RECEIVER

It is not possible to apply MPA directly to RSMA signal detection since the indicator matrix corresponding to RSMA would be a unit matrix (matrix consisting of ones). In this case, the MPA cannot provide good results since corresponding graph contains cycles of length 4. Moreover, the complexity of the algorithm grows exponentially with the number of users.

The drawback of the interference cancellation based on orthogonal projection is that if the number of interferers is high the attempt to map the received signal onto the null space of the interference leads to the distortion of the signal of interest as well.

In this paper, we propose to combine these two methods to create a hybrid receiver of the RSMA signal.

As it was mentioned above, since in RSMA all users collide over each RE, the indicator matrix for RSMA signal comprises unit matrix of dimension *N*x*K*, where *N* is the number of REs over which users are spreading their signals, and *K* is the number of users ($N < K$).

We propose to choose some sparse matrix of size *N*x*K* with good properties (e.g., the corresponding graph should not contain cycles of short lengths and stopping sets) and use it as an indicator matrix. A good way to construct such a matrix could be to use a combinatorial design.

Then, the general MPA described in equations (1)-(10) can be applied. However, before applying calculations corresponding to function nodes (8) the interference coming from interferers designated in the corresponding rows of the indicator matrix **F** must be nullified.

For example, if the RSMA system with 16 users spreading the signals over 12 REs is considered, and matrix **F** represented in Figure 1 is chosen as an indicator matrix, before calculating messages from the function node 1 corresponding to 1st row of matrix F, the interference from users 1, 2, 4, 5, 6, 7, 9, 11, 12, 14, 15, 16 should be nullified. And before calculating messages from the function node 2 the interference from users 1, 2, 3, 5, 6, 8, 9, 10, 11, 12, 14, 16 must be cancelled.

This step can be done with the help of projection based interference cancellation. We propose before calculating messages from the function node *n,* to collect the signatures of users corresponding to zeros in *n*th row of matrix **F**, in matrix of interference **Q** and projecting the received signal **y** onto the null space of **Q** like it is done in (18). However, we propose to avoid excessive noise enhancement and take the noise amplification into account when projecting the received signal onto the null space of **Q**. Due to this, the projection is slightly modified in accordance with MMSE solution:

$$\mathbf{P}_{\mathbf{Q}}^{\perp}\mathbf{y} = \left(\mathbf{I} - \mathbf{Q}(\mathbf{Q}^{H}\mathbf{Q} + \sigma_{0}^{2}\mathbf{I})^{-1}\mathbf{Q}^{H}\right)\mathbf{y}\ , \quad (20)$$

where σ_{0}^{2} is the noise variance.

Then calculation of message from the function node *n* can be done in accordance with (7)-(8) but in space skewed by the projection $\mathbf{P}_{\mathbf{Q}}^{\perp}$, i.e., vector **y** in (7)-(8) should be substituted by skewed vector $\bar{\mathbf{y}} = \mathbf{P}_{\mathbf{Q}}^{\perp}\mathbf{y}$ and matrix **G** in (7)-(8) should be substituted by skewed matrix $\bar{\mathbf{G}} = \mathbf{P}_{\mathbf{Q}}^{\perp}\mathbf{T}$.

The number of users to be cancelled should not exceed *N*. Otherwise matrix $(\mathbf{Q}^{H}\mathbf{Q} + \sigma_{0}^{2}\mathbf{I})$ can be singular.

Taking into account the fact that in RSMA signal all users collide over all REs we can improve the calculation of (7)-(8) by calculating (7) simultaneously for a few components of vector $\bar{\mathbf{y}}$ rather than for just one component with index *n* like it is done in (7). Now, the calculations (7)-(8) are done for all components of vector $\bar{\mathbf{y}}$ corresponding to non-zero elements of column *k* in indicator matrix **F** except the component with index *n*. Actually, it means that the component of vector $\bar{\mathbf{y}}$ with index *n* in (7) should be substituted by vector $\bar{\mathbf{y}}^{[n]}$, where vector $\bar{\mathbf{y}}^{[n]}$ comprises vector $\bar{\mathbf{y}}$ with zeros at the same positions where zeros are located in column *k* in indicator matrix **F** , and one more zero is located in the component with index *n*. And vector $\mathbf{g}^{[n]}$ in (8) should be substituted by matrix $\bar{\mathbf{G}}^{[n]}$. The corresponding LLRs should be summed up. Then this can be written as it is shown in (21).

In fact, calculations in (21) can be considered as a joint ML detection of users corresponding to non-zero elements in row *n* of indicator matrix **F**. If we consider the implementation of the receiver in vector processor, the complexity of calculation (21) is the same as the complexity of calculation (8). And the calculation of message going from the function node in the form shown in (21) provides performance gain. The main complexity of the detector is contributed by calculation of (21), i.e., by the joint ML detection of users. As it was mentioned above, the complexity of the receiver grows exponentially with number of users to be detected jointly with the help of ML algorithm. Due to the sparsity of the indicator matrix **F**, the number of users to be detected jointly can be set to be constant or can grow very slowly. If the number of users to be detected jointly is set to be constant, the complexity of the receiver can be considered to be polynomial.

$$
\begin{aligned}
&\mu_{c_n \to u_k}(j) \\
&= \log \frac{\sum_{\substack{\mathbf{x}^{[n]} \in \mathcal{A}^{d_c}, \\ x_k = a_j}} \exp\left(\sum_{l \in \varepsilon_n \backslash k} \lambda'_{n,l} \mu^{[\mathbf{x}^{[n]}]}_{c_n \leftarrow u_l}(j) - \frac{1}{2\sigma^2} \left\| \bar{\mathbf{y}}^{[n]} - \bar{\mathbf{G}}^{[n]^T}\right.\right.}{\sum_{\substack{\mathbf{x}^{[n]} \in \mathcal{A}^{d_c}, \\ x_k = a_0}} \exp\left(\sum_{l \in \varepsilon_n \backslash k} \lambda'_{n,l} \mu^{[\mathbf{x}^{[n]}]}_{c_n \leftarrow u_l}(j) - \frac{1}{2\sigma^2} \left\| \bar{\mathbf{y}}^{[n]} - \bar{\mathbf{G}}^{[n]^T}\right.\right.} \\
&= \max_{\substack{\mathbf{x}^{[n]} \in \mathcal{A}^{d_c}, \\ x_k = a_j}}{}^{*} \left(\sum_{l \in \varepsilon_n \backslash k} \lambda'_{n,l} \mu^{[\mathbf{x}^{[n]}]}_{c_n \leftarrow u_l}(j) \right. \\
&\left. - \frac{1}{2\sigma^2} \left\| \bar{\mathbf{y}}^{[n]} - \bar{\mathbf{G}}^{[n]^T} \mathbf{x}^{[n]} \right\|^2 \right) \\
&- \max_{\substack{\mathbf{x}^{[n]} \in \mathcal{A}^{d_c}, \\ x_k = a_0}}{}^{*} \left(\sum_{l \in \varepsilon_n \backslash k} \lambda'_{n,l} \mu^{[\mathbf{x}^{[n]}]}_{c_n \leftarrow u_l}(j) \right. \\
&\left. - \frac{1}{2\sigma^2} \left\| \bar{\mathbf{y}}^{[n]} - \bar{\mathbf{G}}^{[n]^T} \mathbf{x}^{[n]} \right\|^2 \right), \qquad j = 1, \ldots, |\mathcal{A}| - 1,
\end{aligned} \tag{21}
$$

The indicator matrix **F** should be chosen in such a way that at least in one row the set of zero elements corresponds to the weakest users if the information about signal power of different users is available at the receiver.

If turbo-equalization processing is used, i.e., detector and decoder exchange the extrinsic information in a few iterations, it is better to change the indicator matrix **F** for each iteration allowing different users being cancelled with the help of projection based method for the same row of indicator matrix in different iterations. This step increases the channel diversity for different iterations. The simple way to obtain the new indicator matrix with the same good properties as the initial indicator matrix is to generate the new indicator matrix by permutation of columns of the initial indicator matrix.

IV. SIMULATION RESULTS

The simulation results are represented in Figure 3. **Simulation results for 6 users over 4REs. QPSK, Code Rate = 1/3..** Simulations were done for 6 users occupying 4 RBs, meaning the overloading factor was 150%. The proposed algorithm, designated in plots by MPA+Proj is compared with Successive Interference Cancellation (SIC), and partial ML algorithms designated by ML3 and ML1. In partial ML algorithm, M users ($M < K$) are detected jointly while interference from other users is considered as a noise. This procedure is repeated a few times until all users are detected. In simulation, each user was detected at least twice. Then, the overlapping estimates were combined. In partial ML algorithm, the decoders' output is not used for the interference cancellation. SIC receiver choses the most powerful user and decodes it first. Then, the bit estimates of this user are mapped to symbol estimates and canceled from the signal taking into account the channel estimates. Next, the same procedure is applied to the next user with highest power. At first iteration, SIC receiver uses partial ML detection, i.e., the most powerful user is detected jointly with other M-1 users ($M < K$). Starting from the second iteration, the interference cancellation procedure relies on decoders' output only. Since the ML detection is used at first iteration only the SIC receiver is vulnerable to the error propagation. Due to this reason only extrinsic information is used for IC.

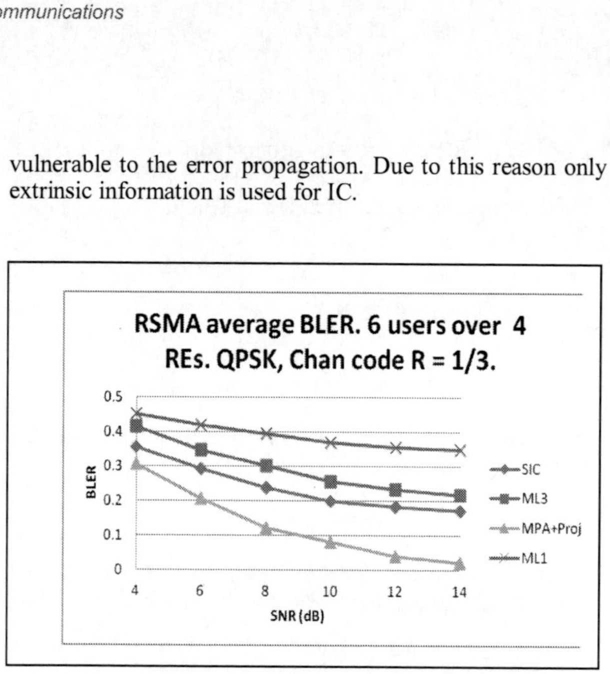

Figure 3. Simulation results for 6 users over 4REs. QPSK, Code Rate = 1/3.

As can be seen from the plots in Figures 3-4, the proposed algorithm provides very high gain for the case of high spectral efficiency. For low code rates (low SE) the gain provided by the hybrid receiver decreases since in this case, all other algorithms start to work quite well.

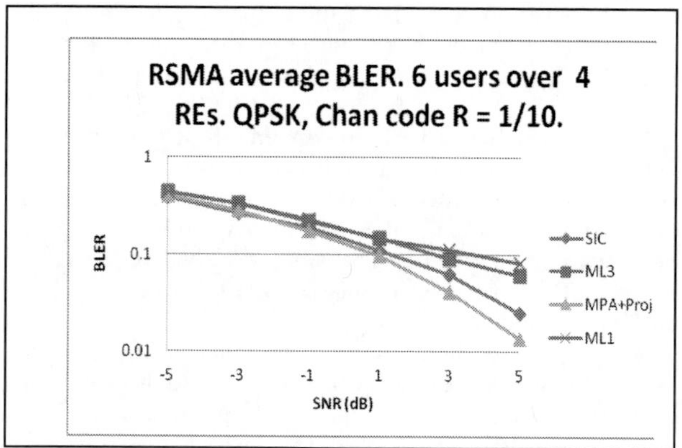

Figure 4. Simulation results for 6 users over 4REs. QPSK, Code Rate = 1/10.

V. CONCLUSION

In this paper, a new hybrid algorithm to detect the RSMA signal is proposed. The proposed algorithm combines MPA and projection based IC and provides significant performance gain in comparison with other algorithms in the case of high SE.

REFERENCES

[1] 3GPP R1-163510 "Candidate NR Multiple Access Schemes," Qualcomm Inc., Busan, Korea, 11th – 15th April 2016.

[2] 3GPP R1-164688 "RSMA," Qualcomm Inc., Nanjing,China, 23rd – 27th May 2016.

[3] 3GPP R1-164689 "RSMA and SCMA comparison," Qualcomm Inc., Nanjing,China, 23rd – 27th May 2016.

[4] R. Hoshyar, F. P. Wathan, "Novel Low-Density Signature for Synchronous CDMA System Over AWGN Channel," IEE Trans. On Signal Proc., Vol 56, No 4, April 2008.

[5] J. Thomas, W. Kober, E. Olson, R. Krumvieda, "Interference cancellation in a signal", WO 03/030440 A1, 2001.

[6] W. Kober, J. Thomas, M. Vis, "Rake receiver for spread spectrum signal demodulation", US 2002/0090025 A1, 2001.

[7] G. Miao, J. Zander, K. W. Sung, B. Slimane, "Fundamentals of Mobile Data Networks," Cambridge University Press, 2016.

[8] Y. Chen, F. Schaich, T. Wild, "Multiple Access and Waveforms for 5G: IDMA and Universal Filtered Multi-Carrier", Vehicular Technology Conference (VTC Spring) 2014 IEEE 79th, pp. 1-5, 2014.

AUTHOR INDEX

International Academy, Research,
and Industry Association (IARIA)
412 Derby Way
Wilmington, DE 19810

ISBN 978-1-5108-4305-9

CURRAN ASSOCIATES INC.
proceedings.com

3rd International Conference on Inventions (ICI 2017)

MATEC Web of Conferences Volume 201 (2018)

Sun Moon Lake, Taiwan
29 September - 2 October 2017

edp sciences